the
crick

Antholo

ASHES

the
cricketer

Anthology of the
ASHES

ALLEN&UNWIN

First published in Great Britain in 2017 by Allen & Unwin

Allen & Unwin
c/o Atlantic Books
Ormond House
26–27 Boswell Street
London WC1N 3JZ

Phone: 020 7269 1610
Fax: 020 7430 0916
Email: UK@allenandunwin.com
Web: www.allenandunwin.com/uk

A CIP catalogue record for this book is available from the British Library.

All images in the picture section are © *The Cricketer* magazine, unless otherwise noted.

Hardback ISBN 978 1 76063 074 4
E-Book ISBN 978 1 76063 827 6

Printed in Great Britain by Bell & Bain Ltd, Glasgow

10 9 8 7 6 5 4 3 2 1

Contents

Introduction

T HE BEST OF the old *and* the new: that is what this book is all about.

The Ashes is one of sport's greatest contests. It has a rich 135-year history (that exact number is subject to debate, of course) and, hopefully, a bright future. *The Cricketer* is the game's best and most-respected read. It is 96 years old and is also looking to the future with confidence. *The Cricketer Anthology of the Ashes* brings these two noble institutions together.

The Ashes were born in 1882 (sort of). England were seemingly in control of a one-off Test at The Oval. They needed only 85 runs to win, but Fred Spofforth famously said, 'This thing can be done', on his way to taking 14 wickets in the match, and the hosts lost by seven runs. A mock obituary was printed in the *Sporting Times*, written by Reginald Shirley Brooks: 'In affectionate remembrance of English cricket which died at the Oval, 29th August, 1882. Deeply lamented by a large circle of sorrowing friends and acquaintances, RIP. N.B. ... The body will be cremated and the Ashes taken to Australia.' Before England capitulated at The Oval, however, arrangements were already in place for the Honourable Ivo Bligh to lead a side to Australia. On the trip, he and the amateurs stayed at Rupertswood, a stately house at Sunbury in Victoria. Rupertswood was home to Sir William Clarke, a wealthy landowner, and his wife is said to have asked that a bail – believed to have been used in the third Test of the series – be burnt, the remains then poured into a terracotta urn and given to Bligh. England won the series 2-1, and Bligh had achieved his objective, to reclaim 'the Ashes'.

The Cricketer opened its doors 38 years later, and we have scoured its archives to assess, and enjoy all over again, a near-century of peerless writing, from greats including the magazine's former editors, Pelham 'Plum' Warner, EW Swanton and Christopher Martin-Jenkins; then we have matched these reports and articles up with new, insightful and entertaining essays from the magnificent Australian writer Gideon Haigh, the magazine's current editor, Simon Hughes, and the rest of *The Cricketer* team, including Huw Turbervill, James Coyne and Jamie Crawley.

Hughes is author of a series of hugely popular books, including the highly acclaimed *A Lot of Hard Yakka*. He is also television's The Analyst on Channel 5's cricket coverage, and on BBC Radio's *Test Match Special*. For this book he has chosen his greatest Ashes XI, with essays on each. These are the great players who have delivered consistently over a number of Ashes series, those who have elevated their game to higher planes when they see the old enemy in their sights. It will be no surprise to you that Don Bradman and Ian Botham made the cut, but many super players have missed out. Haigh was asked to choose his five best Ashes series. Botham's Ashes of 1981 and the 2005 thriller are there, of course, but there are surprise choices, too. Haigh brings these encounters vividly to life.

Turbervill, author of *The Toughest Tour: The Ashes Away Series since the War*, looks beyond Hughes' XI to direct a light on the players who shone briefly in the Ashes. Players like Richard Ellison arrested the attention of an enthralled nation for a short but glorious spell of time. Players who did not quite make the XI, like Steve Waugh, are also in this section. Who can forget him batting on one leg at The Oval in 2001, or defying his critics at the Sydney Cricket Ground in the 2002–3 series?

The Ashes has been a 'family feud', with the United Kingdom and Australia already so intertwined historically and politically. Like all families, though, there have been disputes. Many have been unforgettable. Coyne re-examines moments of diplomacy, politics and controversy. Bodyline was a plan hatched by Douglas Jardine and carried out by loyal foot soldiers from the Midlands and the north – though not Gubby Allen, who refused to bowl it. Cricket perhaps never came closer to the heart of the British or Australian governments than during Bodyline, with the Dominions Secretary meeting Conservative grandees on the MCC committee to try to sort out a mess that resonated as far away as Shanghai. Allen, who became the pre-eminent administrator in English cricket, looms large in the bowling controversies that plagued 1950s Ashes contests, and the grisly D'Oliveira Affair that played out against the 1968 series and remains the biggest stain on MCC's reputation. The often unspoken tension between these ex-amateur administrators and captains, and the professionals sent to do their bidding, finally erupted in the 1970s – through the chuntering quicks John Snow, Dennis Lillee and Jeff Thomson, then the Packer Revolution that has changed everything since. In this section we also hear from *The Cricketer* writers with mysterious monikers – like 'Second Slip', who was the former Test player Frank Mitchell.

Crawley then delves through the magazine's archive to find the boldest, pithiest and most emotive Ashes-inspired writing in its pages. Read both Warner's analysis of English cricket's woes in 1921 after losing the first eight post-War Ashes Tests, and his impassioned exuberance as the urn was regained emphatically at The Oval in 1926. You will find

Swanton's disapproval at the barrage unleashed by Lillee and Thomson in 1974–5 and CMJ's blunt assessment of the sorry state Australian cricket found itself in in 1987. We also see the variety of colourful contributions made by *The Cricketer*'s readers throughout the years – from offering a variety of insights into bodyline, to sharing their exultant joy as the incomparable 2005 series unfolded.

Finally, we have the most detailed statistics section imaginable. You will discover there is an incredible balance to some of these numbers. Australia and England have won 69 series each, for instance (although the former has actually won 130 Tests to the latter's 106). How about this for a stat, though: there have been 533 hundreds and 533 five-fors! There is plenty more where that came from in Section Six of this book.

Although it covers cricket at all levels, *The Cricketer* is steeped in Ashes lore. Douglas Jardine's obsession with Bradman in 1932–3; Len Hutton's 364 at The Oval in 1938; Bradman's invincibility in 1948; Jim Laker's 19 wickets at Old Trafford in 1956; Geoff Boycott's 100th hundred at Headingley in 1977; Botham's brilliance in 1981; Waugh, Adam Gilchrist, Glenn McGrath and Shane Warne's pincer-like grip on the English in the 1990s; Andrew Flintoff surging in on one leg as surgeons hovered in 2009 ... relive these memories and find fresh new takes on the greatest cricket contest of them all.

The Cricketer: a timeline

1921   *The Cricketer* is founded by Sir Pelham Warner, the former England captain and MCC grandee.

1938   EW Swanton makes his first contribution, a report of The Oval Test against Australia.

1960   Swanton becomes editorial director.

1962   Ben Brocklehurst, a farmer and former Somerset captain, joins Mercury House publishers, which acquires *The Cricketer* at his instigation.

1963   Following Warner's death his son, John, becomes editor.

1972   When Mercury House's managing director decides to shut down *The Cricketer* for lack of profit, Brocklehurst buys the title himself, running it with his wife Belinda from their home near Tunbridge Wells.

1973   *The Cricketer* enjoys a spike in its circulation up from 15,000 after absorbing the rival *Playfair Cricket Monthly*. David Frith becomes editor, with Swanton editorial director.

1979   David Frith splits off to form *Wisden Cricket Monthly*, securing a royalty from John Wisden for the name of his new magazine. Reg Hayter comes in as *Cricketer* editor.

1981   Christopher Martin-Jenkins, previously assistant editor to Swanton, becomes editor.

1991   Swanton names his greatest XI from the 70 years of *The Cricketer*: Hobbs, Gavaskar, Bradman, Headley, Sobers, Miller, Davidson, Evans, Marshall, O'Reilly, Gibbs.

2003   The magazine is bought by Wisden and becomes *The Wisden Cricketer*, merging with *Wisden Cricket Monthly*. The editor is John Stern, who stays until 2011.

2010   The magazine is bought by Test Match Extra, with Lord Marland of Odstock and Neil Davidson, the former Leicestershire chairman, principal investors.

2016   Simon Hughes becomes editor, with Huw Turbervill managing editor.

All-Time Ashes XI

Simon Hughes

THERE HAVE BEEN 341 Test matches between England and Australia featuring more than 1,000 players in the 135 years that the Ashes have been contested. It is a bitter rivalry that began when people still travelled about in horse-drawn cabs, life expectancy was 45 and Tinder was something you used to get the parlour fire going. The ancient duel has inspired good men to great deeds and so far 533 Ashes centuries have been scored – and, coincidentally, 533 five-wicket hauls taken, as well as 248 victories celebrated with considerable extravagance. It should be an invidious task choosing just 11 to represent an All-Time Ashes XI in an imaginary match at Lord's against a World XI.

In fact, it is not. The team selected are all universally accepted greats of the game. Their inclusion brooks no argument. There are a few notable omissions, including Herbert Sutcliffe, the only Englishman to have a Test average of more than 60; Harold Larwood – the demon of Bodyline; Jeff Thomson, whose whiplash action and searing pace instilled real fear into opposing batsmen; Clarrie Grimmett, the first man to pass the milestone of 200 Test wickets; and, of course, Ricky Ponting – merciless destroyer of bowlers who became Australia's leading run-scorer. You cannot forget 'Fiery' Fred Trueman either – first man to 300 Test wickets. They are all on the bench. It is only the sheer quality – and longevity – of the men in the final XI who keep them out.

The chosen team – five English and six Australians, including four knights of the realm – offer a tantalising mix of ancient and modern (although none are still playing, unless you can call a three-match series between Warne's Warriors and Sachin's Stars in American baseball stadiums as 'playing'). There are 143 Test hundreds between them and 2,330 wickets. A beguiling all-English opening (batting) partnership of Jack Hobbs and Len Hutton would be a wonderful foil for an all-Australian opening bowling pairing of Dennis Lillee and Glenn McGrath.

Donald Bradman and Wally Hammond, the arch-batting rivals of the 1930s, are automatic picks at 3 and 4 – Hammond's credentials outdoing Ponting – to be joined by Allan Border at No.5. If you are surprised by this and want to argue for Kevin Pietersen, or one of the Waugh twins or the mercurial Denis Compton perhaps, have a look at Border's record. An average of more than 50 (one of only three men to achieve that in the 1980s when the all-conquering West Indies fast bowlers were running amok) and a world-record 153 consecutive Test appearances without ever being injured or dropped. AB was a ferocious fighter from his eyebrows to his toenails.

Just when the opposition bowlers will be praying for mercy, having suffered at the hands of that top five, in walk the two most devastating hitters in Ashes history – Ian Botham and Adam Gilchrist – to supply the turbo-thrust. Imagine being a bowler with these two in the middle and the score 500 for 5. Might be time to call the Samaritans.

But whatever total that group conjured up, there is a quintet of bowlers to make opposing batsmen's lives a misery. Pace, menace and versatility from Lillee, relentless harassment from McGrath, Botham's waspish swing and hostility, Jim Laker to exploit any slight dustiness in the pitch (how he would have loved DRS) and, of course, the superlative Shane Warne, the peerless wicket thief, to tease the batsmen, like a cat toying with a mouse before devouring him when he is ready.

This is a team of men who never countenance defeat; the word is not in their DNA. They have led and inspired their teams to momentous feats that have captured the interest of the world like no other sporting event bar the Olympics and the World Cup. They have given the Ashes its unique flavour and helped make the ancient little urn one of the most coveted trophies in sport.

No.1 Jack Hobbs

Jack Hobbs has the ultimate credentials for being included in the All-Time Ashes XI: he scored more centuries (199) than anyone else in the history of the game and was known as The Master. Twelve of these hundreds were against Australia (second only to Donald Bradman in Ashes records). He was the original run machine. With a colossal 61,760 first-class runs to his name, he is the definition of insatiable. Even Geoff Boycott addressed him as 'sir'.

He was born John Berry Hobbs in 1882 in Cambridge. From an early age he was destined to be a batsman. His father was a professional net bowler at Fenner's, then a groundsman and, finally, an umpire. The ideal combination. Prepare a lovely pitch for your son, bowl him a few in the nets to get his eye in and then offer a grave shake of the head whenever an opposing bowler appealed for lbw in the match. As the first of 12 children, Hobbs also eventually had an entire team of brothers and sisters to practise with. Yet his basic skills were honed alone

– Bradmanlike – by hitting a tennis ball against the wall of a fives court with a stump. He never had any coaching.

He played for Cambridgeshire in his teens and his services were offered to Essex, the nearest first-class county, in 1904. He was rejected so went to join his idol Tom Hayward at Surrey. As it happened, his first Championship game was against Essex. Put straight in to open, he scored 155. Red faces all round Chelmsford, you would imagine. After nine more centuries in the next couple of years he got an England call-up for the Ashes tour of 1907–8 and made 83 in his first Test innings in Melbourne. He had to wait 23 innings for his first Test hundred (against South Africa) but after that reeled them off with elan. By 1911 he had eclipsed the legendary Victor Trumper as the best batsman in the world (although at that stage only England, Australia and South Africa played Test cricket).

With a light and compact build, Hobbs had a high, flowing backlift, great balance, and moved nimbly into position. Joe Root might be a modern comparison. He seemed to know instinctively where the ball was going to be before it was delivered, a mark of most great batsmen. With superb wrists and deft placement, he was exceptionally good on a tricky pitch. He was expert at dabbing an awkward ball short or wide of a fielder and strolling a run, and was prolific off the back foot.

He was a self-deprecating character, though, who permanently shunned the limelight and, if Surrey were going well on a flat track, often gave his wicket away to a toiling bowler and left the field chuckling to himself. According to his first regular England opening partner, Wilfred Rhodes, 'he could have got 399 hundreds if he'd wanted'. The famous writer RC Robertson-Glasgow, who played for Somerset, described playing against Hobbs at The Oval as 'like bowling to God on concrete'.

The First World War interrupted his serene progress to 100 hundreds (achieved in 1923) after which he forged an opening partnership for England with Yorkshire's Herbert Sutcliffe that has no equals. They put on 3,249 runs together and averaged 87 for the first wicket (20 more than any other regular pair in Test history). Their partnership may have been a southern-polish–northern-grit cliché, but they shared 15 century-opening partnerships for England. One of these was a defiant, brilliant 172 on a brute of a 'sticky-dog' at The Oval. The saturated pitch required them to show incredible judgement and fortitude and take many blows on the body, and the partnership was instrumental in England winning the final Test of 1926 and regaining the Ashes for the first time since 1912. (This Test was, incidentally, the first in England that had been extended to a fourth day.)

Off the field Hobbs kept a low profile. He married his childhood sweetheart, was a regular churchgoer and never drank alcohol. When he finally equalled WG Grace's record tally of 125 centuries he celebrated with a glass of ginger beer. He scored 100 hundreds after his 40th birthday and was still playing for Surrey (and going in first and scoring centuries) at the age of 51. He was knighted in 1953 and in 2000 came third (after Bradman and Sobers) in the *Wisden* poll to declare the greatest cricketers of the 20th century. He is the finest opening batsman who ever lived. There is really no argument about that.

★

Hobbs' 1924–5 Ashes tour as summed up by 'Ignotus' in *The Cricketer*.

Hobbs is the master bat of his time, and his reputation had much to lose and little to gain by a further visit to Australia at the age of 42. That he enhanced his reputation – and no one will dispute it – was certainly remarkable. His scores in the Test matches were 115, 57, 154, 22, 119, 27, 66, 0, and 13, and his first-wicket partnership with Sutcliffe of 282 runs in the second match, when the Australians had made 600 runs, was a prodigious effort. In a word, he is indisputably our greatest living cricketer, a batsman pre-eminent in any age and unique in his own generation.

Plum Warner celebrates possibly Hobbs' most significant England innings as he sets up victory in 1926 with Herbert Sutcliffe to regain the Ashes on his home ground.

When England went in again I must confess that I felt anxious. So much depended on a good start. Once again did Hobbs and Sutcliffe prove equal to the occasion, and I can only repeat what I have said of these two batsmen before, that they are even greater, if possible, in temperament than in skill. They are fit men indeed to go in first for England.

Finer cricket on a difficult wicket than Hobbs and Sutcliffe played I have never seen. Much, almost everything, indeed depended on them. If one or both had failed, England might easily have lost five or six men before lunch, for the ball took the spin quickly, and when the sun – which at first hid its face – came out after the first hour, the ball, particularly from Richardson's bowling, kicked up frequently in a disconcerting manner.

But once again the two famous batsmen proved equal to the greatest emergency, and no praise can be too high for what they did. They have made their names immortal in the history of cricket.

Only three runs were made off nine overs from Richardson, and the manner in which both batsmen – and particularly

Hobbs, who took charge for the most part at the end to which Richardson was bowling – gave the rising ball the 'dead bat' was masterly.

I have never seen Hobbs show himself a greater batsman than he did on Tuesday, and Sutcliffe was equally great. Tremendous was the applause when the two men came back to the pavilion at the luncheon interval, with the score at 161 – Hobbs 97, Sutcliffe 53. Almost immediately after lunch Hobbs completed his hundred, and pandemonium broke loose, the game being interrupted for several minutes while cheer after cheer rent the air. In all his long career he has never played a finer or more valuable innings.

That first wicket stand of our most famous pair of 172 made victory almost a certainty for us. Had either of them failed, we might well have been out for a total of 180 or 200.

That they did not fail us at a time of most desperate crisis was only in keeping with their reputation. Never had English cricket known a more dauntless pair: the greater the task the greater their endeavour.

No.2 Len Hutton

There is a terrible old joke that puts into perspective Len Hutton's inestimable value to England. Two Yorkshire neighbours arrive at the Headingley Test but realise they have forgotten their sandwiches. Being a Yorkshireman, one goes back home to get them. When he returns he has a grave look on his face. 'I've got bad news,' he says. ''Ouse has burnt down, wife's run off and kids are in't street in tears.' 'And I've got bad news for thee too,' says his mate. ''Utton's out!'

It is said that northerners mature earlier than people from

the south and, rather like Geoff Boycott and more recently Joe Root, Len Hutton was already the complete player at the age of 22. By this time he had already scored 2,888 runs in a season for Yorkshire and compiled the highest individual Test match score – 364 against the 1938 Australians at The Oval – in just his sixth appearance for England. This effort lasted 13 hours, during which he faced 847 balls, and is comfortably the longest Test innings (by balls faced) ever played. So his immaculate technique and immense staying power were already well established.

He was averaging 67 in Tests when the Second World War interrupted his progress, and a severe injury to his left arm in a training accident inconvenienced him for a while. But after the war he continued his monumental scoring feats – dealing with the twin handicaps of one arm shorter than the other and treacherous uncovered pitches – with sublime footwork and deft touch. He was prolific through the offside – his extra-cover drive was a national treasure – and it was said that his movements to the ball were every bit as slick and certain as Bradman's. He was a pragmatist, too; when asked how do you play fast bowling, famously replying, 'from t'other end'.

As much as his indefatigable batting, Hutton is legendary for becoming the first professional to captain England (in 1952), a post he ascended to despite not captaining Yorkshire who still insisted on having amateurs in charge. Preaching his simple mantras – 'sell thy wicket dear and give 'em nowt' – his promotion had instant results, enabling England to hold the Australians at bay for the first time in two decades in 1953.

The first four Tests of that series were drawn, after which England, thanks to Hutton's determined 82 in England's first innings on a dusty pitch at The Oval, took a precious first-innings lead. Jim Laker and Tony Lock routed the Aussies in the second innings, meaning England needed just 132 to regain the Ashes for the first time in 18 years.

The tension was palpable at a packed ground as Hutton and Bill Edrich set off in pursuit of this modest target, and on 24 Hutton set off for an unlikely third to deepish square leg and was run out. The *Daily Telegraph*'s EW Swanton wrote, 'I have not known a similar moment of complete, quiet, stupefaction.' Edrich and Compton held their nerve, however, and England won by eight wickets, not only regaining the urn but defeating Australia at home for the first time in 27 years.

There was no triumphant street parade or reception at 10 Downing Street (Winston Churchill wasn't much of a cricket fan), but Hutton got his due recognition with a knighthood a couple of years later, Her Majesty the Queen politely overlooking his famous faux pas of asking Australia to bat in Brisbane in 1954–5 when he won the toss. They made 601 for 8 and won by an innings. It was practically the only blot on a magnificent career. Compton called him 'the greatest opening batsman I have ever seen'.

A quiet man off the field, he was not quite as painstaking as chairman of England selectors as he had been as batsman and captain. Having selected Graham Gooch for his first Test in 1975 he asked the debutant if he had ever played against Australia before. 'Well, yes,' replied Gooch, 'you chose me for the MCC XI against the Aussies two weeks ago' [a match in which Gooch made 75]. 'Did I?' said Hutton. 'Sorry, I don't watch much cricket these days.'

★

The Cricketer reports on Hutton's record-breaking innings at The Oval in 1938.

Of Hutton's wonderful innings it is impossible to speak too highly. At the close of the second day's play he had been batting for 11 hours and 5 minutes and 27 4s. On this day he never gave a semblance of a chance, and it was indeed a truly remarkable contribution of skill, concentration and endurance for a player who was only 22 on June 23. It may be urged that Hutton made his runs slowly, but he is nevertheless an extremely interesting batsman to watch.

Gradually Hutton approached Bradman's record of 334 and though he failed to take advantage of a no-ball from O'Reilly a beautiful cut off Fleetwood-Smith, which sent the ball to the boundary, gave him the record. The crowd roared their approval and Bradman raced to shake hands with the young Yorkshireman. The Australians toasted him and the spectators sang 'For he's a jolly good fellow' and cheered again and again.

In 1950–51, Hutton stamped his authority as the best batsman in the post-Bradman world, as seen by Ray Robinson.

Hutton's play won him the rare distinction of being acknowledged by both sides as the greatest batsman in the world. He topped the list of points in a contest for the best player afield. The calm Yorkshireman was the Atlas of England's batting, taking the weight almost unaided in some of the tour's darkest hours. I believe the experiment of making Simpson Washbrook's opening partner in the first two Tests was designed more to give the Notts batsman a start before spin bowling appeared than (as many guessed) to shield Hutton from rip-snorting attack by Australia's high-speed bowlers. Hutton was seldom in doubt against the fast stuff, wherever it pitched, and his driving of Lindwall was one of the highlights of the season. The only times he fell short of his own classic standard were infrequent moments of over-stretched forward play against slow spinners, chiefly Ian Johnson's.

From Brisbane's sticky wicket onwards, Hutton adjusted his play incomparably to every kind of pitch encountered. When he carried his bat throughout England's first innings in the Adelaide Test for 156, nobody else reached 30. As batsman and slipfielder he was on the field for almost 4¾ days of the match – a model of concentration and stamina.

No.3 Donald Bradman

Bradman was a freak. The statistics back that up. A Test batting average of 99.94 that is 60 per cent greater than the next five men on the list (Adam Voges, Steve Smith, Graeme Pollock, George Headley and Herbert Sutcliffe) who all average around 61. The most runs ever made in a five Test series – 974 in his orgy of scoring in 1930 (average 129). A total of 29 hundreds in 80 Test innings. That is a century every 2.75 innings. No other prolific batsman, in history, has managed a century in fewer than every *six* innings (Sachin Tendulkar, for instance, made a Test century once every 6.45 innings. For Ricky Ponting the figure was one in seven). Incredibly, Bradman maintained a similar rate throughout his first-class career (117 hundreds in 338 games which equates to 2.88 innings per hundred). He was literally twice as good as any other batsman who ever lived. And before we infer that Bradman must have therefore been a very selfish player, it is worth also pointing out that 22 of his 29 Test hundreds led to an Australian victory.

That Test average – 99.94 – is tantalising. It is so close to 100 per cent perfection as attained by, say, Torvill and Dean with those 12 6.0s for their Bolero in the 1984 Olympics or Mark Spitz's seven gold medals in Munich in 1970, as to bear comparison with their achievements. But Bradman sustained this astonishing output for *two decades* (interrupted by the Second World War). The 'failure' to finish with an average of 100 gives him just a hint of mortality. A hint.

So why was he so good? He was an entirely natural, uncoached batsman. He famously reared his batting ability round the back of his parents' house, using a stump to hit a golf ball that he bounced off the brick stand of their water tank. The 'wicket' was the laundry door. The ball rebounded off the brick at strange and unpredictable angles. 'The golf ball came back at great speed,' he wrote, 'and to hit it at all with this round stump was no easy task. This extraordinary and primitive idea was purely a matter of amusement, but looking back over the years, I can see how it must have developed the co-ordination of brain, eye and muscle which was to serve me so well in important matches later on.'

It influenced his batting method, which was regarded as unconventional at the time. The MCC coaching manual – a sort of cricketer's bible – recommended that the bat rest on the back toe and be taken back roughly straight towards the stumps while the batsman himself remained still. That was being taught even into the 1980s. Bradman, however, stood with his bat between his feet 'because it was a comfortable and natural position'. Instead of standing motionless as the ball was delivered, he began to move just before it was released. 'It saves a precious fraction of a second and appears to serve the same purpose as a preliminary waggle before your golf swing.'

His backlift went out at an angle in the direction of the slips. It came back round in a loop. It became known as the 'rotation' method. Bradman argued that although this was not ideal for defence, it was best for attacking strokeplay as the movement got you onto your toes and gave your body momentum. He felt that taking the bat straight back was more unnatural and 'virtually eliminates pull shots and cut shots' – his two signature strokes.

The hand-eye co-ordination Bradman developed from his golf-ball games – his 'rotation' method – was fundamental to his success. He learnt how to place the ball with his bat, how to move both towards and back from where the ball bounced to have better control of the shot. It taught him the essentials of watching the ball carefully and concentrating hard – lack of precision playing a fast-moving golf ball with a stump could give you bruised fingers or missing front teeth. It also ensured he used his wrists to keep the ball down (he rarely hit in the air), facilitating that famous quiz question who hit more sixes in Test cricket – Don Bradman or Devon Malcolm? The answer, of course, is Malcolm with seven.

He was famously ruthless, addicted to big scores. Through his career he made one quadruple century, six triples and 37 doubles. It could have been Wally Hammond's fault. After Bradman's remorseless run-making (including two triple-hundreds in his teens) earned him a first Test cap, he was consigned to 12th man for the next Test. He ended up fielding for most of one day as Hammond racked up 251. From then on it seemed to be his mission to outdo anything Hammond achieved. He was merciless on bowlers, never sweated or seemed to suffer from nerves or anxiety. He was never dismissed in the nineties in Tests. His self-belief was total. Even in the Bodyline series, when England went all out to exploit his perceived weakness to short balls on leg stump, he still averaged 56. Nursing a leg injury in his late thirties, he dropped himself down to No.6 in one Test, compiled a six-hour 234 before succumbing to fatigue. 'There's runs out there if only a man had legs!' he said afterwards. He was unstoppable, invincible, impenetrable.

And so were the Australian team he led to England after the war in 1948. They won the Test series 4-0, and went through the entire first-class programme of 30 matches unbeaten (won 22, drawn eight). After his famous duck in his final Test (bowled by Eric Hollies' googly) he finished the tour off with, yes, you have guessed it, three hundreds, before putting his bat away for the last time.

Two factors slightly mitigate his phenomenal achievements. He did not play a single Test outside Australia or England, meaning he was never exposed to the dusty conditions of the subcontinent or the jute matting of South Africa. He also played the first nine years of his Test career with the old lbw Law which declared that you couldn't be out leg before if the ball pitched outside *off* stump (meaning virtually most deliveries bowled by a right-armer). So he played predominantly back, using his pads as a second line of defence. It was spectacularly successful. In his first 52 Test innings he was out lbw only three times – for 18, 167 and 226. The Law was changed in 1937 to allow lbw decisions to balls pitching *outside* off-stump. It did not help much. Bradman was brilliant at exploiting every conceivable facet or nuance of the game. 'Style?' he said quizzically. 'I know nothing about style. All I'm after is runs.'

One could go on. But let's leave the ultimate description of Bradman to the *History of Cricket*. He had, it said, 'a quite abnormally quick reaction commanding immediate obedience from a perfectly co-ordinated body to the message of an icily concentrated mind'. He was the most utterly dominant sportsman in his own field, ever. Exactly, a freak.

★

The Cricketer's 'Second Slip' watches on in amazement as Bradman's staggering achievements in 1930 unfold.

This astonishing player, not quite 22, has demonstrated once again the truth of the old saying that records are made to be broken. Against us at Nottingham he took 131, and, of course, no one has forgotten his 254 at Lord's. Then comes his splendid performance at Leeds, where he showed us no mercy. In the first three matches alone he has beaten all the previous records of his countrymen for the whole series of these games. Nor do we see where he is going to end, for with youth on his side all that is necessary is continued good health. Probably the feature of his play is that he never lifts the balls into the air when driving – the long hop may be occasionally hit off the ground, but as often as not he keeps it on the floor. When one considers the circumstances, that he is a stranger to all the different surroundings of our many grounds, that he has never before played on our wickets, that he ran into such a May as may fitly be described as having been abominable, we cannot but the more wonder.

At the end of the season, with the Ashes back in Australian hands, 'Second Slip' attempts to explain what had just been witnessed.

The young batsman, Bradman – 'Mr Badman' to Sir James Barrie – has indeed broken all records. His 1,000 runs in May was a magnificent feat for a young player coming to this country for the first time. Nor did he ever stop, even to the last match he was making runs. As a rule, batsmen in making these huge scores have luck in being missed, but in Bradman's case it cannot be said that he was a lucky player. Methodical to a degree, with a lightning eye and excellent wrist, he was so quick on his feet that he was able to get well over the ball, seldom, if ever, lifting it off the ground: his record of sixes must be comparatively small. An analysis of his strokes shows that for the most part he was content to place the ball off the middle and leg stumps, cut late and square, and frequently to make an off-drive.

By 1938, Bradman's feats had exhausted all superlatives, as EL Roberts writes in anticipation of that year's series.

Dictionary makers of the future will be faced with the task of finding a definition for a new word – Bradmanism – and perhaps an adequate solution of this verbal problem would be 'an infinite capacity for unlimited rungetting'.

Bradman's name will always be associated in the minds of the cricket public with scoring on a colossal scale. No batsman since WG Grace has made runs in such quantities and with such determined and consistent persistence.

Bradman is Australia's most useful 'twelfth man' because, statistically, he is the equivalent of two good batsmen. Fortunately for England's bowlers he does not have to be dismissed twice in each innings.

The Cricketer's report of Bradman's series winning performances that summer.

> We have exhausted our vocabulary of praise in favour of Bradman. There never has been such a batsman. He wins matches for his side and he saves them as he did at Trent Bridge and at Lord's. And we hold that people are sometimes apt to forget in the glory of his strokeplay that he is the possessor of an exceedingly strong defence. This was his third century in Test matches this season (out of five innings), and his 15th against England, and he is not yet 30. His concentration is as marked as his skill, and his running between wickets amazingly swift. He makes every possible run.

No.4 Wally Hammond

In any other era Walter Hammond would have been the greatest cricketer of his generation. Because his Test career coincided almost exactly with Bradman's (1927–47) he had to be content with second best. A majestic batsman in the classic mould, he was dashing and devastating in equal measure. He bestrode the crease with his bat as Caligula ruled Rome with his sword. When fast bowlers bounced, Hammond hooked. If they pitched up, he drove. If spinners gave the ball too much air he advanced up the pitch and smote them into the distance.

Oddly, Hammond learnt the game in China and Malta, where his father was stationed in the war, and could have played for Kent (where he was born) before ending up at Gloucestershire. Immaculately turned out with blue handkerchief protruding from hip pocket, he cut an immediate dash as soon as he strode to the wicket and set about the bowling with regal authority, cover driving with a flourish and specialising in a back-foot drive which sent the ball scorching past the bowler. In his (and Bradman's) first Ashes in 1928–9 he scored 905 runs (then the record for a Test series) at an average of 113.

Bradman, of course, upstaged this in the next Ashes (with his aggregate of 974 in 1930) and, in a way, Hammond created Bradman, or at least his superiority complex. A 20-year personal duel commenced, in which Hammond can only claim to have scored one victory – his 336 not out against New Zealand in 1933 (including 10 straight sixes), which was the new highest Test score and had eclipsed Bradman's 334 in 1930. In every other way (Test wins, number of centuries, captaincy of his country) the Australian had him trumped.

The last of these issues – the captaincy of his country – was an absurdity. After Douglas Jardine was relieved of his post, Hammond was the obvious man to take over. He was reeling off 3,000 runs in a season for Gloucestershire and numerous double- and triple-centuries, but he was a professional, so the 'rules' didn't allow him to be captain. He filled the void in his life by bedding a lot of women. It was said that Hammond had two ruling passions – his cricket bat and his genitals (he was not the first premier batsman that this applied to and he certainly wasn't the last). But taking wickets as well with his lively fast-medium bowling and snaffling catches in the slips (820 in his first-class career – the third most ever by a fielder) he *was* the English team. So for the 1938 Ashes he relinquished his match fees, became a director of a tyre company and was put in charge.

After a drawn first Test at Trent Bridge, in which Bradman, also now captain, defended stoutly for 144 not out, Hammond produced a command performance at Lord's. His

240 – taking just five hours and including one rifle crack of a straight drive which rebounded off the pavilion wall and came straight back to the bowler – was said by the cricket historian CLR James to be the greatest innings he had ever seen. But Bradman defied England again with another defeated century and Australia went on to retain the Ashes. At least Hammond had the consolation of finally overtaking Bradman's tally of Test hundreds with his 22nd (also an English record) against West Indies in 1939.

But it was to be his last major Test innings. He played less frequently for Gloucestershire in 1946, the first season after the war, yet still topped the English first-class averages for the eighth successive time (with 1,783 runs at an average of 84.9). But his messy divorce, covered unsympathetically by the press, caused him to withdraw and he became alienated from the England team, despite still being captain. He was also infuriated by Bradman's decision not to walk on 28 in the Brisbane Test of 1946–7 (he went on to make 187) and the relationship between them, which was at best grudging, deteriorated significantly. Hammond retired from first-class cricket soon after the tour. He finished with 167 centuries and 50,551 runs, the seventh most of all time.

Batting throughout his career with great style and panache, he was in many ways the antidote to the more clinical Bradman. Len Hutton said, 'I'd prefer to see an hour of Walter Hammond than eight hours of Bradman.' That would make a more than worthy epitaph.

★

On his death in 1965, Hammond's monumental 1928–9 tour of Australia was recalled by wicketkeeper George Duckworth.

Hammond hardly played a game without leaving his imprint as batsman, fielder or bowler. His first Australian trip under Chapman in 1928/9 is freshest in my memory although he was outstanding in his next two visits. His long association at the wicket with Jardine and his cover driving was so fierce against Grimmett that two fielders were deployed on the boundary edge at deep extra cover. On this tour Hammond would split his fielding activities with Patsy Hendren. After occupying the slip position early in the day he would go into the country after tea 'for exercise' as he called it. But he later justly earned the title of the game's greatest slip fielder and there was no more electrifying sight than to see Hammond on an English sticky wicket standing only a yard away from the wicketkeeper and catching everything.

While not on the same level, and overshadowed by other events, Hammond was mightily impressive on the 1932–3 tour, as Plum Warner reviews.

WR Hammond stands by himself as the best allrounder in the world today. He is indeed a glorious cricketer who is at his best as a batsman when playing a forcing game, which is his natural bent. To an exact sense of timing he adds great physical strength, and, when he makes up his mind to hit, the ball literally flies off his bat. A beautiful off-side player, his back strokes were as hard and as clean as his forward or driving strokes – and when he was in, cover point, mid-off, and extra cover were kept very busy indeed. To their credit be it said that they deprived him of many runs. On the on-side his stroke play is far stronger and more varied than it was. An easy style, quickness of foot and wrists of steel made him most attractive to watch even when he was scoring slowly.

One of the most dramatic moments in the Test matches was when Wall sent his off-stump flying in the first innings at Melbourne. He had begun with a couple of 4s, and looked about to play a big innings, and on his dismissal such a shout went up as I have never heard on any cricket ground in the world. There were 63,000 spectators present, and for several minutes they yelled and cheered and waved their hats and handkerchiefs. The almost frantic rejoicing was a rare compliment to a great batsman.

Hammond was also a valuable bowler, and in the second innings of the first Test bowled four or five overs as good as anything Barnes ever sent down, during which he got out McCabe and Richardson, when wickets from our point of view were needed. His fielding, too, in the slips and on the leg side, to Larwood, reached something like perfection. Everything Hammond does on the cricket field bears the hallmark of a natural genius. A fine cricket brain completes the ideal cricketer.

No.5 Allan Border

Fast-forward to the modern day. Well, the era of bouncers and helmets and a higher-octane brand of cricket anyway. Through great change in the game, a decade of West Indian dominance and the advance of one-day cricket, Allan Border reigned supreme. A tenacious left-hander oozing fighting spirit, he was one of only three batsmen who played throughout the 1980s – what one might call the black and blue era given the number of very fast bowlers (and dodgy pitches) around – to have a Test average of more than 50. The others were Javed Miandad and Viv Richards, who was obviously spared having to face his own fearsome pacemen. It is some achievement.

Border will not be in many people's lists of great players. He was an unspectacular left-hander, one of those who seems not to play many memorable shots, but you look up and he already has 40. He was busy at the crease and quick to spot a short ball which he despatched through the offside with a blur of arms and a belligerent intent. His shots were often crude but they sent the ball skimming across the outfield and his cut was ferocious.

Getting into the Australian side for the first time when it was decimated by World Series Cricket in 1978–9, he started at No.6 but soon became the regular No.3. His returns were decent, but this was in a poor Australian side so they went mainly unnoticed. But it was a measure of his growing reputation that he was usually regarded as the key wicket in the 1981 (Botham's) Ashes and after he was out the innings often fell away.

A loyal foot soldier rather than a born leader, he was made captain of the Australians after Kim Hughes' tearful resignation in 1984, but his team twice sacrificed the Ashes (in 1985 and 1986–7). He was gaining invaluable experience playing for Essex, however, making bucket-loads of runs and helping them to the 1986 County Championship title.

More importantly, he was observing Essex captain Keith Fletcher's methods and forensic knowledge of county players and he used these to critical effect in the 1989 Ashes. He joined forces with the ex-Australian captain Bobby Simpson (as coach) and discarded his previous jovial demeanour. He was soon nicknamed Captain Grumpy for his prickly attitude, but set the tone with a succession of feisty innings and presided over a triumphant tour, winning the series 4-0. (He had also taken the critical wicket of Mike Gatting – reverse sweeping – in the 1987 World Cup final to give Australia their first ever global title.)

The West Indies remained unconquered home and away, until the classic Adelaide Test of 1993. Australia were one Test up with one to play and needed 185 to win the fourth Test and seal the series. This was their chance. They collapsed to 144 for 9, but then Tim May and Craig McDermott forged a valiant 10th-wicket partnership. But with two runs to win, McDermott gloved Courtney Walsh behind and Australia had lost by one run. The series was now level 1-1 but, to Border's dismay, Australia were blown away in the final Test in Perth by Curtly Ambrose and Ian Bishop and lost by an innings. Border suffered the ultimate ignominy of a pair in the match.

He continued to offer granite-like substance to Australia's middle order for another two years, becoming the nation's leading run-scorer during an unbroken sequence of 153 Test appearances, the longest by any player in Test history. Allan Border was a survivor; AB stood for Aussie Battler. Australia's player of the year is now presented with the Allan Border medal in recognition of his huge contribution.

★

Border was a bright spark for Australia in the 1981 series with hundreds in the final two Tests. Tom Graveney was particularly impressed with the left-hander.

> To me the man Australia had to thank for their great improvement was Allan Border, surely the best batsman on either side. I have watched a great deal of cricket in my life and I don't think I've seen anyone pick up the length of the ball any quicker than Allan. This is the most important thing in making batting a much less complicated business.

When waiting for the ball to be bowled to him, Border stands still: this may sound simple, but it is amazing how few of today's players in fact do stay steady. Because of his picking the length, Allan is a fine player both off the back foot and when he is driving. To put it in a nutshell he makes a single movement whatever stroke he is playing. If the ball is pitched up, his right foot goes to the pitch of the ball and when it is short his back foot goes behind the line. If I had a son young enough, I would tell him to watch and copy Allan Border because he was the most accomplished player in the series.

In his final Ashes series, Border registered his highest Test score in the match that sealed a third successive Ashes win. Richard Hutton reports.

Australia's captain takes time to find his touch these days, and with Boon being similarly restrained by a better spell from Caddick, Australia were limited to 98 from 33 overs in the final session.

Bicknell's dedication to line and length earned him a 90-minute spell on the second morning. He bowled as well as anyone against Border, who again availed of a lengthy playing-in period. After losing Boon, Border and Steve Waugh launched their partnership with care against some steadier England bowling and a gradual but visible deterioration of the bounce. Thus England's fate was sealed, and as if to underline the hopelessness of their cause, Thorpe was introduced as a sixth bowler when McCague's stamina was impaired by some severe treatment from Border.

The day, a miserable 40th birthday for Graham Gooch, had become one for the record books. Border and Waugh were playing with a clinical precision of Bradmanesque proportions. It was therefore entirely appropriate that on resuming on the third morning and reaching 200 Border's score became the highest by an Australian at Headingley other than Bradman's two scores of over 300 in the 1930s.

No.6 Ian Botham

Beefy. One word that invariably silences loud Australians. From the day in 1977 that a 21-year-old Ian Botham got into a fight with Australia's hard man Ian Chappell they could not handle him. He pummelled their bowlers and routed their batsmen and took blinding catches and drank them under the table. He bedded their women, too. Well, definitely one anyway. He rampaged across the Australian psyche for almost two decades. He battered them into submission. He won the mother country bragging rights over her upstart offspring. He was so vigorous and audacious and outspoken Australians thought he was one of them. That is an Aussie's ultimate mark of respect.

It is 40 years since Ian Botham's Test debut, at Trent Bridge in July 1977. It feels like yesterday, helped by the advent of YouTube, of course. The slim physique, the nervous grin, the loping run, the lively action, the exploratory wide delivery outside the off-stump, the drag-on by Greg Chappell and the exultant celebration, the first of 383 such exuberant dances down the pitch in his 15-year Test career, this one in front of the Queen, who had made a rare visit to Nottingham. Just to please Her Majesty he took four more wickets that day – emboldened by the words of his county captain Brian Close before the match: 'Don't let those Australians intimidate you,' he said. Not long afterwards he was intimidating them. He was like a character from *Boy's Own*.

Was Botham a batsman who bowled, or a bowler who batted, asked the former Indian player and commentator Sanjay Manjrekar one day. It is a good question that is often asked of allrounders. Andrew Flintoff was definitely a bowler who batted (though he desperately wanted to be regarded the other way around). Jacques Kallis was a batsman who bowled. Garfield Sobers, too (despite starting in Test cricket as a bowler who batted No.8). Botham? A bowler who batted. Just. Why? Mainly because he took his bowling slightly more seriously. He applied himself to the task of taking wickets, of working batsmen over. He wanted to bowl. Often when he was on a roll you could not get the ball off him. Batting was his relaxation. It was fun.

This is not to say he didn't take batting seriously. He had a very good basic method, played straight, watched the ball carefully. He had the ability to hit good balls for four, rising on his toes to strike short deliveries on the up, carve them over cover or clonk them back over the bowler's head. No one can make 14 Test hundreds – yes, FOURTEEN – as many as Marcus Trescothick and Allan Lamb and more than Peter May, John Edrich and Tom Graveney – and not be an excellent batsman.

He was daunting to bowl at. The railway sleeper of a bat was wielded above his shoulders like an axe ready to be brought down with crunching intent and deposit a misdirected ball over the ropes. Or even a well-directed one. You knew he had the power to humiliate you. In one Sunday League game in 1983, Somerset needed 15 to win from the last over bowled by Middlesex's fearsome West Indian quick Wayne Daniel. Botham only got the strike with three balls to go and 12 needed. He hooked an attempted bouncer for six, missed the next with a wild swipe and then boomed the final ball, a low full toss, into the crowd over deep square leg. And yet

I also saw him block for four hours on the fifth day against Pakistan at The Oval in 1987 to save the game and the series.

But his bowling was special, particularly when he was young. He bounded friskily to the wicket, landed strongly at the crease and unleashed questioning, searching, demanding deliveries, full of length, swinging late one way, or the other, at good pace – mid-80s at least – jumping wide of the crease for a variation, purveying the odd mischievous slower ball – which we all copied – and saving rib-jarring bouncers aimed under the armpit for tailenders. Geoff Boycott liked those. 'They don't like 'em in there!' he said. Botham was always prospecting for wickets and he celebrated each prize with elated satisfaction.

He gave most of his energy to his bowling, meaning he didn't have that much left for his batting. That is why he tended to play swashbuckling-type innings despite having the technique to bat in more measured fashion. He just did not have the physical, or mental, reserves to play long, drawn-out innings. And batting (and spectating) would not have been such fun if he had.

His other great attribute was his self-belief. This – a deep-seated conviction that nothing was impossible and that he was always right – came out in all sorts of ways, from the type of practice he indulged in (hardly any) to the pre-match team talks, to the insistence on 'one more over', the overcoming of career-threatening injuries, the ability to take out leading members of the opposition and getting them completely wrecked while he was able to front up the next morning as fresh as a daisy, and the pronouncements on subjects he knew nothing about, invariably terminating a losing argument with a good-humoured but emphatic 'well, how many Test wickets did you get then?'. Once, at Durham, the team met to discuss a one-day match and went through the opposition's strengths player by player.

Botham listened for a while but eventually had had enough. 'Look,' he said, 'if we do our jobs, they can't do theirs.' He was right. The match was won comfortably.

He was Australia's great tormentor. England never lost a series against them in which he played a full part. It carried on even after he departed Test cricket. He waited until Australia visited Durham in 1993 to announce his retirement from the game. He looked outside the window at the imminent rain. 'Look at that approaching thunderstorm,' he said. 'There's that much metal in my body now if I get struck by lightning you'll all die!' When play got underway he treated them to a cameo with the bat then watched gleefully from slip as Durham bowled Australia out and made them follow on.

With an hour or so left for play on the final day he came on to bowl for the last time. Australia were 50 for 1, David Boon and Matthew Hayden at the crease. A young Steve Waugh, the next man in, was on tenterhooks as the great man lolloped to the crease. He went through his complete repertoire.

'Cor blimey!' said Allan Border.

'What's he tried now?' asked Merv Hughes, lying down.

'One that Boony couldn't reach,' Shane Warne said.

'He'll get him in a minute, you bet!' retorted Hughes.

You could feel the reverence in their voices.

And then, after 11 eventful but unusually fruitless overs, he was done. He kept wicket for a few minutes – in no pads and batting gloves for some reason – and then the match was over and he left the field to a standing ovation. 'That's part of our childhood gone,' said Chris Scott, Durham's wicketkeeper. He was right. Botham was a hero, a colossus, omnipotent. Such was the esteem in which he was held that he could call Australians 'convicts' and they would actually agree with him.

★

In *The Cricketer*'s 1981 Annual, Somerset's Peter Roebuck paid tribute to Botham, recognising better than anyone the crucible that his teammate had been through, to come out the other end with a bigger smile on his face than ever.

> With his luck and fortitude, Ian for long bestrode the cricket scene, making hay while the sun shone. He batted majestically, fielded brilliantly and bowled incisively.
>
> His bowling perhaps showed the attraction of the man, all burly determination and bold variation. His action was full of bounce, his deliveries full of nip and his eye wicked with defiance. An unpredictable handful for batsmen; an optimistic, vigorous cricketer, sometimes brilliant, apparently utterly out of his depth at other times.
>
> He strode from success to success, dominating international cricket. It seemed as if it could never end. Yet quite suddenly it did. In 1980 Ian experienced sustained failure for the first time, and it did not rain, it poured.
>
> Suddenly he was under attack from all quarters. Newspapers said he was overweight. He was prevented from playing soccer for Scunthorpe. His name hit the headlines for speeding and on assault charges. As England's new captain he was heavily criticised for his lack of form and worst of all in Trinidad in 1981 for his 'irresponsible' swipe at Viv Richards' gentle offbreak. Suddenly Ian's every move was subject to close scrutiny and intense analysis. Where before his indiscretions were tolerated as a part of his Viking spirit, now his failures were held up and scorned.
>
> As captain of England he resembled a caged tiger. Eventually the wheel came full circle to everyone's delight. Botham

resigned as captain, aware that his reign was over anyhow. Suddenly he blossomed again, winning three Test matches and the Ashes for England by a series of devastating performances. His batting was more mighty, more majestic than it had ever been before. His bowling recovered much of its wit and sparkle and, at last, he was catching flies on the slips again.

No doubt Brearley did much to stimulate this revival, encouraging Ian to open out his personality to have the courage to risk all again. Perhaps Brearley might have, when Botham holed out off Richards that infamous time, rebuked Ian not for hitting out but for holding back.

Now Keith Fletcher is captain and it will be surprising if he is not deeply grateful for the support of cricket's boldest buccaneer.

In his finest performance with the bat post-1981, Botham set England on the way to victory at Brisbane in the first Test of 1986–7, as Christopher Martin-Jenkins describes.

Botham entered the arena bare-headed, confident and almost patronising to all young Australians around him. He was not beaten, so far as one could detect, all day, except when occasionally he slogged, and missed. He played himself in with patience and some 20 minutes before lunch suddenly unleashed a formidable volley of strokes hitting three effortless fours in one over from Reid, a straight drive and two chipped to midwicket off his toes.

The roles were reversed for a short while after lunch with Gower starting to play altogether more solidly, his off-side strokes going to mid-off rather than gully and runs being picked up fluently off his legs, while Botham struggled to retrieve his timing. But Gower, who had already played a couple of his famous swivel-footed pulls through midwicket, was well caught attempting another.

Botham was on 62 when this happened and Border now settled for a policy of giving him singles to a deep-set field, meanwhile attacking his partners. It seldom pays to offer the initiative to any batsman and Botham certainly wasn't complaining. Whilst Emburey was at the wicket he scored a good many twos by dabbing the ball well short of the eight boundary fielders and when DeFreitas joined him runs soon began to flow again from both ends.

Botham reached his hundred shortly before tea with a cut and a straight drive for twos off the first two balls of an over from Hughes and he celebrated by hooking the next one for six, then hooking and on-driving three more crashing fours in the next three balls – 22 from one over and all this off a local Brisbane boy! It was a shame indeed that fewer than 8,000 people were there to see him.

He wins the fourth Test, and with it the Ashes, with the ball. Here's CMJ again.

Having been 83 for 3 at the end of an exhilarating morning's cricket before a crowd of heartening proportions, 58,203, Australia lost their last seven wickets for only 33 runs as Small, with an inspired piece of seam bowling, and Ian Botham, running in off only 12 paces and varying his pace cleverly, scythed through the middle order with almost embarrassing haste.

Dean Jones, in a stylish and confident innings, was comfortably the highest scorer, but if there were two more important wickets than his they were those of Marsh and Border, the two men with the tightest techniques. Both fell to Botham, one hooking, the other cutting. The Botham hex on Australia? It certainly seemed as though neither batsman would have played so rash a stroke against another bowler. But it was impossible not to admire Botham's determined and intelligent bowling in conditions which called on the bowlers to hit the pitch with the seam and wait for the batsman to edge the ball. In addition, of course, Botham had only recently recovered from his torn muscle under the ribs and was still unable to let himself go without pain.

No.7 Adam Gilchrist

Adam Gilchrist was a game changer in a macro as well as micro sense. Not only did he frequently convert ordinary totals into imposing ones with his rapacious strokeplay but he completely transformed the thinking about the wicketkeeper/batsman's role in Test cricket. After the consistent damage he inflicted, every country began seeking buccaneering, impudent batsmen who could keep wicket. Gilchrist was the catalyst for the emergence of players like Geraint Jones, Matt Prior, Mark Boucher, Brendon McCullum, MS Dhoni and many others in both international and domestic cricket. The days of keepers who batted at No.8 and cobbled together a useful 30 were well and truly dead. Gilchrist not only raised the bar. He built a completely new frame.

When he was first selected for Australia's Test team he made an instant impact. Having scored a run-a-ball 81 against Pakistan on debut, he came in to bat in his second Test with Australia on the ropes at 126 for 5, chasing 369 for victory.

Gilchrist set about a bowling attack that included Waqar Younis, Wasim Akram and Shoaib Akhtar, scorched to 149 not out (from 163 balls) and Australia surged to a four-wicket victory.

His arrival in the Ashes was similar. Having savaged England at Edgbaston with 152 in the first Test (I recall one straight six into the stand which Richie Benaud on commentary summed up as 'That's up with us!'), he rubbed salt in the wound on a tricky Lord's surface in the second Test with a breakneck 90 and England were soon 2-0 down. His frisky 54 at Trent Bridge rescued Australia from 94 for 6 and earned them a narrow lead. It was enough for Australia to clinch the Ashes in just 11 days of cricket, the fastest ever. England had surrendered the Ashes for the seventh series in a row. There were calls for the ancient urn, which resided in the Lord's museum, to be transported down under for good.

Reaping the benefit of opening – highly successfully – in one-day internationals (he made 16 one-day hundreds) Gilchrist was the second new ball destroyer, striding in at the fall of the fifth wicket around the 80th over to completely wreck the bowlers' hopes of a quick amputation of the tail. The harder ball might deviate more, but it also went faster off the bat. Holding the blade unusually high up the handle for maximum leverage, he wielded it like a samurai sword, slaying a tiring attack which had already had to deal with Hayden, Langer, Ponting and the Waughs, with lightning hands and nimble feet.

England had a plan for Gilchrist in 2005, and it involved Andrew Flintoff going around the wicket and angling the ball into him then taking it away in the air. It worked brilliantly and he did not manage a single fifty in that series. It was one of the main reasons England regained the Ashes that year. But Gilchrist exacted bitter revenge 18 months later when he pulverised England's attack for an astonishing 57-ball hundred – one shy of Viv Richards' Test record – on his home ground in Perth. Four times in two overs he deposited Monty Panesar onto the bank at deep midwicket and Australia ran amok with 527 for 5 dec. It was another Ashes-sealing performance.

Gilchrist finished his Test career with 18 hundreds and an average of 47, superior to many frontline batsmen who have been labelled 'great'. And we have not even mentioned his wicketkeeping which was slick and agile and dovetailed beautifully with Shane Warne's wiles. The air was forever rent with a gravelly 'bowled Shaayne!' from behind the stumps when the leg-spinner was on song, which he invariably was. It must have been fraught being a batsman against that Australian side. But it might have been even worse being a bowler.

★

By 2001, England must have thought they'd seen all the ways Australia had of beating them. Enter Adam Gilchrist, as Dermot Reeve reports.

The lead was only 42 when Adam Gilchrist joined Damien Martyn at the crease. The pair had to fight hard as both Gough and Caddick found movement in humid conditions. But battle they did. A brilliant 160-run partnership followed, ensuring the strongest of positions.

In desperation Hussain turned to Butcher, who soon dismissed Martyn thanks to a splendid catch by Trescothick. Butcher then dismissed Warne, Lee and Gillespie in double-quick time. Gilchrist then lit up Edgbaston with one of the most devastating displays of clean hitting seen in a Test arena. Runs scored overtook balls faced for the world's best ever batsman/

wicketkeeper as he added 63 for the last wicket with McGrath, who contributed one run.

Hussain in particular looked shell-shocked and did not know where to place his fielders. All on the boundary for Gilchrist was the smart move but you had the feeling that England's leader did not want to go completely on the defensive. In the end Gilchrist holed out to long-on showing total commitment to the team cause and left the field to a standing ovation from a stunned audience.

Peter Roebuck profiled Gilchrist later on in the summer, taking a look at what lay behind the run-a-ball path of destruction being blazed through England's bowling attack.

Adam Gilchrist was booed on his first appearance for Western Australia, was booed again when first wearing his country's colours in a 50-over match, and for a third time upon walking out to bat in his baggy green Test cap. On each occasion he was taking the place of a favourite. Yet he did not show any hesitancy nor yet resentment at the reaction of the uninformed. None of it left its mark upon him as he set out to convince his tormentors of his merits.

He is a magnificent cricketer, capable of taking the place of a tried and trusted craftsman like Ian Healy and leaving the team stronger for his inclusion. He is ambitious, too, and moved across the Nullarbor in search of opportunity. Nor is he quite as genial as his appearance indicates, as he can produce barbed comments upon the field, though it is usually Ricky Ponting and Shane Warne whose fingers are found in the pie.

He is a formidable competitor and it is no coincidence that Australia have won so many matches in his brief career. Often he has been the difference between the sides, anyhow alongside Steve Waugh and Glenn McGrath.

Of course comparisons with Sir Garfield Sobers are ridiculous. Yet he does have the same swing of the bat and refusal to be contained by opponents or the game itself. No less tellingly he has turned the jeers into cheers. Throughout he has approached life and cricket as if good news were just around the corner, the birth of a child or eight draws upon his coupon. Often he has been right. Optimism has a power of its own.

No.8 Shane Warne

Australian heroes were meant to be hard men with gimlet stares, barrel chests and bristling moustaches who devoured meek English bowlers as if they were a piece of tenderised steak or singed their eyebrows with vicious 90mph bouncers accompanied by a string of expletives. Then into the Ashes' midst strolled a bleached-blond beach bum with a silver stud earring and fat fingers. Who was this dude?

Just the best wrist spinner who ever played the game, that's all.

The smoking, drinking, pizza-loving Warne was one of the first intake at the Australian Cricket Academy, newly established after the embarrassment of losing the Ashes in 1987. They were in fact seeking an antidote to the venom of the West Indies fast bowlers. Instead of fighting fire with fire they thought they would use smoke and mirrors and believed this chubby leg-spinner might be up for it. 'Spins the ball like no one I've ever seen,' said former Australian leggie Jim Higgs to the academy director Jack Potter, 'but he has a problem with discipline ...'

Within a year, and after just four matches for Victoria, he was making his Test debut. It was an inauspicious start. After two Tests against India he had 1 for 228. He returned to the academy, got fitter and was selected for the Australian tour of Sri Lanka. When Allan Border threw him the ball and he took 3-0 in 13 balls to give them a 30-run victory, they began to see what they had invested in.

Most of the cricket world saw it, too, a few months later when he produced the ball of the century – his first delivery in an Ashes Test – to Mike Gatting. Never mind the occasion, the moment, the victim (a well-known devourer of spinners) or Graham Gooch muttering down the other end that if it was a cheese roll it would not have got past him. The speed, the flight, the dip of the ball sending it veering outside the leg stump, the perfect length and the degree of spin were astonishing.

Those were his primary assets. Strong fingers and powerful shoulders gave the ball a real tweak. That was where the 'dip' came from. It was almost as instrumental in his wicket-taking as the spin and the variations. Many times during his career a right-hander would attempt to clip Warne through the legside and chip a straightforward catch to midwicket. It looked like a soft dismissal. But it was that unexpected curve in towards the batsman's legs – generated by the amount of spin – causing him to overbalance slightly, resulting in the lifted shot, that brought about the dismissal.

But allied to his basic raw materials were two other crucial ingredients. Exceptional control for a man who turned the ball as prodigiously as he did. He conceded just over two an over throughout his Test career. That would be outstanding for any bowler. For a leg-spinner it was exceptional, and only partly due to the general absence of wrist spinners in the modern game. He hid all his variations within a suffocating blanket of accuracy. And he had a very agile mind, able to read a batsman's methods and intents, and counter them.

In this regard he was ably assisted by his friend and mentor, Terry Jenner, aka The Spin Doctor. Jenner, a former Test leggie himself, had fallen on bad times when Warne emerged, but the two forged a symbiotic relationship. Jenner used all his experience and nous to give Warne's natural skills sophistication, and their burgeoning relationship pulled Jenner out of the abyss.

I watched them at work before a Test against West Indies in Adelaide. They were bowling at Matthew Hayden in the nets. Jenner, who though in his late fifties could still land a decent leg-break, went wider of the crease to the left-hander to create a different angle. 'I used to do it when I bowled against Sobers,' he said. 'You bowl the same ball, but from a different place and you might get an edge or a miscue.' Warne practised this variation for a while until he was happy with it.

On the first day of the Test the next day, Warne was on in the 17th over. He was bowling to Brian Lara. Fourth ball he went a bit wider of the crease and Lara, looking to drive but, getting his angles wrong, poked a catch to mid-on. An over later, Warne went wider of the crease again to the left-handed Shivnarine Chanderpaul and he edged to slip. After the celebrations, Warne turned to the commentary box where Jenner, and I, were sitting, and gave him a thumbs-up. 'Marvellous bowling by Warne,' said Jenner on air, 'he planned for that.' This was the source of one of Warne's favourite sayings: 'It's not what you bowl so much as how it got there.'

He began with a leggie and a googly and a top spinner and learnt the back-spinning flipper which earned him a few glorious wickets, notably Alec Stewart stepping back to cut and seeing the ball snake wickedly along the ground. He had funny names for many of his deliveries. A favourite was the pickpocket delivery which stole behind the batsman's body and bowled him around his legs. Gradually injuries reduced his repertoire to the leggie and the straight-on slider, but exploiting umpires' greater enlightenment after the invention of Hawk-Eye, they were all he needed. All he had to do was spin a couple, then the batsman would be playing for the turn, get his pad too far over and be pinned lbw by the slider.

Small adjustments of wrist position, seam position, foot position. That was all he needed. Warne was so simple, yet so devastatingly effective. His bowling was pure theatre, from the walk in, 'decisive but nonchalant, like somebody sliding up to whisper sedition in your ear ... The ball commenced its journey mysteriously in his left hand before being imperceptibly slipped into the right ...' (Gideon Haigh in *On Warne*), through his 'unimprovable' action to his skipping follow-through. He conned fine batsmen with sleight of hand. He made tailenders look like newborn foals on roller skates. Do you remember the amazing delivery to Andrew Strauss in 2005 that pitched almost off the cut strip, spun at right angles and bowled him leg stump as he shouldered arms, making Michael Slater on TV guffaw in amazement? Warne was a commentator's dream and a batsman's nightmare.

He became comfortably the leading wicket-taker in Ashes Tests (with 193) and finished with 708 Test wickets. If DRS had been introduced during his career he would have been the first to a thousand. And all achieved with twirling fingers and a flashing smile and the ball travelling no faster than a moped.

★

Warne's 'Ball of the Century' to Mike Gatting, as described by Richard Hutton in *The Cricketer*.

If Warne's first ball was a 'loosener', England must have been quaking in their boots at the thought of what was coming next. In its trajectory it ducked into Gatting so that on pitching it was wide of the leg stump by a good foot and turned viciously out of the rough to clip the outside of the off-stump, leaving the batsman aghast and rooted to the spot.

Eighteen months later, Warne registers his Test-best figures of 8 for 71 at the Gabba, as Mark Nicholas reports.

Ashes cricket is liberally sprinkled with marvellous bowlers who have illuminated the contest for the old urn and tormented the old enemy. None, though, can have captured cricket's soul in quite the way that Shane Warne has done, or can have had such a single hand in renovating an art long forgotten and much mourned.

Australia won the first Test match of this eagerly awaited series because for the most part they were the better, slicker team, and because in the wonderful Warne they have a glittering jewel who transfixes the opposition with his variations and renders them mute with his accuracy. His dismissal of the confident-looking Alec Stewart during the England second innings with a wicked flipper left the mouths of the gripped Gabba wide open with its effect. It convinced the watching world that Warne had virtually everything in his box of tricks and Bill Brown, the one Australian skipper left from the days before Bradman, confirmed as much by saying that only Clarrie Grimmett of all the leg-spinners that he had seen could live with the young, charismatic Victorian.

Warne did his worst damage on the final day when his long spell of attrition, resulting in the seventh-best Australian figures of all time, broke the back of England's spirited resistance.

So England needed 508 to win and the bookies offered 300-1 against the possibility. More likely they had five sessions and an hour to survive and when Stewart was bamboozled by that flipper and Atherton was adjudged lbw straight after lunch to a flighted, slower leg-break the bookies seemed sage, not just with the 300-1 shot but also the miserly 10-1 they were offering against the draw.

But the organised, restrained Hick and the neat, calm Thorpe hung on ... and hung on. They kicked Warne away with remorseless discipline and pulled at anything short with vengeful power. As the watching maestro Barry Richards observed, 'they played as well as anyone could have against Warne in these conditions'.

England were 211 for 2 and fighting. That the dream died barely mattered. England, save Gooch who batted with masterly defence until a rush of blood in mid-afternoon did for him, were pulled this way and that by a fabulous bowler who is inspiring a new generation of cricket fanatics. At times, on the worn, last-day pitch, Warne was unplayable and at other times the sheer intensity of his performance overwhelmed his opposition.

Australia paid homage to the Man of the Match, the blond beach bum with the silver earstud who turned his hand to leg-breaks and captivated a nation.

No.9 Jim Laker

In a different way from Shane Warne, Jim Laker was an unlikely-looking cricket hero. Inconsequential in appearance, with a sly grin and rounded shoulders, he was a Yorkshireman of few words (slightly ironic given his success as a commentator in later years). He started life as a batsman and fast bowler in the Bradford League and only turned to off-spin when stationed in Egypt during the war (where presumably there were not too many green, bouncy pitches).

After the war he was recruited by Surrey to form a long and lethal spin-bowling partnership with Tony Lock. As did Warne he had strong fingers and unerring accuracy. He could land the ball on the proverbial sixpence. He also had superb flight, persuading the ball to drift away from the right-hand batsman and then spin sharply back.

He had one other advantage. The lbw Law had been changed in 1937 to allow leg-before dismissals to balls pitching outside off-stump, coinciding almost exactly with Laker's conversion to off-spin. Life had been tough for that type of bowler before, as batsmen just used their pads to block anything turning back onto the stumps. This change opened up a whole new realm.

Laker began to induce a sort of hypnosis on batsmen on turning tracks. In a Test trial he took 8 for 2 in 14 overs. He regularly took hat-tricks. He loved bowling with five men round the bat as batsmen, suddenly deprived of their lbw security blanket, poked and prodded uncertainly. He snapped up 166 wickets in 1950 at an average of 15 apiece, and passed 100 wickets comfortably every season at paltry cost. He took each wicket with barely a reaction, just a little shrug and a turn on his heel to take his sweater from the umpire. He was a passionless exterminator.

If England were undecided whether to focus their energies on seam or spin at the start of the summer of 1956, their mind was soon made up at The Oval when Surrey played Australia and Laker took all 10 wickets in the first innings. Dry turners it was going to be. At Old Trafford, venue for the fourth Test, the pitch was a shaven, reddish surface instead of the grassy one they had encountered against Lancashire earlier in the tour.

England managed 459 on it batting first. Until the effects of the heavy roller wore off, the Australian openers were untroubled. But as soon as Laker was introduced, and produced a peach to the talented left-hander Neil Harvey that pitched leg and hit off, paralysis set in. After Lock had dismissed Burke caught at slip, Laker wreaked havoc. He took 7 wickets for 8 runs in 4 overs. The Australians, mostly backfoot players, were mesmerised by Laker's immaculate control and subtle variations of length. Two were bowled and one lbw on the back foot; two were caught close in pushing forward too hard at the ball, and one was stumped. Only Richie Benaud tried to attack and was caught at deep mid-wicket. They were 84 all out and Laker had taken 9 for 37.

Ian Johnson, the Australian captain, suggested that they had been 'trapped on a stinker, the fellows were angry and the batting blew up'. But May, his opposite number, saw it differently. 'The pitch was not that bad. Jim just dripped away at their nerves, realising that they had got a little obsessional about him and the wickets.'

Laker had a very deliberate method, moving smoothly to the crease in what John Arlott described as 'a constabular stroll' and then, bowling mainly around the wicket, pivoting on his front leg to get plenty of drift away and spin back.

Australia were asked to follow on before the close of the second day and the groundsman asked Johnson which roller he would prefer. 'Please your effing self,' the captain growled. Again they made a solid start (Laker took one wicket with a full toss) but torrential rain and squally showers permitted only 90 minutes' play over the next two days, with a rest day in between. Australia crept to 84 for 2.

On the fifth day the pitch was so saturated it was unresponsive for most of the first session, and Australia got through to lunch unscathed. But the sun was drying the surface and eventually balls began to pop and turn. Four wickets had gone down for 16 runs (all to Laker). Benaud hung around for a while with McDonald, and Laker and Lock swapped ends and then were rested.

After tea Laker was back on from his favoured Stretford End and, once he had snared McDonald caught at short-leg and bowled Benaud on the back foot, the end was swift. When wicketkeeper Len Maddocks was lbw playing back to a half-volley, it was all over, England had won the Ashes and Laker had become the first bowler in Test history to take all 10 wickets in an innings, giving him 19 for 90 in the match. No one had ever even taken 18 before (or since), at any level of cricket. And what did he do? He spun round, casually shook hands with the non-striker, slung his jumper over his shoulder and meandered off to the pavilion for a fag.

It was the ultimate virtuoso performance, without par in sport, and all the more amazing as Laker's spin twin Lock had bowled 69 overs in the match (to Laker's 68), beaten the bat constantly and taken just one solitary wicket. After doing various interviews, Laker eventually got away from the ground at about 8pm for the long drive home. He stopped halfway for a snack at a pub in Lichfield where his wickets were being replayed on TV. Not a soul recognised him. He was married to an Austrian who did not know much about cricket, and when he arrived home she said, after fielding many congratulatory telephone calls: 'Jim, did you do something good today?' And that is how he preferred it.

★

Laker's Match – the most outstanding bowling analysis in Test cricket history, as Bill Bowes describes.

It was amazing, almost unbelievable. In 35 minutes since tea Australia had lost 8 wickets for only 22 runs. In 22 balls Laker had taken 7 wickets for only 8 runs and had finished with an analysis of 16.4-4-37-9. And this, mark you, on a pitch where England had just scored 459, and on a day when England had added 152 runs in 140 minutes to their overnight score.

The last shower of rain fell at Old Trafford just after 5am and the ground staff, working from 6am, had the pitch and outfield ready for play within 10 minutes of the scheduled time for the start.

Good defensive batsmanship could save the day for Australia. 30, 60, 90 minutes went by and still the batsmen defended to splendid purpose. No matter how May rang his bowling changes they had the reply.

Unfortunately for them the sun came out during the break and ... it seemed obvious that there was now a little bit of help for the spinners. Twice in Lock's first over to Craig he beat the bat with deliveries turned and lifted slightly. Twice in his first over to McDonald Laker also beat the bat. And in his third over of the afternoon Laker began to strike. He had Craig, who had batted almost 4¼ hours for 38, lbw.

McDonald went to his 50 by hitting Lock, who still tended to pitch short, for two 4s and a 2 in one over. But in Laker's next over at the other end, Mackay obligingly repeated his stroke of the first innings and edged a ball to slip where Oakman made the catch.

Miller defended grimly for 15 minutes before, drawn forward by Laker, he missed and was, like Mackay, out for a duck. The next batsman, Archer, was out to the second ball he received for the third duck in succession.

Benaud and the magnificently subdued McDonald put a temporary end to the England jubilation. They defended until tea-time when Australia, still with a chance of saving the day, were 181 for 6.

Laker, however, with a tea interval rest for his spinning fingers, came into the fray refreshed. Once again he began to strike life out of the pitch and he ended McDonald's 337 minutes' defiance by making him edge a catch to Oakman in the leg trap.

A few minutes later he bowled the defiant Benaud, and Australia with only two wickets to fall had 90 minutes to play ahead of them.

For 20 minutes Lindwall and Johnson defended, but then came Laker's ninth victim with Lindwall also caught in the leg trap. Laker had now got 18 wickets, a truly great performance.

With almost bated breath the crowd watched Lock bowl his succeeding over, and Oh, what a cheering broke out when Laker got Maddocks lbw! For the second time this season he had got all 10 wickets against Australia. Magnificent. It had been Laker's match.

No.10 Dennis Lillee

Ask any batsmen from the 1970s which bowler they least liked to face and the answer would be Dennis Lillee. Joel Garner was harder to score off, Colin Croft more physically dangerous, Jeff Thomson was faster, Michael Holding more slippery. But none of them had Lillee's sheer wicket-taking mastery in all conditions. Lillee had a permanent killer instinct. Lillee was the Terminator.

There is a brilliant clip on YouTube of him bowling to Viv Richards in a domestic cup semi-final between Western Australia and Queensland in 1976. Western Australia had been bowled out for just 77. Strolling out to open for Queensland on a glorious afternoon in Perth, Richards must have imagined a quick and easy 40 not out would do the job. But Lillee had other ideas. He tore in to bowl, sending down an uninterrupted succession of vicious bouncers at a startled Richards, some of which only just missed his maroon-capped head, before ripping out his off-stump with the last ball of the first over. Richards wandered off looking visibly disturbed. Lillee reduced Queensland to 34 for 5 and they were summarily dismissed for 62. He, of course, was man of the match.

Despite a hirsute, straggly-haired appearance that made him look as if he had just strayed away from a Credence Clearwater Revival gig, Lillee exuded menace. Tall and strong, he had a long, marauding run-up, a superb sideways action, front arm braced, fingers outstretched, wrist cocked and a rapid delivery – once timed at 96mph – that naturally swung away from the right-hander. But allied to that he was clever. He could detect a batsman's weaknesses in an instant and had numerous tools at his disposal to exploit them.

Not only could he swing the ball – mainly out – but he could cut it, too, running his fingers down one side to bowl a brilliant leg-cutter. He varied his pace cleverly, saving his energies often for a bouncer carefully directed at the rib cage rather than wastefully over the head. 'I try to hit a batsman in the rib cage when I bowl a purposeful bouncer, and I want it to hurt so much that the batsman doesn't want to face me any more,' he said. He changed his position on the crease to create different angles. He read pitches expertly. If you thought reverse swing was invented by Pakistan you thought wrong. Lillee discovered it on abrasive Australian surfaces in the early 1970s. It was he who taught Imran Khan how to do it.

England had already had painful experiences of the tearaway Lillee in the early 1970s and a slightly refined version in 1972, but after he sustained a serious back injury they weren't expecting his rebirth as a calculated assassin in 1974–5. This was the horror series from which every England batsman returned with glazed eyes and vacant expressions looking as if he had been at war. And in a way they had. There was bombardment from both ends. Lillee was fast and mean and precise from one end. He knew how to nail an opponent. He was a ruthless executioner. Jeff Thomson was faster, looser, ultra vicious. Like a human torpedo. He was a random exterminator. They took 58 wickets between them in that series, coining the familiar phrase – Ashes to Ashes, Dust to Dust, If Lillee don't get you, Thommo must – and Australia won the rubber 4-1.

The list of Lillee's most frequent dismissals in Tests reads like a Who's Who of batting – Viv Richards (9 times), David Gower (9), Graham Gooch (8), Geoff Boycott (7) and he continued to torment England for another six years, until partially tamed by Ian Botham's command performance in 1981. He still took 39 wickets in the series, though, and soon afterwards went past Lance Gibbs' Test wicket record of 309. The scorecard entry 'caught Marsh b Lillee' appears 95 times in Tests, more than any other combination. He could be a dangerous lower-order batsman, too, and a provocative presence generally, deliberately winding up captains, opposing batsmen and umpires. He was all that a quick bowler is meant to be: fast, mean, rough, tough and terminal.

★

In his diary of the 1975 season, Tony Lewis singles Lillee out among Ian Chappell's outstanding side.

> Lillee is a man who would be in any side in the world. Apart from the enormous courage involved in his fightback to fitness after those stress fractures of the spine, he has other qualities. He is aggressive, physically and verbally, which is absolutely essential in the fast-bowling game: he can take 'stick', as he did in the Prudential competition against the West Indians, and come back snorting fire. Yet he has learnt the true art of bowling which lifts him far above the ordinary. Variation of pace, length and line are all under his control. His presence has made the Australian side of 1975 a memorable one.

David Frith, meanwhile, celebrates Lillee's fortitude to still be bowling at all.

> There have been faster bowlers than Dennis Lillee, but not many. There have been more hostile fast bowlers, but not many. Spofforth, Constantine, Charlie Griffith, Andy Roberts, Jeff Thomson – all have brought menace, even terror, to the bowling crease. Lillee concedes nothing to any of them.
>
> He is one of the great fast bowlers of the twentieth century, possessing a full set of gear changes, a knowledge of aerodynamics, equal to Lindwall's, an abundance of stamina and determination, and more courage than is given to most.
>
> He needed that courage in 1973 and '74 when he set about achieving one of sport's most impressive comebacks. The four stress fractures in the lower vertebrae would have finished many a career. Lillee, having dramatically bowled his way to fame, was faced with six weeks in plaster and a long and

gruelling fight to full fitness. He withstood the punishment and handsomely repaid those who had worked with him and believed in him. At the end of the 1973/74 season high hopes were at least as high as the highest of his notorious bouncers.

England arrived next season to defend the Ashes in six Test matches. In the first Test, a new extermination firm was formed: Lillee and Thomson. England's batsmen at Brisbane would just as happily have had their chances in the company of Leopold and Loeb, or Browne and Kennedy, or, at the end of the day, Burke and Hare. It was devastating, still fresh in memory.

Australia's opening pair took 58 wickets in the series out of 108 that fell to bowlers – this despite Thomson's withdrawal through injury halfway through the fifth Test and Lillee's after six overs with a damaged foot in the final match.

The full force of this controlled cyclone was felt in the 1975 series, though England's sleepy wickets absorbed some of the energy. This is when Lillee's other bowling skills asserted themselves. As in the 1972 series, when he took a record 31 Test wickets, Lillee beat batsmen by change of pace and with his wicked awayswinger. Rod Marsh and the ever-expectant slips cordon did the rest.

No.11 Glenn McGrath

If Dennis Lillee was the archetypal Seventies paceman, Glenn McGrath was a next-generation Nineties upgrade. He was a superior model in every way – taller, thinner, sleeker, more energy efficient, more reliable, better value for money with higher productivity. McGrath was a wicket-taking machine. He might have been born in rural New South Wales, but he could have been manufactured in Munich.

Indeed, after his rough-edged early days when he was an out and out quick, he became almost mechanical. There was his robotically straight approach to the crease, a rhythmic, small-stepped stride-pattern building to a slight jump inwards at the stumps, left foot landing practically in front of leg stump. The bowling arm was bolt upright, taut as if infused with steel, propelling a metronomic line and length on or just outside off-stump. He never gave batsmen an iota of width. Height and long levers generated extra bounce and unexpected pace. There were no frills or deviations. Just relentless battering at the obstacle until it gave way. He was a bowling Dalek.

Like a sophisticated laser, he targeted the leading member of the opposition and hunted him down. He dismissed Michael Atherton 19 times, Brian Lara 15, Nasser Hussain and Sachin Tendulkar eight. Jacques Kallis averaged 9.83 against him. He hounded them with mean lines and menacing stares. He was a man on a mission and he wouldn't give up until it was completed. The man known as Pigeon for his skinny legs had phenomenal staying power.

The hint at humanity was in his temper. Occasionally when things didn't quite go his way, or he bowled a bad ball, he would temporarily lose it. He would storm back to his mark or down to fine leg, effing and blinding, the complexion reddened with annoyance. There was some Irish fervour in there somewhere. It was amusing to watch him berating himself on the boundary – chuntering and gesticulating – unless you were the batsman about to negotiate his next over.

A merciless interrogator on his home tracks, extracting extra life and zip and constantly asking the batsman difficult questions, he was even more effective abroad where he could recalibrate his aim to a marginally shorter length. He took 87 wickets in England (at an average of 19.34). He exploited the Lord's slope brilliantly, rumbling in from the Pavilion End and landing the ball precisely just outside off-stump. Some deliveries would jag down the slope, others would not. He was uncertain which way the ball would move, but the batsmen were clueless. On his first visit to the Home of Cricket he took 8 for 34, on his second 8 for 114 (in two innings) and on his third – in 2005 – 9 for 82 (also in two innings). Who can forget the way in that 2005 game, that he blew away England's top five (including his 500th Test wicket) for 21 runs – the ball constantly bursting through batsmen's defences – after Australia had been rumbled for 190? If he hadn't stepped on that ball in the second Test at Edgbaston – ruling him out of two Tests – England would never have regained the Ashes.

McGrath and Shane Warne enabled Australia to boss the game from any situation. If there was any assistance in the pitch, they would find it. If there wasn't they would impose a sort of paralysis on the scoring, denying the batsmen runs, reeling off maidens, Warne tossing balls unhittably into the rough, McGrath rounding off a monotonously accurate over with a high, unreachable bouncer. When they were in their pomp – between 1999 and 2005 – Australia won 19 Test series and lost just one (the dramatic encounter in the subcontinent when India won in Calcutta after being made to follow on).

In 2005 McGrath eclipsed Courtney Walsh's tally of 519 Test wickets to become the most successful fast bowler of all time. He almost managed to take more Test wickets than he scored runs, which says as much about his terrible batting as it does about his terrific bowling. He was a ruthless assassin. Anyone unfortunate enough to have to open the batting against him deserves our utmost sympathy.

★

Halfway through the 1997 Ashes, Richard Hadlee analyses what he likes about Glenn McGrath, who was on his way to 36 wickets in the series.

Glenn McGrath epitomises simplicity in an excellent bowling action. He isn't a typical Australian fast bowler, like Lillee, Thomson or McDermott, who all had physical aggression and a presence. Glenn has a more subdued manner which is effective for him. His performance can be adversely affected when he tries to become overly aggressive. Control of mind is therefore critical to him.

Glenn McGrath is an excellent role model for young fast bowlers. He has a straight, gradually accelerating approach to the crease, with good forward momentum. He bowls close to the stumps, which increases his chances of lbw decisions, a high action at delivery to help the ball bounce, good control of the ball at release for swing and seam, admirable line and a nice follow-through.

McGrath maximises his height at delivery through a short delivery stride – the longer the stride, the lower you get. Standing as tall as you can at delivery is important. Fast bowlers with a long delivery stride and back-foot drag might find it difficult to get the ball to bounce off a length. It is more a case of bowling the ball along the pitch instead of into it.

Andrew Miller pays tribute to McGrath on his retirement after the 2006–7 whitewash.

He was not the quickest nor the most cunning. He lacked the extreme height of the West Indian pacemen who ruled before his arrival and the unrestrained menace of Dennis Lillee and

Jeff Thomson. He would swing the ball only rarely, while his movement off the seam was nothing more than just enough.

But McGrath had an unrivalled ability to sweep through cracks. McGrath's *modus operandi* was more focused and more ruthless: he promised, and invariably delivered, the most rigorous search of a batsman's abilities. Every player he came up against knew exactly what he was about to undergo but that did not make the ordeal less exacting. Mike Atherton, who fell to McGrath 19 times in Tests (the worst record by a Test batsman against a specific bowler), admitted as much in the first chapter of his autobiography.

Just as Atherton was nothing without a viable technique, so McGrath's single greatest asset was his fantastically functional bowling action – a frill-free masterpiece of biomechanics. The simplicity was beguiling: it made the extraordinary look ordinary.

His rhythmical run-up would leave him loaded with momentum as he hit the crease, his braced front leg ensured he used his full height with no need for a knee-jarring leap, his perfectly cocked wrist meant complete mastery of seam position. Simplicity begets simplicity. No wonder he was still going strong at 37.

The Five Greatest Ashes Series

Gideon Haigh

1932–3

'Never once did he flinch; it is admitted by our opponents that he out-generalled his adversary; having once got him on the run he mercilessly kept him there, and who shall blame him?' Thus, as the English summer of 1933 impended, 'Second Slip' of *The Cricketer* reviewing Douglas Jardine's recent accomplishment in leading England to a 4-1 Ashes victory in Australia.

The answer would shortly be forthcoming: reviled by Australians already, Jardine would prove too hot for England's cricket establishment to handle. And in this the most influential voice, although he hesitated to raise it publicly, would be 'Second Slip''s boss, Pelham 'Plum' Warner, who had been Marylebone Cricket Club's tour manager, and an anxious observer of deteriorating relations between England and Australia. 'Second Slip''s triumphalist verdict on the Bodyline series is thus a fascinating first draft of a history still to reach a final version despite many and varied retellings.

A sense of vindication was pardonable. Jardine's team were pitted against the wonder of the cricketing age, Donald Bradman, whose average after 19 Test matches had mushroomed to 112.29. Withering fast bowling assailing leg stump by Harold Larwood, reinforced by Bill Voce, Gubby Allen and

Bill Bowes, transformed the crease into a shooting gallery and Bradman's teammates into collateral damage. But in the first flush of victory, who cared to quibble, especially as 'Second Slip' would have been working off distant impressions formed from a press coverage sanitised for English readers? The 4-1 margin appeared to brook no argument, even if the match reports were obliged to echo some of the off-field rancour, involving, as it did during the third Test, *The Cricketer*'s editor.

There was a tremendous uproar when Woodfull was unfortunately struck over the heart, and the Australian captain's refusal to talk to PF Warner, who had gone to the dressing room to sympathise with him, on the grounds that the England team were not playing cricket in the proper spirit owing to the employment of leg-theory, only added fuel to the fire. Subsequently Pelham Warner stated that the incident between himself and Woodfull had been settled amicably by Woodfull apologising to him. Woodfull, however, denied the apology, but pointed out that it was not a personal affair with Warner but his disapproval of the methods of the English bowlers.

Those 'buts' and 'howevers' notwithstanding, Warner was clearly caught out in a lie, reflecting his discomfiture at the querulous telegrams whizzing back and forth between his Australian hosts and Marylebone, and at dealing with Jardine whom he thought 'half-mad' and whom he felt 'made cricket impossible'. 'What can I do?' he asked his old Australian friend Clem Hill during one bout of hand-wringing hereabouts. 'You can come down off the fence for a start, Plum,' retorted Hill. But Warner never did, as evinced by his own evasive and emollient notes on the series, when finally he committed some thoughts to paper, while claiming it would 'be improper, both on public and private grounds, to discuss, at the present moment, the controversies which arose in Australia', and shrinking from comment on England's bowling methods on grounds it was 'sub judice'. His verdict that Jardine was 'one of the best captains on the field England has had' studiously side-stepped Jardine's demeanour off the field, and his private belief that 'DRJ must not captain again'.

From a contemporary vantage, the match reports in *The Cricketer* enable appreciation of the Ashes of 1932–3 as a series unfolding in real time rather than a controversy visible only in murky hindsight. After all, after two Tests, the series was all square: Bradman had made a duck and century; England had erred in Melbourne by going without a spinner, and in Adelaide slipped quickly to 37 for 4, at which point the home side probably had its nose ahead. England, in the vernacular, 'batted deep', and had the resources to regroup; as throughout, Australia's tail took contrastingly little shifting. England's players, the professionals at least, were united behind Jardine; Australia's admired their captain Bill Woodfull, but differed over his stoical response to Bodyline. As the series was discussed in high diplomatic councils, local tempers boiled. Larwood's timeless story was of overhearing a little Australian girl quiz her mother: 'But Mummy, he doesn't look like a murderer.'

The Gabba has been a dry gulch for away teams in the last decade or two, but on England's first visit it was a scene of celebration. Larwood's clean bowling of a skittish Bradman and a perplexed Ponsford in the same over, leg stump each time, must rank for drama and impact with any Test hat-trick; Jardine's 83 minutes without a run attest his monumental self-denial. England were flowing as Australia were ebbing. The fourth and fifth Tests were won with soaring sixes, the widening gap between the teams reflected in that the visitors prevailed in the last match despite dropping no fewer than 14 catches.

In hindsight, the Bradmano-a-mano duels with Larwood loom largest. No bowler had bowled so fast or threateningly on Australian soil; no bowler would ever so get beneath Bradman's skin: the local hero fell to Larwood four times, and clearly had Larwood on his mind when dismissed on the other three occasions. Yet who would have guessed when they walked off together at Sydney, Larwood injured, Bradman out, that the former was leaving a Test field for the last time, while Bradman's career had more than 15 further years to run?

The Cricketer's contemporaneous reporting illuminates some other frequently forgotten feats: the all-round contributions of Wally Hammond and Hedley Verity; the left-handed grit of Eddie Paynter and Maurice Leyland; the grim rivalry of the ascetic Jardine and the feisty Bill O'Reilly. Jardine faced almost 800 balls in the series for fewer than 200 runs; O'Reilly bowled a third more (eight-ball) overs than anyone else in the series, more than a third of them maidens. Jardine's admission to O'Reilly that his bowling made him feel 'like an old maid defending her virginity' reveals dry humour behind the deep tenacity.

The description of Stan McCabe as applying 'death or glory' methods during his defiant, undefeated 187 in Sydney took on additional resonance with the injury that befell Bert Oldfield two months later in Adelaide. *The Cricketer* reported Oldfield simply as 'struck' and simultaneously absolving Larwood of responsibility, almost as though as he crumpled to the ground he cried: 'Don't worry, Harold, it's not your fault.' Yet perhaps never in a Test series has mortality seemed such a possibility, so uncompromising was the bowling, so ill-equipped and barely protected the batsmen. With a hint of disapproval, *The*

Cricketer felt inclined to mention that 'several Australian batsmen wore chest-pads as well as thigh pads'.

This all played well with a victory dinner at the Dorchester Hotel on July 19 1933, at which MCC president Lord Hailsham exalted Jardine as 'the best captain in the world'. But as it happened, MCC was even then commencing a slow but deliberate volte-face in order to assuage Australian concerns about their next tour of England, with Warner's full, if always confidential, approval. 'The real trouble is Jardine,' wrote the editor of *The Cricketer* to a friend in Australia. 'Is he to be capt[ain]? At present I say "No" unless he makes a most generous public gesture of friendliness and then I am not sure I would trust him … But, please, keep my own opinion on DRJ to yourself.' As it happened, to Warner's great relief, Jardine pre-empted any decision by announcing in March 1934 that he had 'neither the intention nor the desire to play cricket against Australia this summer'. With that, and a long official colloquy that deplored 'direct attack', Bodyline was consigned to the past.

Or so the authorities hoped. If they got their short-term wish for the continuance of Ashes cricket, they never quite eliminated the sense of slightly shabby administrative connivance. Bodyline has gone on to be discussed and debated, positions shifting unpredictably. Even Jardine reflected on the degree of luck involved, confiding in John Arlott: 'You know, we nearly didn't do it. The little man was bloody good.'

Sensitivities have altered, too. In 2002, MCC president Ted Dexter decided to hang Jardine's portrait at Lord's less conspicuously, apparently anxious not to upset antipodean guests. Yet Australia and England remain the best of enemies; fast bowling has lost much of its shock value; captaincy with a 'plan' that unswervingly pursues victory is much admired. Every eighth respondent to a 2016 poll by *The Cricketer* deemed Jardine to be England's greatest captain; his win ratio of 60 per cent is unchallenged among those who have led their country in 15 Tests or more. Nearly 60 years after Jardine's death blame has given way somewhat, to something rather closer to credit.

★

The most infamous Test series in cricket history began in Sydney with a comfortable England victory against a Bradman-less Australia. Stan McCabe stepped up in the Don's absence with a frenetic 187 not out. *The Cricketer*'s 'Second Slip' – former England Test player Frank Mitchell – reports.

Woodfull won the toss and although Ponsford made a determined stand until after lunch, Australia's first four wickets fell for 87. In the next two hours, Richardson and McCabe carried on to 216. As the sting of the attack lessened, McCabe began to score freely with strong on strokes, cut behind point, and good drives.

With Wall as his partner, McCabe by 'death or glory' methods scored with delightful freedom and hit up 60 in less than an hour before the innings closed. McCabe batted four hours and hit 25 boundaries.

England moved doggedly to a healthy first innings behind centuries from Sutcliffe, Hammond and Pataudi, before Larwood followed up his five-for in the first innings with another in the second.

Larwood was the outstanding figure of the England attack. His 49 overs for 10 wickets was a herculean effort. He stuck to his heavy duty with a great heart, although troubled by a strained left side in the second innings. At one stage he had only two fieldsmen on the off side, and his control was as impressive as his pace. It was clear that the Notts fast bowler would be a match-winning factor for as long as he continued in this form. Australia's steady and persistent bowling was better equipped with spin types, but contained nothing approaching the dynamic influence of a Larwood. In one spell Larwood bowled 10 overs for 17 runs and four wickets.

Bradman returned in the second Test, recovering from a first-ball duck in the first innings to march to a heroic unbeaten hundred which proved the difference in a low-scoring match. England capitulated before Australia's spinners in the final innings, exposing Jardine's decision to go into the game without one.

Winning the toss again, Australia scored a laborious 194 for 7 before stumps. Bradman went first ball, when he tried to hook a short one from Bowes, and touched it in to his wicket.

England's reply [of 169] was all the batsmen deserved for their display. Sutcliffe headed the list, but his 52 was the most scratchy innings he has ever played in Australia. The outstanding bowler was O'Reilly, who mingled leg-breaks, 'wrong-uns' and over-spinners. Varying his pace and making the ball come off at different heights, O'Reilly earned his wickets.

The England bowlers fought back splendidly, and at the close of play appeared to have put their side in a favourable position. Australia's only consolation in a second innings of 191 was an impressive 'come back' by Bradman, who scored 103 not out, in three hours, while eight wickets fell at the other end. This was a different Bradman – not the dasher with audacious strokes, but a batsman fighting grimly to save his side from collapse, and to regain his confidence and certainty. Viewed from every angle of batsmanship, this innings must be ranked for merit as probably the greatest Bradman has played.

England's sudden collapse came as a shock. Sending the ball into a good breeze, O'Reilly gained in flight and turn by slackening his pace. The leg-break which beat Sutcliffe early broke almost the width of the stumps. The spin of some of Ironmonger's deliveries was aided whenever the ball pitched on a part of the surface worn by bowlers' feet.

One-all and on to Adelaide, where England begin badly but recover to a par position. Bodyline then comes to a head when both Woodfull and Oldfield are badly hit by short balls from Larwood. England then bat themselves into a dominant position, before Australia, as in the first Test, crumbled in front of Larwood's onslaught.

The match began in perfect weather, and, although there had been some rain the day before play started, the wicket appeared to be in perfect condition, when England began batting, but it was quickly apparent that the ball was kicking. England could not have made a more disastrous start. Lunch was taken with the score at 37 for 4 – a desperate position.

After the interval Leyland attacked the bowling splendidly, and with Wyatt defending with great skill, England gradually recovered. The Yorkshireman played magnificent cricket for his runs. He made some beautiful hooks off Wall and also drove very hard. Defending with the greatest skill, Wyatt also punished any loose balls with great severity, claiming three sixes and three fours. Before lunch the ball was inclined to kick, but after the interval the wicket dried a lot and played easily.

Seldom, if ever, has a Test match even been played under such unpleasant conditions. There was a tremendous uproar when Woodfull was unfortunately struck over the heart, and the Australian captain's refusal to talk to PF Warner, only added fuel to the fire. Every time Larwood set his field for the leg-theory the crowd created a scene. There was a further uproar when Oldfield was struck by Larwood, but the Australian wicket-keeper quickly let it be known that the bowler was in no way to blame … but when O'Reilly took Oldfield's place, the crowd booed every time Larwood bowled.

Eddie Paynter is the hero in the decisive Test of the series, as he comes to the wicket straight from his hospital bed to help England to a narrow first innings lead. Australia were once again dismissed cheaply, and appropriately it was Paynter who hit the winning runs in England's run chase.

For the first time during the series Australia made a really good start, the first wicket not falling until 133. Jardine made numerous bowling changes, and continually altered his field. With Bradman in, he put Larwood on and set a leg field, and the batsman was undoubtedly uncomfortable, but he managed to survive.

England fought back in great style on the second day, and Australia lost much of their initial advantage. Larwood began with his leg-theory, and by clean bowling Bradman and Ponsford in one over put his side in a much better position. Bradman, who hit 11 fours, was out trying to cut a ball on the leg stump, while Ponsford went too far over and made no attempt to play the ball which hit his leg stump.

So far from consolidating their position England had to fight extremely hard for runs. Some very fine bowling by O'Reilly kept the batsmen very quiet and the England wickets fell at regular intervals. When the sixth wicket fell at 216, Paynter, to the surprise of everybody, came out to bat. He had come straight from hospital where he had been sent owing to an attack of tonsillitis and would certainly not have batted if England had not been in such a grave position. His pluck made him a great favourite with the crowd, who cheered him to the echo.

Requiring 160 runs for victory, England lost Sutcliffe in Wall's second over. Jardine concentrated entirely on defence and at one point was in 83 minutes without making a run. The second wicket had put on 73 invaluable runs when Jardine was lbw after batting two hours and 12 minutes. Leyland continued to bat extremely well and just when it looked as if Leyland would remain to the end he edged a ball into the slips. Playing a grand innings for his side he was in for three hours and 42 minutes and hit nine fours and one five. Paynter came in and made the winning hit by hooking McCabe for six.

With the Ashes safe, England closed out the series with another comfortable victory back at Sydney.

Writing in *The Cricketer* on his return from Australia, editor Plum Warner appraises the performances of the two most central figures in England's victory.

D.R. Jardine is one of the best captains on the field England has had for many a long day. An acute observer and thinker, his management of the bowling and placing of the field were admirable, and he demanded and obtained a high standard of fitness and discipline. Brave and tenacious, he would never ask anyone to do anything which he would not attempt himself. Never did anyone leave anything less to chance, and his keenness and determination were immense.

The matter being *sub judice*, this is neither the time nor the place to discuss the problems which his adoption of the leg-theory raised – and the hostility shown by the Australians to this type of bowling. It is sufficient at the moment to say that he was unswerving in his attitude, and that he bore the 'barracking' of the crowd and the criticisms of the papers with calmness and dignity.

H. Larwood may well claim comparison with any fast bowler of any age, his run up to the crease, action, delivery, and follow-through being models of rhythm and swing ... I cannot recall a more accurate fast bowler. He had such complete control of the ball that Allen stood nearer in at forward short-leg to him than any short-leg had ever before ventured to stand, and escaped injury. His bowling was undoubtedly the chief factor in the recovery of the Ashes.

1954–5

In the mid-1950s, Australia was controversially the location where Britain trialled its new nuclear arsenal. Its equivalent on the cricket field was Frank Tyson, whose nickname, 'Typhoon', evoked his primal and devastating pace. Though his time would pass quickly, fast bowlers for decades afterwards were judged by reference to him. Was this or that new lad as quick as Typhoon? Nobody was realistically judged as coming close.

Every captain fantasises about the capacity to blast his opponents to smithereens; few are gifted the opportunity to do so. Leonard Hutton dreamt of it longer than most. He remembered Bodyline, of reading that Bradman had been bowled first ball in Melbourne by his Yorkshire mentor, fast bowler Bill

Bowes. He knew, as England's numero uno for 15 years, what it was like to bear the brunt of a new ball at velocity, how it corroded technique and wore nerves. As the *Orsova* conveyed his Marylebone Cricket Club to Australia in September 1954 he was gratified that his selectors had taken his word that pace held the key to success down under.

England were defending Ashes won by the odd Test the year before and Hutton had no illusions about their challenge: his conviction, based on two prior tours involving one win and eight defeats, was that visiting teams needed to be a quarter better than Australia man-for-man to make up for the disadvantage of alien conditions. The hosts would have the services of Ray Lindwall, Keith Miller and Bill Johnston, speedy and shrewd; only the yeoman Alec Bedser in Hutton's attack had a comparable record. Yet Tyson impressed him from the first: a 'conscientious and intelligent man' who focused his mind while walking back to his mark by reciting Wordsworth, and who en route pounded the *Orsova*'s decks to get fit for the forthcoming days in the sun. Hutton said afterwards that he knew his team were in with a chance during a tour match when Tyson hit Neil Harvey on the shin, and the batsman had to unbuckle his pad to rub the blow.

In fact, Hutton got slightly ahead of himself by sending Australia in at the Gabba in the first Test with a four-man pace attack on a pitch whose green tinge proved deceptive. Over the next eleven and a half hours, England gave up 8 for 601, Tyson 1 for 160 of these, and Australia prevailed by an innings and 154 runs. Hutton, a droll man, remarked that pitches were like wives: one was never sure how they would turn out. Undismayed, he doubled down by omitting Bedser, blunted by the toll of years and an attack of shingles, from the starting XI for the second Test at the SCG, only to find his team 7 for 88 after three hours at the crease. England were lucky to restrict their first-innings deficit to 74 runs.

The match, even the rubber, appeared to pivot on a point in the visitors' second innings. Scrabbling desperately to extend England's lead, Tyson turned his back on a bouncer from Lindwall that left an egg-sized lump on the back of his head. 'When he came out of his concussed state,' recalled Hutton, 'I swear there was a new light in his eyes, as if a spark had been kindled deep down inside him.' When Australia began its chase for 223, Tyson came down like a wolf on the fold, his 6 for 85 giving him 10 for 130 for the match, and presenting England with victory by 38 runs: for the rest of the series, Hutton believed, Tyson was 'as fast as any bowler in the history of cricket'.

For others, the tour was also a triumph. Twenty-five-year-old Peter May and 21-year-old Colin Cowdrey anticipated their emergence as the axis of English batting and leadership for the rest of the decade; even without the supplanted Bedser, the attack was as complete as any sent to Australia, with Brian Statham a tireless trier into the wind, the economical Trevor Bailey and Bob Appleyard giving no quarter at medium pace, the mercurial Johnny Wardle purveying subtle left-arm slows. Denis Compton played several useful innings; Godfrey Evans contributed gymnastic catches, bouncy bonhomie, and in due course the winning runs. Twenty-four-year-old Tyson, however, would prove the difference between the sides, quiet and cerebral off the field but implacable on it, slightly stooped but with shoulders so powerfully broad that they almost looked too wide for doorways. Bowling off a new run-up, truncated and streamlined in consultation with the former England fast bowler turned coach Alf Gover, he took 13 of his 28 wickets at 20 unassisted; his bouncers were sparing but effective, their threat usually sufficient in these pre-helmet days.

A photo sequence of Tyson taken soon after in New Zealand by Willie Vanderson of Fox Photos sums up fast bowling at its most physically explosive: the follow-through shows him flannels billowing, receding hair on end, rotation completed so that the front arm is trailing behind him like a banner, airborne despite boots that look better suited to deep-sea diving. Few, too, have better described the pleasures of their craft than he in *A Typhoon Called Tyson* (1961), where he wrote that 'to bowl fast is to revel in the glad animal action, to thrill in physical power and to enjoy a sneaking feeling of superiority over the mortals who play the game'.

The most opaque episode in the series came in the third Test, and was immortalised by cricket-loving Harold Pinter in the scene in *The Birthday Party* (1958) in which Stanley is peppered with unintelligible questions by his mystery interrogators McCann and Goldberg. 'Who watered the wicket in Melbourne?' might have bounced off Stanley, but not so long before everyone in cricket had had a theory: just when the pitch seemed in danger of disintegrating, a fortuitous and quite illegal surface moistening over the rest day closed its cracks for a couple of sessions. A famous photograph, taken even as a mortified Melbourne Cricket Club was denying all responsibility and talking of mystery water tables, shows players peering curiously at the inscrutable pitch after play resumed – blame has subsequently been pinned on a groundsman anxious about soaring temperatures inflamed by menacing bushfires carried on desert winds. Perhaps fortunately, England was the chief beneficiary of the slight easing in batting conditions. By the time Australia was set 240 to chase, the cracks had reopened, the ball was rasping through at various heights, and Tyson was irresistible: his 7 for 27 culminated in a 51-ball spell of 6 for 16. The fall of the last wicket on the stroke of lunch on the last day left the stands with tens of thousands of stunned fans and caterers with tens of thousands of surplus meat pies.

The caravan that wore its way to Adelaide now had a certain momentum. A further unruly Australian collapse here yielded England its first victory in a series in Australia since Bodyline, and a win with certain similarities: the combination of unyielding captaincy and extreme pace, the fightback from early defeat and the trend of growing supremacy, even the brave omission of a storied great (Bedser's counterpart in 1932–3 had been Maurice Tate). A further likeness lay ahead: like Larwood, Tyson would settle in Australia, first in Melbourne, later on the Gold Coast.

By now, Hutton felt like 'the jockey on a runaway Derby winner': Australia was saved a 1-4 flogging, in fact, only by Sydney's worst flooding in 50 years, which ensured a sodden inconclusion in the final Test after the hosts had followed on. Pickings had been lean for the batsmen of both sides, with only five centuries in toto. But Australia was left to lament a second consecutive Ashes defeat that in 1956 became a third, thanks this time to spin, with Jim Laker irrepressible as an injured Tyson was confined to a solitary Test.

The Australian captain in the latter two series, off-spinner Ian Johnson, never quite shook off suspicions that, as Ray Robinson hinted in his cool appraisal for *The Cricketer*, he was the pick of a conservative establishment too squeamish to promote Keith Miller to the role. Australia's next great captain was in Johnson's ranks in 1954–5, even if Richie Benaud's 148 runs at 16.4 and 10 wickets at 37.7 hardly suggested it. But, however powerful it may be for a period, no force is ever permanent.

★

Fresh from regaining the Ashes after a 20-year drought in 1953, Len Hutton's England went to Australia with a particularly strong side, spearheaded by one seriously fast bowler in Frank Tyson. Ray Robinson reports.

By the third Test match it became clear that Australia had no counter to the high-speed bowling of Tyson and Statham. Tyson, with his purposeful stride and obvious shoulder power, and Statham with his rhythmic run and flexible arm, made an unforgettable sight which never failed to stir me. They desolated Australia's batting in a way not seen since Larwood and his fellow bowlers ravaged it in the Bodyline Tests 22 years earlier. As far as memory can be trusted over such a span I believe that Tyson is as fast as Larwood was then. As a pair he and Statham are the swiftest I have ever seen in action for England. In the rubber they took 46 wickets of the 80 wickets shared by nine English bowlers.

So Hutton carried the day with fast bowling. On the Saturday in Melbourne all except two of the 27 overs from the higher end were bowled by Tyson and Statham, so the batsmen were allowed no respite from the fast bowling, though Hutton contrived to give each bowler half-hour rests between turns of three overs or so at the crease. After a suggestion that he was keeping the total overs a day low, so that the fast bowlers could keep the pressure on the batsmen, Hutton explained that two of his bowlers were almost newcomers to Test cricket and he felt it his duty to see that they received the utmost guidance he could give in placing their fields for the various batsmen.

England is envied for possession of two such batsmen as the vice-captain PBH May and MC Cowdrey, whom Hutton rightly classes as the two best batsmen in the world under 25. After the innings defeat in the first Test, England's hopes were faint on the third day of the second Test when the third wicket in the second innings fell with the side still 19 runs behind. The 116 partnership by May and Cowdrey was the turning-point of the whole series. May was the first of the team to score a Test century. He is the noblest straight driver in international cricket, equally punishing off front foot or back. Cowdrey's batting, as solid as his build, is remarkably mature for an undergraduate of 22. The Oxford captain's chin never strays far from his shirt collar and I have never seen anyone else play so close to his front leg, the stanchion of his defence and his powerful driving, patient and well-placed. He often spare half-volleys but wickets were always precious when he came in. In the Melbourne Test innings in which Cowdrey scored 102 the other batsmen managed only 80.

Australia had the opening bowling combination of Lindwall and Miller in only two of the four Tests that decided the rubber. Miller missed the second Test because of a swollen knee and Lindwall the fourth because of a calf injury. It is impossible to calculate the difference this made. At 35, Miller is still unrivalled as an allrounder for a big occasion but the amount of bowling he does will have to be tapered off if he is to do himself anything like justice as a batsman. In looking past this inspiring cricketer for captain, the Australian Board of Control did not give their team the best chance of wresting the Ashes from England. The board's invidious decision placed Ian Johnson in an unenviable position. His task was not eased by repeated published reminders that a number of critics thought the wrong man was leading Australia. Though he lacked Miller's flair, I thought Johnson did fairly well. On the main count, he could not be held to blame for his batsmen's failure to cope with high-speed bowling, which he himself faced resourcefully and resolutely.

Australia were helpless in the face of the most devastating performance of pace bowling ever seen, as CB Fry discusses.

A few weeks ago television subjected the Prime Minister of all Australia to quizification by four eminent newspaper men; and the leader of the panel invited Mr Menzies to give them, laymen as they were, his views on the debacle of Australian cricket at Adelaide and elsewhere and the phenomenal success of our Frank Tyson.

The connection was that there had been adroit and even crafty questions addressed to Australia's Prime Minister on Formosa and the China Seas. Typhoons are phenomena of those wide waters.

Needless to say the politician was a match even for the journalists in the art of dialectic. He glanced the difficult question to leg in Prince Ranji's best manner but was ready with a straight drive for the fast one they pulled on him. Trust Mr Menzies. He is one of the best judges alive of the great game and a master of phrasing.

About Mr Frank Tyson, he said first 'please don't forget Statham; they worked in company'. He said that he classed the pair as equal to the best fast bowlers he had ever seen, for example, McDonald and Gregory, Larwood and Voce and any rival names, if any.

Let us consider the difference that real fast bowling makes in first-class cricket. I write as one who was still active in big cricket when anything approaching real pace was a rarity, when the appearance of a Larwood found all sorts of hero-batsmen walking in front of their stumps, missing the ball and being hit on their thighs and in their ribs and squealing for legislative protection.

No laudator piffle about this. After the Larwood–Jardine flurry and fuss in Australia in the thirties I saw a Test match at Nottingham played on an innocuous red-marl wicket when five of the best Australian batsmen, Woodford, Ponsford and Co., were walking in front trying to play Kenneth Farnes' fairly fast stuff away to leg and in the process being hit by the ball on their thighs. Why? Because they had been brought up on nothing faster than fast-medium bowling at which they had found convenient to push forward and walk around so as to persuade the ball away towards the onside between mid-on and the umpire, which they found easy to kill with leisurely back-play; which they could leave alone or cut at will outside the off-stump.

Yes, my hearties. But you meet a Larwood, a Lockwood or a Tyson and you cannot amiably defend or attack in that comfortable fashion. The genuinely fast bowler, the Typhoon, is on you all too quickly. You have scarcely time to play a stroke at all. You have to be keen as a razor and swift as a snake in order to counter real speed. The batsman who does not lift his bat from the blockhole in good time, who crouches over his handle, who does not stand tall and commanding, finds himself snatching at a save-me-somehow stroke, edging or missing the high-riser and too late in blocking the one that keeps low.

No, sheer pace is for the batsman, if it is sheer enough, a separate problem. A problem that can be mastered but not without toughness and grit and resolution, not without intelligence and aptitude; not without something more behind your effort and the half-baked maxims of the average 'coach', not without an alert determination to counter-attack the dynamics of the human catapult who is attacking you.

Is Tyson the fastest ever? That is a useless question because no one can say. Pure academics. But really fast he is by any standard.

1972

Five being an odd number, Ashes series are implicitly directed towards a decisive outcome. Yet every so often, one has finished with honours even, including consecutively in 1965–6 and 1968, each, rather wearyingly, featuring three draws. The Ashes of 1972 belongs in a subtly different category, the touring team having been uniquely compelled to come back twice from deficits: played out, as John Arlott put it, 'at full competition without acrimony' and providing 'constant surprise and suspense', it is in some respects a forgotten classic of the Test genre, owned by nobody. Yet although Ian Chappell's team were to leave the trophy behind, their spirit and skill heralded a resurgence in Australian cricket after a period of austerity. With the addition of a few moustaches and the exposure of a little more chest hair, this was the team that would lead the decade, the names of Chappell, Lillee, Marsh, Stackpole, Edwards, Walters and Mallett et al. coming trippingly from the tongue.

In advance of the tour, Australian Test selector Neil Harvey told Chappell that he had been charged with 'a team of goers' – this was by way of consoling him for the non-selection of Australia's most experienced batsman, Bill Lawry, and pace bowler, Graham McKenzie. If some choices yielded little, they were all decisively forward-looking, and on which the captain was free to place his stamp. Just as well, perhaps, that he had one. Grandsons of a former Australian captain, Victor

Richardson, Ian and his brother Greg liked their cricket with a touch of flair and a philosophy of selflessness. England, meanwhile, was cannily captained by Ray Illingworth, and contained many of the players he had led successfully while recapturing the Ashes 18 months earlier. After 31 wickets at 23 against Australia away, John Snow would take 24 wickets at 23 against them at home, a noteworthy double.

The Australian campaign began inauspiciously. At Old Trafford, they extended to 12 their streak without an Ashes victory, suffering an 89-run defeat, mainly by losing all 10 first-innings wickets for 74. The 25-year-old South African émigré Tony Greig marked his Test debut with 57, 62, 5 wickets for 74 and a crucial slip catch. But Snow's 8 for 128 was matched by Lillee's 8 for 106, and the game's highest scorer, with 91 from 111 balls to complement six catches, was the pugnacious Rod Marsh. The emerging dynamic was of experience versus energy, and at Lord's it veered back violently.

The second Test ranks as one of the most extraordinary of all. In 1970, West Australian Bob Massie had come to England to try his luck, taken three expensive second XI wickets at Northants, and not been offered a contract. Now, in dim and muggy conditions, he swung, swerved and slanted the ball every which way, transfixing batsman after batsman from the Nursery End, from round the wicket as well as over: by early on the second day, he had become only the third bowler to claim eight Test wickets on debut.

In defiance of Snow, Ian Chappell made a militant half-century and Greg Chappell a poised and controlled century, with their parents, brother Trevor and long-time coach Chester Bennett in the crowd. Greg would regard his 131 in 373 minutes as the best innings of his career: in conditions demanding vigilance in the V, it took him three hours to strike the first of his

14 boundaries. In the middle, he counted his runs in silent 10s; at intervals, he would sit away from his teammates so as not to let his concentration slip. In more light-hearted but hardly less crucial vein, Marsh hit two sixes and six fours in 50.

Massie then proved even more effective and hypnotic in the second innings, breaking through every time Ian Chappell was on the point of resting him. All 16 of his wickets, for 137 in 60 overs, were bowled, lbw or caught behind the wicket. Never again would Massie obtain such parabolic movement – he would play five more Tests for only 15 further victims. But his figures at Lord's remain the best by a pace bowler in Anglo-Australian annals. Just as amazingly, Australia's eight-wicket victory was its first Test win of the decade. It was celebrated with such gusto that Lillee at a royal reception a few hours later introduced himself to the Queen with a time-less: 'G'day.'

Still slightly spooked by Lillee and Massie, when the third Test began at Trent Bridge two weeks later, Illingworth responded to another overcast morning by sending the visitors in, only for hundreds by Keith Stackpole and Ross Edwards to build Australia an unassailable advantage. Eventually, Australia set England 451 to win in 561 minutes in the final innings. 'Outplayed, outmanoeuvred and outclassed,' as Arlott put it in the *Guardian*, the hosts needed all their professional aplomb to ensure a stalemate.

Reporting for *The Cricketer*, John Woodcock described the fourth Test at Headingley as 'one of the most controversial Test matches of recent times' – if anything, this was an under-statement. In freezing damp before the match, curator George Cawthray's alarmingly piebald pitch was stricken with a fungus called Fusarium. The result was a surface that every so often produced something unplayable and otherwise generated the mainly untimeable. Not since Old Trafford in 1956 had 22 yards more closely resembled no man's land, 22 of 31 wickets falling to spin over the game's eight hectic sessions. Illingworth's first innings 57 was the match's only half-century, the 104 he added with Snow for England's eighth wicket one of only two partnerships worth more than fifty. Derek Underwood, in conditions tailored to his insidious left-arm deceptions, claimed 10 for 82 from 51 overs, ensuring that the Ashes remained in English custody. After the match, Cawthray's dubious surface was lugubriously dug up – as far as Australians were concerned, one game too late.

Beginning on August 10, the fifth Test at The Oval was the first in England to be televised live in Australia; it would round out, too, the first Ashes captain's diary, being kept by Ian Chappell for publication as *Tigers Among the Lions* (1972). The cricket fully lived up to its expanded global audience. Lillee, his walk back a hearty 44 paces, his run-in as untamed as his hair, hurled himself into the fray on the first day, and with three wickets in four balls reduced England to 7 for 159. They were revived by an irreverent partnership between Alan Knott and Geoff Arnold of 81 in 69 minutes, but Australia after two early losses took control, in the person of the brothers Chappell. For the first time in a series dominated by the ball, a session passed without a wicket; for the first time in history, brothers each scored a century in the same innings of a Test match. In six years of first-class cricket, the pair had only once added a hundred; now they added twice that, in just over four hours, and Australia secured the lead for the loss of three wickets. Underwood kept England's arrears to 115, but England then lost three wickets in erasing it.

With the match to be played to a completion, the fluctuations never ceased. Dropped catches impeded Australia's progress; the second new ball expedited it; Knott and the tail again proved hard to remove. With 10 for 181, Lillee's series record grew to 31 wickets at 17.7, an Australian record to that time; gate receipts, meanwhile, swelled to a world record of more than £250,000. Australia began the sixth morning, the last of the series, needing 126 with nine wickets in hand – on a wearing wicket against Underwood, harder than it sounded. They lost three wickets for five runs in 25 minutes; they went a quarter of an hour without a run; another wicket at this point and 1-3 defeat would have been distinctly possible. Injuries to Illingworth and Snow tilted the balance back. With positive, perky strokes either side of lunch, Marsh and Paul Sheahan put on the 71 necessary to square the series, a widely published photograph of their excited, arm-in-arm dash for the pavilion at the end symbolising the strides their cricket had taken.

If later Australian cricket sides would at times invest too much in machismo, this one, as Woodcock noted in *The Cricketer*, was respected for courtesy as well as competitiveness; it even got on with its manager Ray Steele, who admired the captain's 'basic down-to-earth attitude and freedom from humbug'. 'We're a young team and this tour has done a great deal to teach us how to play under variable conditions,' said Ian Chappell after the series. 'The team should be better the next time we meet England in our own country in 1974/75.' By then they were without the retired Stackpole and the faded Massie, but the volatile Jeff Thomson and the reliable Max Walker had joined Lillee in a to-die-for pace unit. England were also sans Illingworth, curtly sacked in September 1973 despite a record of 12 Test wins and only five defeats. Two-all, then, belied the teams' funicular fates: well-matched as they were for the summer, they were trending in opposite directions.

★

A topsy-turvy series in which England had just enough tricks up their sleeve to retain the Ashes, but Australia could claim a win on points, as the side that would define the next generation of Australian cricket came into its own. John Woodcock reports on each of the five Tests, starting at Old Trafford.

Every seam bowler worthy of name must have coveted his chance to try his arm at Old Trafford in the first Test Match. With the ball moving all over the place for the first four days England more or less had to win, and they did so in the end by 89 runs with two and a half hours to spare.

In recent times the seamers have never had it so good. In four innings only 877 runs were made, and there would have been fewer still had the catching been better.

Arnold's luck as a cricketer changed when he was preferred to Lever, Price, Shuttleworth or any of the others who might have shared the new ball with Snow. His length and direction were exemplary, and he moved the ball about in Australia's first innings in a way that could have confounded anyone you care to name, from WG Grace to Geoffrey Boycott. With the weather generally overcast both sides had an equal chance to exploit the conditions. Lillee's 6 for 36 in 16 overs on the fourth day is an indication of this.

Australia's collapse on the last morning, when they lost 6 wickets for 90 runs, was reminiscent of those which enabled England to win the Ashes in Australia on their last tour. As Stackpole showed, in a fine innings of 67, and Marsh and Gleeson in an unexpected partnership of 104 for the ninth wicket, there was much less in the pitch than there had been on earlier days which could not be countered by resolution and a good technique. First Greg Chappell, then Watson, and finally Walters got themselves out by playing carelessly.

Marsh's wonderful hitting – he struck Gifford for four sixes in his three overs – and Gleeson's stubborn defence, as well as the bowling of Lillee and Stackpole's batting, had given Australia reason to hope for better things at Lord's.

The second Test would become known as Massie's Match thanks to a quite unbelievable performance by Australia's Bob Massie on debut. One-all.

The second Test match at Lord's produced a succession of riddles. How could an Australian side without a Test match victory for two and a half years have won it in conditions that were so peculiarly English? How, on a pitch that was described as being 'as good as any you'll find in Adelaide', could England, in their second innings, lose 9 wickets for 86 runs in 55.2 overs?

How could Bob Massie, in his first official Test, achieve the truly wonderful figures of 16 wickets for 137 runs (only Jim Laker and SF Barnes have ever taken more wickets in a Test match) when he was rejected by Northamptonshire a year or two ago after he had been there on trial?

It was indeed an extraordinary match, and when it was over a series which had looked to be in England's pocket after Old Trafford was suddenly wide open. Massie carved out a place for himself in cricket history by making the most of the atmosphere, which was heavy and humid for the first three days, and by confounding England's batsmen by bowling round the wicket at them. England went into the match with two fast bowlers (Snow and Price) when what they needed was at least one top-class swing/seam bowler. Tom Cartwright, had he been playing, might have been the answer to Massie. Even so, Snow's 5 for 57 in Australia's first innings was excellent.

Greg Chappell's 131, which pulled Australia round from 87 for 4, in reply to England's first innings total of 272, was scarcely less vital than Massie's bowling. It was a superbly judged piece of batting, and technically of the very highest quality. Without it Australia's chances of making a fight of the series could well have collapsed – like England's second innings. This was a terrific match for Western Australia, whose four representatives all had a major hand in Australia's victory.

England were still shell-shocked when they got to Trent Bridge, but where an easy-paced wicket made for a fairly routine draw.

Upon winning the toss for the third time in the series Illingworth put Australia in to bat in the hope of finding some help for his seamers. It was an understandable decision, even if it was influenced by doubts about facing Massie and Lillee at the start of the match. When the pitch was found to contain none of the juice that Illingworth had hoped for England were in trouble, and this was made worse by a succession of dropped catches, on the first day. Stackpole, who made 114, was let off twice before he was fifty. But with the pitch playing as flawlessly on the last day as on the first, all was well in the end.

By the finish, in fact, England could feel that they had got the better of Massie, temporarily at least. In the second innings he took 1 for 49. In three innings before that he had taken 20 for 180. Gleeson posed no particular threat, and as Australia pressed for victory in the fourth innings Lillee rather lost his rhythm. All this could be seen as an encouraging sign for the rest of the series. It meant, too, that there were visions of

England winning at the start of the last day, when they needed another 341 runs. At lunch, with 210 minutes left and eight wickets standing, they were still 251 runs short; and when Smith and Parfitt were both out to Lillee, armed with a new ball, they applied themselves to making a draw of it, which, you could say, was really all they had ever done.

England win at Headingley amid claims that the pitch had been tampered with in an effort to nullify Lillee and Massie.

England retained the Ashes at Headingley in one of the most controversial Test matches of recent times. They won at five o'clock on the third day, after bowling Australia out for 146 and 136 on a pitch as bare as a ballroom floor. The match-winner was Underwood, who, in his first Test appearance of the summer, took 10 wickets for 82 runs in 52 overs. The top score for either was Illingworth's 57 in England's first innings. For him the match was a personal triumph, whatever the state of the pitch.

Whichever side Underwood had been playing for would almost certainly have won. When the ball is turning, even as slowly as it was at Headingley, he is the best in the world. This was what made the Australians so suspicious. Without saying so, some of them thought it was a 'fix'. Personally I believe that the grass was taken off not to suit Underwood but to prevent a repetition of the accident, earlier in the month, in which Boycott had his finger smashed by Willis. Had the grounds-man taken less grass off we should no doubt have had a more evenly balanced match, giving the Australians less cause for complaint.

On the afternoon before the Test it was obvious for all to see that the pitch was to be a burial ground for fast bowlers. Just as it was obvious, when Illingworth and Underwood began to turn the ball on the first morning of play, that it was to be a battle of the spinners. On the first afternoon, in two hours and five minutes, Australia lost 6 wickets for 40 runs in 39 overs. On the second morning, in two hours' play, England lost 6 wickets for 69 runs in 33 overs. On the third day Australia were bowled out in 56.1 overs. England, needing 20 to win, lost Edrich and could be thankful that it wasn't 150 they needed.

Australia square the series at The Oval. John Woodcock senses that there's something to Ian Chappell's promising side.

Only the bigots will have felt that Australia's victory in the fifth Test match, leading to a drawn series, was a bad thing. The Oval groundsman produced a pitch which lasted well, and the Australians, true to their word, proved themselves just the better side in these conditions. It was a wonderful Test match; either side could have won until towards the end of the final partnership – between Sheahan and Marsh.

In the fourth innings Australia needed 242 to win. They had got 100 for 1 when Illingworth sprained his right ankle so severely that he never bowled again. With the ball turning by then this was the last thing England wanted. Even so, Australia slumped to 137 for 4 early on the last day, which later became 171 for 5, so that England yielded bravely.

As usually happens when one side is on the way up, the other on the way out, Australia got better as the series went on and England did not. Although not particularly successful in the two matches in which he played, or convincing against Lillee, Boycott's absence was a great loss to England. He could have made the difference between victory and defeat at The Oval, just as Massie could have done for Australia in the first

Test, had he been bowling in those freakish conditions at Old Trafford. All things considered – not least the Headingley pitch – 2-2 was a pretty fair result.

1981

One in nine workers were unemployed, and inflation was 16 per cent. There were convulsive riots in more than a score of cities and towns, and uproar everywhere, whether it was Irish paramilitaries detonating bombs and sinking ships, female peace protesters thronging Greenham Common or civil servants striking over public-sector austerities; even the marriage of the Prince of Wales and Lady Diana Spencer, seemingly fairy-tale, would end unhappily. Yet for cricket, the year 1981 retains a magical ring. Perhaps no series has so often been replayed, a guaranteed crowd-pleaser thanks to its arc of adversity and deliverance, mysterious chemistry and spontaneous brilliance, England and Australia. Had the unavailable Greg Chappell toured rather than his younger brother Trevor, the balance may have been otherwise. As it was, two teams otherwise well-matched man-for-man were separated by a single cricket phenomenon, Ian Botham.

Summer began with Botham at bay, his joyless year as captain of England a contrast to the three barnstorming all-round years before it, when he had averaged 40 with the bat, 18 with the ball. The patience of selectors had thinned, and his commissions were being handed out one at a time. His Australian counterpart, 27-year-old Hughes, could take some confidence in the experience of his star elders Dennis Lillee and Rod Marsh, and the promise of prodigies like Allan Border and Terry Alderman.

For Botham, the experience soon soured further. Hughes sent England in at Trent Bridge where Lillee and Alderman shot them out for 185 and 125, and Border battled almost six hours to secure a five-wicket victory. Then, beneath the gaze of the game's governors at Lord's, Botham picked up an ignominious pair in a drawn match that left him without a win in a dozen Tests as captain. He felt, in his words, 'like a 200-year-old', and stepped down before being pushed.

To go forward, England's selectors walked back, tapping Botham's predecessor Mike Brearley. Grizzled and cerebral, 39-year-old Brearley was Botham's opposite in almost every respect, including natural talent, his average from 35 previous Tests an unflattering 23.6. Yet for Botham he had always been a talisman: Brearley was 'someone I admire both as a person and a captain and whose judgement I respect'. For his own part, Brearley felt 'ready for the call'. He had been undergoing psychoanalysis since September 1979 as part of his training in that career; what he was to accomplish over the next four Tests demonstrated extraordinary capacities in sympathy and insight.

For the first three and a half days of the third Test at Headingley, England's improvement was difficult to discern. In conditions in which their seamers should have excelled, Australia passed 400; their batsmen then lasted barely 50 overs, and were forced to follow on. Their only source of satisfaction was Botham, who in nearly 40 overs took 6 for 95, and from 54 balls made 50. But after the rest day, gloom continued to descend: just after 3pm, with England 7 for 135 in its second innings, still 92 runs in arrears, the new electronic scoreboard quoted odds on Australia of 1-4, on a draw of 5-2, and on England of 500-1. So outrageous were they for a two-horse race that Lillee and Marsh could not forbear a £10 flutter with Ladbrokes.

Botham was still at the wicket at tea, a subdued 39 from 87 balls, but had no plans to linger – he had been one of several England players to check out of their hotel that morning. Lillee and Alderman, who had so far carried all before them, were tiring. Botham took them on, in company with Graham Dilley, a tailender but with pretensions; the field scattered; there were no-balls, overthrows, misses, mishits and confusion. Botham's first 50 took 57 balls, his second just 30, composed of 11 fours and a soaring straight six. Dilley's 56, slightly more sedate but often handsome, helped in the addition of 117 runs in 80 minutes.

England were still only 25 in credit when Dilley fell, but No.10 Chris Old and No.11 Bob Willis kept Botham company while a further 104 were added in 85 minutes. Having been within a few tailend wickets of an innings victory, Australia found themselves 20 hours later commencing an awkward fourth-innings chase, and to Botham lost an early wicket. Still there was no logic to what followed. At 1 for 56, Australia needed 74 for victory with nine wickets left: the sun was out; neither time nor the pitch were a factor; lunch beckoned, and after that a 2-0 lead. When Bob Willis switched to the Kirkstall Lane End, he had not taken a wicket for more than 40 overs, had been plagued by no-balls and ill health. Suddenly, with the wind at his back, he struck thrice, the ball lifting vehemently. Suddenly, Brearley felt, England might even be favourites.

The momentum shift was complete. Australia's subsidence continued after the break, until seven wickets had fallen for 19 runs in barely an hour's elapsed time, with Willis bowling almost in a disassociated state – he stood aloof from celebrations, stalked back and stormed in as if on a two-speed conveyor belt. With Australia 55 runs from victory, Lillee and Bright suddenly scored 35 in four overs, but a sharp catch and a pinpoint yorker quelled their brief uprising, rounded Willis' figures out at 8 for 43, and made for an 18-run victory margin – Lillee and Marsh experienced perhaps sports betting's most rueful £7,500 collect.

Restored to form and fortune, Botham would make the summer his own. The fourth Test at Edgbaston teetered for three days without so much as a half-century, until Australia stood 46 from victory with six wickets remaining. But when a ball from John Emburey turned and bounced on the gritty Border, Brearley backed his intuition and turned to Botham, who took 5 for 1 in 28 deliveries, fast, straight and true.

The fifth Test at Old Trafford stood in a fine balance on its third day as England, after securing a 101-run first innings lead, found themselves in the doldrums of 5 for 104 in 69 overs. Again Botham broke the game open, with 118 in 123 minutes and two moods: an initial reconnaissance of 28 in 53 balls, followed by a spectacular of 90 in 49, largely at the expense of the second new ball. A record six sixes sailed into an ecstatic crowd. Of a partnership with Botham of 149, Chris Tavare eked out 28, in among Test cricket's third slowest Test half-century.

Having collapsed in their previous two fourth innings, Australia showed commendable pride: Graham Yallop made a fluent hundred, Border a stoic one, and England needed 136 overs to secure a 103-run victory and the Ashes. But what had started so promisingly would haunt the luckless Hughes thereafter. Lillee and Marsh fumed at his occasional naivety; he was excoriated by the Australian press, as Botham had been by the English; there would for the Australian be no happy ending, his career finishing just over three years later in tears of disillusionment. Of Botham, meanwhile, there was now no stopping. His match figures in a drawn sixth Test at

The Oval, 91-22-253-10, were those of a man newly glutton-ous for the game.

Half a dozen Tests gave the players of 1981 almost unprec-edented scope: Botham's 399 runs at 36.3, 34 wickets at 20.5 and 11 catches stretched from horizon to horizon. There were other giant feats, too: Border's 533 runs at 59 includ-ing a period where he was not dismissed for 11 hours, while Alderman and Lillee claimed 81 wickets between them in 636.4 overs, including 157 maidens. The averages, however, spoke only an approximation of the truth, for they showed Brearley as contributing only 151 runs for eight stays at the crease. Sometimes claims for captaincy can be fanciful, romantic, credulous. Without Brearley's faith and sang-froid, however, there would almost certainly have been no English fightback, no Botham bounceback, and no legacy of 1981 to celebrate all the years since.

*

'Botham's Ashes' began with a low-scoring Australian victory in Nottingham. Pressure was heaped on under-fire England captain Ian Botham, and, after a draw at Lord's, his posi-tion had become untenable. *The Cricketer* editor Christopher Martin-Jenkins reports as the most extraordinary tale of redemption unfolds.

At Lord's on the gloriously sunny evening of July 7, Ian Botham resigned a captaincy which would in any case have been taken from him after 12 Tests in charge. His record in 13 hectic and traumatic months was eight draws and four defeats. His succes-sor was also his predecessor, Mike Brearley, who lost three of his last four Tests as captain, in Australia in 1979/80.

The original choice of Botham at the age of 24 was a gamble which always seemed likely to fail. Ironically, it was on Botham's brilliance as an allrounder, but especially as a match-winning bowler, that many of Brearley's successes as a captain were based. Before he became captain Botham scored 1,336 runs at an average of over 40 in his 25 Tests and took 139 wickets at an average of 18. During the next 12 games he scored only 276 runs at an average of 14 and took 35 wickets almost twice as expensively as before.

Alec Bedser, along with his fellow selectors, and Brearley, who had recommended Botham as his successor last year, must take the responsibility for thrusting a raw, young ser-geant-major into the role of a commanding officer for battles against a superior enemy. Botham was their key player and it was obvious enough that his responsibilities off the field would tax him greatly. That such a dynamo should have been worn down so soon, even if he can be recharged, is a tragedy for English cricket. If a more experienced man – Fletcher, Boycott or Willis – had been given the task, each might have been just as dramatic a failure, but the consequence of English cricket would have been much less damaging. Mr Bedser, for whom one feels almost as much sympathy as the young man he helped to choose, said that Botham might be back as captain of England in 12 months. It was a characteristically loyal statement by a kind-hearted man but it overlooked the evidence: although Ian Botham has many qualities, a flair for leadership is not yet one of them.

Mike Brearley is called out of international hibernation, and Botham, freed from the heavy burden, powers England to the most sensational turnaround ever seen in sport.

Ian Botham, magically transformed in his first match away from a captaincy which had weighed more heavily than Frodo's ring, stole the third Test from Australia in two hours of thunderous driving. Coming in at 105 for 5, with England still 122 behind, his brilliance, bravado and, in Kim Hughes' words, his 'brute strength', gave England's bowlers 129 runs to play with. At 56 for one their cause seemed hopeless but Bob Willis took eight of the last nine wickets, Mike Gatting and Graham Dilley held crucial catches and the daylight robbery was completed amidst national rejoicing.

The astounding turnabout in a momentous day's cricket began shortly before tea [on the fourth day] when Bob Taylor was caught off a glove at short-leg to make England 135 for seven, still 92 behind. By tea, Botham and Dilley had taken the score to 176 for seven. Between tea and the close Botham added a further 106 off his own bat out of the 175 runs added in 27 overs. John Woodcock rightly compared [Botham's] spectacular piece of controlled hitting to Gilbert Jessop; Peter West remarked that it was as if the village blacksmith had taken charge of a Test match. Botham himself, launching his sixteen-stone frame at the ball with joyous abandon, just smiled his way through one of the most amazing innings of all time. Murderous drives and square cuts brought him 19 fours in his personal century, reached off 87 balls: he also stepped three paces down the pitch to drive the fast-medium Alderman straight for six.

Dilley outscored Botham with a series of rasping off and cover drives. He never seemed to move his feet – nor, very often, did Botham – but luck had changed sides with a vengeance and both players seemed either to middle the ball or to miss it altogether.

With his Test career in doubt for the umpteenth time, Willis, of the big heart and vicious bounce, gave it everything he knew. Brushing aside the cost of regular no-balls, he bowled at fierce pace to a shorter length and a straighter line than in the first innings. And suddenly Australia's foundation crumbled. Chappell deflected a mean bouncer with his glove in front of his face; Hughes edged another lifter low to third slip; and Yallop fended off to short-leg, where Gatting held a fine low catch. These wickets fell in the space of 11 balls from Willis and at lunch it was 58 for four.

Old, with his meticulous accuracy, had taken over from Willey before lunch into the breeze and at 65 Border went back to him, misjudged the bounce and played onto his stumps. Three runs later Dyson shaped to repeat the cracking hook he had played off Willis in the previous over and this time went through with the stroke too early, gloving it to Taylor.

Marsh hooked Willis off the top edge to a deep fine leg where Dilley judged the catch brilliantly, a yard in from the boundary rope. Had it been a six ...

Lawson quickly touched Willis to the admirable Taylor but Lillee and Bright bravely reversed the surging tide. Bright hit two legside fours in one over from Old, Lillee two on the offside off Willis. In four overs they added 35 and suddenly in this frantic match only 20 were needed by Australia. Willis had the sense, at this stage, to change his hitherto successful policy of bowling and as soon as he did so Lillee spooned a ball towards mid-on. Gatting was slow to sight it but, just in time, ran in and held the ball low to the ground.

Alderman walked out with 20 still needed, and Brearley brought on Botham to give the match what he felt would be the appropriate finish. However, it was the inspired Willis who knocked out Bright's middle stump with a full length to complete the victory that had saved a moribund series.

Botham, now on a roll, wins the next Test for England with the ball ...

England's rousing victory in the fourth Test at Edgbaston was seen at the time as being quite as remarkable as the one at Headingley. In fact, it was much more predictable, even with Australia needing only 151 to win on a reasonably comfortable pitch, because this was always an even match between two sides of similar ability, likely to have a tight finish. At Headingley, Australia had been in total control, England 500-1; at Edgbaston, the bookmakers seldom risked more than two to one against any result. This made it a gripping, tense encounter, made more enjoyable by the old-fashioned weather in which it was played.

England took the fourth wicket at 87 when Yallop tried to turn Emburey against the spin and edged to silly point. But the crucial wicket came at 105 when Border, who had put away any rare short balls from Emburey and resisted all other temptation, received one which really popped and turned to give short-leg a simple catch. 105 for 5!

Marsh, who cut his first ball from Emburey for four, was in harness with Kent when Brearley called up Botham to take over at the City End from Willis, who had taken too much out of himself in his morning spell. Brearley might have turned instead to Old, or to Willey, who never got a ball in the match. But he has faith in Botham and, thanks to Brearley, Botham has rediscovered faith in himself. At once he began to pound in at the batsmen with quite irresistible force. Marsh let emotion outweigh reason and was late and across the line as he drove furiously at a full-length ball. Botham's next delivery was fast and kept low. Bright was late on it and palpably lbw. 114 for seven!

Botham finished off the innings now with the surge of a champion. The slow, draining tension of the afternoon turned into euphoria for the home team and their supporters, despair for all Australians. Lillee chased a very wide ball and Taylor caught him joyfully at the second attempt. Kent, the last authentic batsman, drove desperately towards mid-on and was castled via his pads; Alderman missed his first two balls and was bowled by the third. In 28 balls Botham had taken five wickets for one run.

... and then the one after with the bat.

When Botham came in, England's lead was 205. He played himself in sensibly but had begun to flex his muscles already when the second new ball was claimed by Hughes at 151 for five. Suddenly, it was mayhem. In the next over from Lillee, Botham hooked two sixes over backward square-leg, clubbing the ball high on the bat from just in front of his unprotected head. Next he square cut superbly and drove back over Lillee's head with awesome force. 22 runs came from the over. Another superb drive over Alderman's head was followed by perhaps the best stroke of all, an apparently effortless pull yards over mid-wicket into a delirious crowd.

Australia's fielding never wilted but there was no stopping Botham ... he moved from 28 to 100 in 37 minutes, reaching the landmark off his 86th ball with a sweep off Bright, his fifth six. He celebrated with a classical straight-drive over the sight-screen. No one in Ashes Tests had ever hit six sixes before. Only Jessop (off 75 balls at The Oval in 1902) had scored a hundred off fewer balls. Only Jessop can, indeed, be compared with Botham for destructive hitting.

Australia restore some pride in the drawn finale at The Oval. CMJ captures the mood of the stunned spectators perfectly with his emotional summary.

There may never be another series like this. England's victory must have had the same effect on the impressionable young of Britain as did those of 1953 and 1956 on those born during or just after the war. Another generation will remember 1926, a lingering few 1902. Many adults have become only temporary slaves to the most lovable and demanding of games this summer, but the younger converts are probably inspired for life. From Headingley in mid-July to The Oval at the end of August it was like living through an extended honeymoon. Those of us who love cricket felt light-headed and wanted everyone to share our enthusiasm.

2005

Even now it can be a little difficult to believe that the events of the 2005 Ashes series took place. Look up and down the Australian team that Ricky Ponting led and it is hard to spot a weakness: Matthew Hayden and Justin Langer; Damien Martyn and Michael Clarke; Adam Gilchrist, for heaven's sake. That's before you're even at perhaps history's greatest bowling combination, Shane Warne and Glenn McGrath. The cricketers of the next rank slot there only by comparison, from Jason Gillespie and Brett Lee to Michael Kasprowicz and Shaun Tait. England? Michael Vaughan was guarded by two solid openers, Marcus Trescothick and Andrew Strauss, and could place his own new ball with an honest toiler in Matthew Hoggard and a professional enigma in Steve Harmison. Then, well: Ashley

Giles? Geraint Jones? Ian Bell in his first series and Simon Jones in his last? And a year out, what could have been said of Andrew Flintoff, who at the time averaged 25 with the bat and 40 with the ball, and Kevin Pietersen, who had played three county seasons as a batsman after arriving from South Africa as an off-spinner? Perhaps Mystic Meg saw it coming; cricket's cognoscenti saw little reason to imagine other than a continuation of a decade of Australian cricket hegemony.

Even on the last day of the series, Australia could have found a way to clutch the Ashes back. Pietersen offered several chances in a tentative first half-hour at the crease, including a decidedly catchable edge to his county captain Warne at slip. But then, with one bound, he was free, and has ever a Test been drawn so ecstatically? In preserving England's 2-1 series lead, Pietersen muscled his way to 158 in 187 balls, scattering seven sixes in the festive crowd. It was as if Dunkirk had been relieved by the Light Brigade.

As in 1954–5, as in 1981, England had yanked that lead first from a deficit. When the team lined up for the first Test at Lord's, expectation was palpable. The teams had duked out two excellent one-day series, skewing first England's way then Australia's. The early exchanges were willing and sanguine, Harmison hitting the helmeted heads of Hayden and Ponting, opening a boxer's cut beneath the latter's eye. At tea on the first day, England had bowled Australia out for 190, and walked in to a standing ovation. By stumps, they were themselves a bedraggled 7 for 92, McGrath reinforcing his lethality from the Pavilion End, and setting a pattern of high hopes and false dawns that the series would follow. Pietersen, on his Test debut, stood tall midst the chaos, albeit that he also dropped three catches; otherwise it appeared that Australia had the answers regardless of the questions. As the visitors completed a 239-run mauling on the fourth day, England's chance of an ambuscade appeared to have gone.

Hereabouts, however, England broke a pattern that had dogged them in Ashes cricket for 20 years – a tendency to fragment in adversity. The axis of captain Vaughan and coach Duncan Fletcher was strong. They made no change to their team; nor did Australia intend to, until obliged by an extraordinary accident, McGrath on the morning of the second Test at Edgbaston turning an ankle during the warm-ups. To a home team looking for reasons to believe, it felt like an auspice. Unexpectedly, perhaps even a little contemptuously, sent in, they surged to 1 for 132 at lunch. Attack, for so long an Australian prerogative, was proven a game two could play. Only Warne, who responded to England's cut with thrusts of his own, looked capable of slowing them down. He took 4 for 116 from their first-day score of 407 in less than 80 overs, a kaleidoscopic day's cricket.

Having hit five of England's 10 sixes in his 68, Flintoff set to demonstrating the expansion of his all-round prowess. He approached as directly as Jonah Lomu running for a try line and kept at his task like Pete Sampras in a five-setter, while radiating a relish for the contest that recalled nobody but Botham. And as with Botham, others rallied round him, as even tough competitors took just a step or two back. Wickets were shared as a 99-run lead was secured, which Flintoff expanded with a further 73, this time with four sixes. Warne's 6 for 46 kept Australia in the game, and with the glimmer of a 2-0 lead.

Edgbaston was suspected as England's noisiest ground; it was on the third afternoon that it secured it. When Flintoff was thrown the ball, he was cheered to the echo; when he bowled Langer with his second ball, the noise was like a sonic boom; when he nicked off Ponting in the same over, there had been quieter concerts by Metallica. Every time Australia threatened to consolidate its chase for 282, England found a way. After Flintoff had caught Gilchrist and trapped Gillespie, Harmison bowled Clarke with the day's last ball, bowled 40kph slower than the penultimate delivery and landing on a perfect yorker length. Australia began the final morning needing an unlikely 107 from its last two wickets, yet Warne and Brett Lee began as if there was nothing inconceivable about it – suddenly it was England leaking runs to all parts.

The last hour, as Lee and Kasprowicz added a happy-go-lucky 59, transfixed fans in both countries, a turfed catch at third man as the target loomed in sight taking on the look of history in the making. The caught-behind decision against Kasprowicz with three runs needed was an error also, if discernible only on replay, the glove at the instant off the bat. But Billy Bowden's crooked finger had made it one-all, and filled the next three Tests with possibilities.

England did everything in the third Test at Old Trafford but win. McGrath returned to the colours, bowled Vaughan with a no-ball, and watched him storm to 166 out of 444. Only Warne stood in the way of Simon Jones' confounding spell of reverse swing, which melted Australia's middle order like an HG Wells heat ray; the nominal task of 423 for victory enticed Australia less than the assignment of batting 108 overs for safety, itself a kind of psychological concession.

By now, a sort of cricket mindedness had seized England as not since 1981. Tests were still carried forth by free-to-air television; football had yet to flood all corners of the media and the Olympics to seize the patriotic heights. At the whiff of an exciting final day, patrons drove for miles and queued for blocks, those who succeeded in obtaining admission admiring and cursing a masterful innings from Australia's captain.

Ponting stood fast for almost seven hours, hitting 16 fours and a six in 156, and if he did not make batting look easy at least he made it appear practical. But Vaughan urged his teammates to look to the Australian balcony after Lee and McGrath had survived the final four overs. The Australians were celebrating, he said – celebrating a draw. That was a newly vulnerable quarry.

Nothing in this series, however, was immune to a kind of reversion to the mean. England made their best score at Trent Bridge, dominating the Test almost from the get-go, especially once Flintoff conspired with Geraint Jones in the biggest partnership of the series, 177 from 235 balls, then Vaughan boldly enforced the follow-on. Ponting then worked himself into a fine fury when run out by a dead-eye substitute fielder, Gary Pratt, whom he suspected of lurking with coach Fletcher's intent.

Yet Australia sold themselves dearly and struck back inexpensively, England turning a final chase for 129 into a limp, thanks as ever to the irrepressible Warne. For long minutes deep in the fourth day, as England wavered at 7 for 116, it again appeared possible that the tourists might strike back from the brink of defeat and ensure the Ashes' safe-keeping. Hoggard hit a half-volley through cover to ensure at last that they did not.

Two hundred years after England had expected every man to do his duty, their cricketers bore something akin to the same burden – a Test match, perhaps the last of its kind, followed by a decided proportion of the English public. The Australians were a troubled team, many of their key players neutralised, albeit that Warne's shadow seemed to lengthen at each passing session. The darkness in this late-summer fifth Test, however, would work to England's advantage.

Flintoff upped the tempo once Strauss built the base on the first day. And although Australia made their best start of the series in reply, Langer and Hayden both making centuries, rain and bad light immediately began draining the Test of the time necessary to force the conclusion they needed. Just when they were poised to break free, too, Flintoff interposed, monopolising the ball from the Pavilion End with unflagging pace and hostility: interrupted by an overnight and lunch break, he bowled 18 consecutive overs and took 4 for 38. The title of a popular retelling of the series, *Is It Cowardly to Pray for Rain?*, originated in the other English instinct at this time to seek respite in the clouds. The Australians bought good-humouredly into the burlesque, wearing sunglasses when England began their second innings as spectators raised umbrellas. As on the last day at Edgbaston, many fans would have been made happiest by barely any cricket at all.

No one present will ever forget the final day. Pietersen had batted well during the series without quite playing the innings his talents justified; but for Warne's butterfingers at slip, he might have failed to again. After lunch, however, he mocked the solemnity of the occasion, as the stripe down the middle of his hair proclaimed his look-at-me individuality. The Australians never gave up, but were assuredly weary, even Warne, whose 76 overs in the match earned him 10 for 246 – and just as there can hardly have been a more spifflicating innings in the cause of a draw than Pietersen's, there can never have been a greater performance in a lost series than Warne's. With 40 wickets at 19.93 and 249 runs at 28, he was like a team of his own.

Many of the Australian team that walked off that day at The Oval would hang around to wreak a conclusive revenge 18 months later in Australia. The wheel might pause but it never stops – which is, in its way, the story of the Ashes.

★

Simply the tensest, most exciting Test series ever. *The Wisden Cricketer*'s contributors report on each unbelievable episode with eyes wide and mouths gaping, starting with Gideon Haigh at Lord's.

Plans for battle are notorious for never surviving contact with the enemy. England's plan in this Test lasted longer than most in recent memory – a whole two sessions – but by the end of four days was as battered and bedraggled as any since 1989.

The plan depended on a lot going right and to begin with much did. Stephen Harmison tenderised Australia's top order with bowling that seldom arrived below the waist, and seemed to centre on the sternum, then polished off the tail with 4 for 7 in 14 deliveries.

Anything Harmison could do, however, Glenn McGrath could do better. In his fourth over, he removed Marcus Trescothick then Andrew Strauss with deliveries that went down the slope; in his seventh, eighth and ninth respectively, he bowled Vaughan, Bell and Flintoff. It was high-quality seam bowling against batting of deepening diffidence and the continuation of a remarkable renaissance.

No single game can set at nought the progress of two years but Australia were not so impressive in this match as England were acutely disappointing. 'They won't give up, this lot' is a comment which Australians have heard often this summer. 'They're different. They're fighters.' But if this was the first battle, what on earth is war going to look like?

To the second at Edgbaston. Scyld Berry reports on a Test match already then making serious claims as the greatest ever played.

Has there ever been a more exciting match? The drama at Edgbaston began before the start, when news that Glenn McGrath had injured his right ankle in practice swept like a bushfire, interrupting radio programmes. It continued – at four runs an over and in front of capacity crowds who played their part in the action – right through until the climax, which really was like a Greek play, nobody knowing what the gods would decide.

Australia were behind from the moment Ricky Ponting sent England in on a flat pitch which only offered seam movement if the ball was very full, i.e. driveable. When McGrath was carried off with torn ankle ligaments, why did the captain not play to his strength and bat. He had no doubt decided to bowl in advance; changing plan would have been a vote of no confidence in his new seam attack. From the moment Brett Lee found as little deviation as a sniper's bullet, England sensed they could level the series.

It will always be a different game for England if Marcus Trescothick can survive the new-ball bowlers until Shane Warne comes on. Trescothick's 77 before lunch gave England the advantage which for the rest of the game was like an edged chance to Geraint Jones: it looked as though they might let it slip but never actually lost it. With McGrath absent and the openers going after Warne, Australia leaked runs at both ends and England's first innings 407 was their highest on the opening day of a Test since World War Two. In the match England hit 16 sixes – one sixth of their run aggregate, an amazing proportion. Yes, the boundaries were short but it was the same for both sides, and Australia managed only two.

The crowd was not quite so wildly patriotic as it is when the Birmingham Test is staged at the proper time, the last week of the university term, but it did its part in rousing Andrew

Flintoff to the status of a world-class allrounder. He had done serious bowling before but this was the first Test in which he scored substantial runs against the best: 141 off 148 balls.

Flintoff's next contribution was his bowling. To dismiss Australia in only 76 overs on a flat, slow pitch was an outstanding effort achieved largely by reverse swing. Flintoff took four wickets in four balls spread over Australia's innings: two tailenders in successive balls and then, in his first over of the second innings, Langer and Ponting. He later called it the best opening over he had ever bowled, and rightly. He reverse-swung the ball both ways at ferocious pace and had Ponting in trouble every ball.

It all seemed over on the third evening when Australia lost Michael Clarke in the extra half-hour and ended on 175 for 8, still 107 short. If nothing changed, it would be impossible for the tailenders to reach 282. But something did change: England's tactics. On the last morning Vaughan relied on his two heavyweight fast bowlers Harmison and Flintoff. They bowled Bodyline and yorkers, in other words very straight. The normal line of just outside the off-stump went out of the window. Aggression usurped thought and the runs flowed, not only from the many shots to leg but from the leg byes and byes down leg side, and the no-balls. Harmison bowled a full toss wide of off-stump which Lee – battered and bruised under England's assault – must have climbed into a thousand times since in his sleep but which he only pushed to deep cover for one. Kasprowicz had been shovelling every short ball to leg but *in extremis* he did not attack. He went for caution or survival, ducked, and only gloved down the leg side. And say what you like about Geraint Jones but he never shirks a challenge.

If there were any doubts that the series had caught the attention of the whole country after Edgbaston, they were well and truly cast aside by five remarkable days at Old Trafford, as Paul Coupar describes. England dominate, but Australia survive.

About once a decade an English Test match lights up the nation, and the glow radiates far beyond the boundary. Suddenly loud phone calls on trains seem less annoying and getting out of bed less a chore.

Such games are normally a rare pleasure, but by now it was clear this was no normal summer. As the match spiralled into the realm of fantasy on the Monday, around 15,000 fans were turned away. The Channel 4 coverage drew over 7.7m viewers, a seven-year peak. On London's Underground, so recently a place of fear, passengers were happily distracted as drivers announced score updates.

As Vaughan rightly said afterwards, England won almost every session. Edgbaston showed his side could compete; this showed it was no fluke. Australia's fielders missed seven chances, and they relied on two legends of the game – Shane Warne and the Manchester rain – to survive. It was another judder in the tectonics of world cricket.

Andrew Miller sees England go 2-1 up at Trent Bridge with another dominant display. Shane Warne's force of personality makes England sweat for every run in their run chase, as more than eight million viewers cower behind the sofa.

There was something eerily familiar about England's fourth innings target of 129. Twenty-four years earlier, in the spiritual precursor to this last Ashes nerve-shredder, Australia had themselves been left 130 to win after enforcing the follow-on and fell 18 runs short in a match that would echo down the ages.

As England's No.9, Matthew Hoggard, shambled out to join Ashley Giles with 13 runs still required, history beckoned one way or another. A packed house sick with nerves cheered every run as if it was a Cup final winner but eventually Giles prodded Shane Warne through midwicket to end the agony.

Despite [Australia's] best endeavours a target of 129 was none too forbidding, especially once Marcus Trescothick had steamed the score to 32 for 0 after five overs. But Warne, more certain of victory than any Englishman in the ground, struck with the first delivery of each of his opening overs. Andrew Strauss followed via a TV referral and when Ian Bell hooked Lee to deep backward square leg, England were 57 for 4 and as deep in the mire as Australia (58 for 4) had been at Headingley all those years ago.

Flintoff and Kevin Pietersen calmed the nerves but Lee, in a searing spell of vicious adrenalin, extracted both in consecutive overs before Geraint Jones swished Warne to mid-off in a fluffed attempt to break the shackles. But into adversity strode the diffident figure of Hoggard. Lee over-pitched as he searched for another yorker and out of the screws came the sweetest cover drive that Trent Bridge will ever witness. The demons had been vanquished and suddenly England dared to think the unthinkable.

A finale worthy of everything that had gone before it. Warne and co. take England to the wire, but Kevin Pietersen comes of age on an unbelievably tense final day at The Oval. Match drawn, Ashes regained. Tim de Lisle rejoices.

A Test series already famous for its pulsating drama demanded one last twist. The Oval supplied several. Ten hours were lost to the weather, and yet, with two sessions to go, a result was on the cards, and the most likely was an Australian win. But a display of dazzling audacity from Kevin Pietersen, and of yeoman solidity from Ashley Giles, kept the bridge. At some unidentifiable moment after 4pm on Monday, September 12, England did what some had thought they would never do. They regained the Ashes.

It didn't quite go all the way: a fourth cliffhanger was too much to ask. But the capacity crowds that queued patiently each day were repaid with rich entertainment. They saw the advantage swing from Australia to England to Australia to England to Australia to England. They saw Warne and Flintoff, the two superstars already inked in as men of the series, stretch themselves even further. And when that duel ended abruptly, its place was taken by a furious dogfight between Pietersen and Brett Lee.

Saving a Test match used to be a matter of seeing out time, cutting out risk, and being quite prepared to bore the anoraks off the crowd. With his 158, Pietersen tore up that idea and opted for a form of defence that looked suspiciously like head-long attack. The destiny of the Ashes ended up in England's least safe pair of hands. Somehow, it worked. And so the Ashes were regained not warily or watchfully, but with the fearless instinctive cricket that England had played all summer.

The final morning had it all: ebb (fluent start by Vaughan and Trescothick), flow (near-hat-trick by McGrath), thrills (Pietersen's sixes), spills (Pietersen dropped twice) and sudden brilliance in Adam Gilchrist's catch and a pair of wonderballs from Warne to Trescothick. When England lurched to lunch at 127 for 5, Australia were favourites. Consecutive deliveries hit

Pietersen in the ribs and nearly decapitated him. After lunch Pietersen got both mad and even, taking 35 off 13 balls from Lee. Bouncers were hooked into a gloating crowd; a 96mph length ball was flicked for four in a frenzied blur. Seldom had fire been fought with such fire.

Diplomacy, Politics, Controversy:
Five Ashes Flashpoints

James Coyne

T O ME, THE Ashes is a bit like the meeting of two relations with a great deal in common, but who prefer to emphasise their differences. There was a time – barely a quarter of a century ago – when English and Australian gentlemen sat in smoke-filled boardrooms at Lord's and the MCG and together decided the fate of the world game. The explosion of India's cricket and the liberalising of their country's economy from the 1980s onwards means this no longer happens. Meanwhile, the ICC has evolved from a subcommittee of Lord's into a world body – even if its standards of governance are not what they should be – regulating rules of conduct, appointing umpires and divvying up broadcasting revenues. This has removed some of the potential flashpoints between old foes. And, in this globalised T20 franchise age, English and Australian players are probably closer together in thought than ever. But England and Australia are still among the big three cricketing boards, and the Ashes remains the one sure-fire money-maker in Test cricket. Where there's money at stake, there's room for bust-ups, as has always been the case through the long history of cricket's greatest rivalry.

The Bodyline fallout

The Bodyline crisis is the touchstone for Anglo-Australian disputes. It has inspired books, plays, a range of chocolate biscuits, and a particularly one-eyed Australian TV series in the 1980s. Yet, at a time when cricket yearns for social and cultural relevance in Britain, it is sobering to be reminded that a dispute on the field of play threatened to have a materially negative impact on relations between two friendly countries. In an English context perhaps only the Mike Gatting–Shakoor Rana incident of 1987–8 comes close: in both cases, the dispute threatened to scupper a trade deal between the UK and a Commonwealth ally. That is diplomatic pressure that cricket administrators find hard to withstand.

On Saturday January 14 1933, during the third Test at Adelaide, Australia captain Bill Woodfull was struck under the heart by Harold Larwood, bowling to a conventional field. After Woodfull was out for 22, Australia's 12th man Leo O'Brien bumped into the England team manager, Pelham Warner – also editor of *The Cricketer* – and told him that his captain was in a bad way. Warner knocked on the door of the dressing room to offer his commiserations. It was then that Woodfull, calmly and politely, offered his famous rebuke. 'I don't want to see you, Mr Warner. There are two teams out there; one is trying to play cricket and the other is not.'

Warner had intended the conversation to be private, but it turned out to be the spark for a diplomatic dispute unprecedented in the history of cricket. Various Australians have been suspected as behind the leak. Warner was sure it was Woodfull's opening partner, Jack Fingleton, who had strong links to the media. But Fingleton claimed, years later, that Don Bradman gave the story to the *Sun* reporter Claude Corbett. 'I got a ring on the phone that night at our hotel,' Corbett is said to have told Fingleton. 'It was Don Bradman. We arranged a rendez-vous on North Terrace and, while we sat in his car, he told me all about the Warner–Woodfull incident. It was too hot a story to run on its own, and I gave it to all the press.' Bradman flatly denied his role in this, accusing Fingleton of continuing his ven-detta against him. For his part, O'Brien maintained that only he, Alan Kippax, Jack Ryder and Ernie Jones had witnessed the incident. Warner claimed in the ensuing furore that Woodfull had expressed regret for the incident, but Woodfull refuted that. 'I did not apologise to Mr Warner for any statement, I merely told him there was not anything personal between us. I strongly repudiate any suggestion I tendered an apology to Mr Warner for any statement I made.'

Later on that feverish Saturday, Larwood's Bodyline partner Bill Voce required treatment, and a message went out on the public address system appealing for medical assistance. A record crowd of 50,962 for the Adelaide Oval, assuming it was for Woodfull, let out a cacophony of jeers. Some chanted: 'One, two, three, four, five, six, seven, eight, nine, OUT, YOU BASTARD! Go home, you Pommie bastards! Bastards! Bastards! Bastards!'

When play resumed after the rest day, Bert Oldfield top-edged Larwood into his head, fracturing his skull. *Wisden* reflected: 'The majority of spectators completely lost hold on all their feelings.' Police ringed the boundary, fearing a full-scale riot. An England fielder is said to have turned to George Hele, one of the umpires: 'George, if they come over the fence, leave me a stump.' Hele shot back: 'Not on your life, I'll need all three myself.' The South Australia board were so concerned about serious unrest that an armed guard was placed in the middle overnight.

It was presumably this fear of public disorder that prompted the Australian board to fire off a cable to MCC after the fifth day. It was read out immediately to the assembled press in Australia.

All the crucial cables were published in *The Cricketer*'s 1933 *Spring Annual*:

The Australian Cable of Protest (January 18 1933)

Body-line bowling has assumed such proportions as to menace the best interests of the game, making protection of the body by the batsman the main consideration.

This is causing intensely bitter feeling between the players as well as injury. In our opinion it is unsportsmanlike.

Unless stopped at once, it is likely to upset the friendly relations between Australia and England.

That first Australian cable was incredibly forthright. Their state of alarm was, in hindsight, completely understandable. But they also seem to have dashed the message off in a hurry, with only five of the nine board members present at Adelaide. The rest were scattered across the country. Laurence le Quesne wrote: 'The absent members were merely asked to approve the sending of a telegram of protest that they had not seen.' Their message also assumed a deal of knowledge about the action in Australia, which English audiences had not adequately seen. Had they had longer to think about it, the board might have reconsidered the use of the term 'body-line' – coined during the series by the journalist Hugh Buggy – although their intention could well have been to distinguish it from the usual 'leg-theory' MCC would have been familiar with. And a charge of 'unsportsmanlike' bowling was a huge accusation to make against the MCC's touring side.

The day before the cable was sent, Australian board secretary William Jeanes had sought out Warner and his assistant Richard Palairet to ask them to abandon the bodyline tactics; Warner responded that on-field decisions were the purview of the captain. Jeanes, knowing what Douglas Jardine's response would have been, did not bother to consult him. Warner suggested the Australians run any message past him before sending on to Lord's; this they declined to do. Woodfull had asked the board to take action, and presumably gave the cable his blessing; Bradman and Fingleton did not, while vice-captain Vic Richardson thought it was best for Australia to suck it up and retaliate in kind. (Ahead of the second Test, Woodfull had refused to countenance doing so.) A press campaign to select Eddie Gilbert, the indigenous fast bowler from Queensland who had hurt Jardine in a tour game, went unheeded.

There was no air mail between the UK and Australia until 1934, meaning letters took weeks to arrive. (Warner had written to MCC secretary William Findlay around the first Test, making clear his displeasure at the implications of Jardine's tactics, but this was not known at the time.) Newsreels were limited to a few seconds of footage. Photographs showed the extent to which Jardine was packing the legside and Larwood and Voce were digging it in, but could not adequately convey the drip-drip water torture of the prolonged assault. Kippax, for whom the bombardment had been too much in the first two Tests, was dropped from the side, and provided BBC radio summaries for the rest of the series. While hostile to bodyline – he co-authored a book after the series called *Anti Body-line* – he was careful to keep his commentary factual and unsensational. And the 15-minute summaries for Poste Parisien radio by former Australia all-rounder Alan Fairfax – perched on a booth on the Eiffel

Tower – were 'disguised by euphemisms and omissions', reckoned David Frith in *Bodyline Autopsy*.

The timing of a day's play in Australia has always been problematic for the English press corps and their deadlines. For that reason, hardly any national newspapers bothered to send out a correspondent in 1932–3; many relied on reports from the Reuters agency. Their man was Gilbert Mant, who maintained Reuters' reputation for scrupulous factual reporting in his coverage. EW Swanton had been with the *Evening Standard* for five years, but was not sent on the tour, punishment, he believed, for failing to get his copy in on Herbert Sutcliffe and Percy Holmes' record stand at Leyton in June 1932. Instead the *Standard* sent Bruce Harris, who was primarily a tennis reporter; on the boat out to Australia he had to ask one of the touring party what style of bowler Hedley Verity was. Harris struck up a friendship with Jardine, and did not really question his tactics.

The *Star* had the great batsman Jack Hobbs as their guest columnist, but neither did he oppose Jardine. Warwick Armstrong, who oversaw Australia's 1921 Ashes triumph – still fresh in many English memories – was critical of bodyline in the *Evening News*. It was not lack of sportsmanship that he was unhappy with, but, rather, a tedious diet of short balls which took out of the equation many of the game's most crafted deliveries and strokes, and an unnecessary denuding of Larwood and Voce's great skill as bowlers. As for reports of unrest and 'barracking' from the crowds, this was nothing new in MCC eyes: they well remembered protests along these lines by Percy Chapman on the 1928–9 tour; and even Warner's team had been hissed off the field in 1903–4.

A letter by Sydney Snow – of Sydney, no less – to *The Cricketer* underlined the lazy assumptions some felt were being made in England:

Sir, I am sure it is the wish of all cricket enthusiasts that the unfortunate controversy between the MCC and the Australian Board of Control should be disposed of and forgotten as soon as possible, but the reply sent to Australia by the MCC is not likely to have the desired effect. The main source of the trouble, so called 'body-line bowling,' has been lightly passed over in reply and particular stress laid on 'barracking.' 'Body-line bowling' is the cause, 'barracking' the effect, and it is the cause which must be eradicated.

Australian resentment at the tactics employed – 'within the law' as they undoubtedly are – first became manifest in the match against an Australian XI in Melbourne in November, and reached fever point in the third Test in Adelaide. These tactics, in Australian opinion, rather resembled the prize ring, not cricket as we know it.

With all respect I do not think the majority of the English public, who quite naturally support Jardine and his men, really know what so-called 'body-line bowling' is – it has been confused with leg-theory, which is entirely different. One wonders what the effect on the spectators at Lord's would be if Constantine, Griffith and Martindale indulged in an hour or two of the same type of bowling as Larwood and Voce employed in Australia!

Whether intentional or not, balls were pitched by them less than half way down the wicket, and flew over and round the batsman's head. Such balls were never anywhere near the stumps. This is a point which is apparently not yet realised here.

Until some action is taken to rid the game of the unpleasantness introduced by the new bowling methods – this action can and should be taken by the players themselves – I entirely agree with the MCC that it is in the best interests of cricket that the Tests should be discontinued, very regrettable as such a step would be.

THE CRICKETER ANTHOLOGY OF THE ASHES

The MCC's response was more carefully constructed, yet unbending. As far as they were concerned, both the Woodfull and Oldfield injuries occurred when Larwood was bowling to an orthodox field. And it did not take long for them to use their trump card: the Ashes' status as a guaranteed money-maker. The takings for the 1928–9 series had been £75,324 (1932–3 eventually made £70,352). Neither board wanted the financial hit that two cancelled Ashes Tests would have caused.

The MCC Reply (January 23 1933)

We, Marylebone Cricket Club, deplore your cable.

We depreciate your opinion that there has been unsportsmanlike play.

We have fullest confidence in captain, team and managers, and are convinced that they would do nothing to infringe either the laws of cricket, or the spirit of the game.

We have no evidence that our confidence has been misplaced. Much as we regret accidents to Woodfull and Oldfield, we understand that in neither case was the bowler to blame.

If the Australian Board of Control wish to propose a new law or rule, it shall receive our careful consideration in due course.

We hope the situation is not now as serious as your cable would seem to indicate, but if it is such as to jeopardise the good relations between English and Australian cricketers, and you consider it desirable to cancel remainder of programme, we would consent but with great reluctance.

The Australians' Second Cable (30 January 1933)

We appreciate your difficulty in dealing with this matter without having seen the actual play. We unanimously regard 'body-line' bowling, as adopted in some games in the present tour, as opposed to the spirit of cricket, and unnecessarily dangerous to the players.

We are deeply concerned that the ideals of the game shall be preserved, and we have therefore appointed a committee to report on the means necessary to eliminate such bowling from Australian cricket, beginning with the 1933–4 season.

We will forward its recommendation for your consideration and hope for your cooperation in their application to all cricket. We do not consider it necessary to cancel the remainder of the programme.

The Australians had conceded significant ground. The dreaded word itself had acquired inverted commas. But the Australians had not dropped their charge of 'unsportsmanlike' tactics. And there were worries, in both Britain and Australia, of the wider consequences. While events were unfolding at Adelaide, the office of the Governor of South Australia, Sir Alexander Hore-Ruthven, was approached by two proprietors of the *Adelaide Advertiser*, and the general manager of the shipping firm Elder Smith, asking him to quell the unrest.

Hore-Ruthven, himself British, was in England on holiday, and went to the Dominions Office to meet JH Thomas, a cabinet minister in the national Labour government. Thomas arranged to meet four members of the MCC committee – the Earl of Dartmouth (late of the Privy Council), Sir Stanley Jackson (a former Governor of Bengal), Viscount Bridgeman (a past Conservative Home Secretary) and Sir Kynaston Studd (Lord Mayor of London) – at Downing Street on February 1. Alas, records of this meeting, and any departmental files concerning Bodyline, have never been traced, so we may never know if Ramsay MacDonald's cabinet did discuss the crisis, as has been claimed. But Thomas did say that no issue caused him more trouble in his time in the Dominions Office. And at a lunch event ahead of a tour of North America by the Nottingham entrepreneur Sir Julien Cahn, Thomas quipped: 'All I can say is, don't take Larwood with you to Canada.'

Many believe the tour was saved because of an intervention by Warner on February 1. He pressed ET Crutchley, head of the British Mission in Canberra, to use his influence to bring about a retraction of the 'unsportsmanlike' accusation. Crutchley contacted the Australian prime minister, Joseph Lyons, who is said to have warned Allen Robertson, the cricket board chairman, that if they did not back down there was a danger that the conversion of an Australian loan in London might be imperilled. Robertson despatched board officials to meet Warner, and the two sides reached a compact.

The MCC Reply (February 2 1933)

We, the committee of the Marylebone Cricket Club, note with pleasure that you do not consider it necessary to cancel the remainder of programme, and that you are postponing the whole issue until after the present tour is completed.

May we accept this as a clear indication that the good sportsmanship of our team is not in question?

We are sure you will appreciate how impossible it would be to play any Test match in the spirit we all desire unless both sides were satisfied there was no reflection upon their sportsmanship.

When your recommendation reaches us it shall receive our most careful consideration and will be submitted to the Imperial Cricket Conference.

The Australians' Final Cable (February 8 1933)

We do not regard the sportsmanship of your team as being in question.

Our position was fully considered at the recent Sydney meeting, and it is as indicated in our cable of January 10.

It is the particular class of bowling referred to therein which we consider not in the best interests of cricket, and in this view we understand we are supported by many eminent English cricketers.

We join heartily with you in hoping the remaining Tests will be played with the traditional good feelings.

Resentment lingered, however, in Australia and further afield. Hore-Ruthven reported that some Australians were refusing to buy British goods in the shops as a result of the affair. Soon afterwards, *North China Daily News* reported: 'It is remarkable how this Bodyline business has militated against Australia in certain quarters in the Far East. This may seem far-fetched, but it is nevertheless a fact that Australians engaged in business in Hong Kong and Shanghai have been embarrassed by it. I know of several deals lost to Australians because of it.'

When he reported back to Lord's, Warner let it be known that he thought the tactics would lead to popular resentment in England. He later wrote: 'The question was not understood in this country. Very few people had seen bodyline in full blast, and I was of the opinion that, if let loose in England, the pavilion critics would condemn it and that in a short while spectators would begin to leave the ground.' Several of the key figures in Australia were summoned to meet Lewisham and Findlay; not, though, the two senior members of the touring party thought most opposed to bodyline, vice-captain Bob Wyatt and opening bowler Gubby Allen. The Australian suggestion to give umpires the power to call no-ball, then remove the bowler from the attack if a delivery was aimed to injure a batsman, was initially rejected by MCC.

Heading into the 1933 English season, Arthur Carr, county captain of Larwood and Voce, vowed to employ bodyline when it suited. Then, in the Varsity match at Lord's in July, Cambridge University's Ken Farnes bowled fast leg-theory with four short-legs at the Oxford tail. This was the first that English audiences had seen of bodyline at first hand. A joint letter to *The Times* from Sir Home Gordon and Lord Suffield expressed 'regret that the tactics seemed to savour those employed in the Australian Tests, which would destroy the whole charm, spirit and enjoyment of the game'.

A few days later at the Old Trafford Test, West Indies quicks Learie Constantine and Manny Martindale bowled bodyline against England – as Sydney Snow had foreseen – and Nobby Clark replied in kind. Wally Hammond required three stitches to a gaping wound inflicted by Martindale. Fingleton claimed MCC had a hand in it: 'I am credibly informed that the West Indians bowled bodyline in that match on an agreed understanding with some influential members of the MCC who wanted to see what that theory was like.'

In county cricket, Middlesex and England batsman Patsy Hendren took to wearing a three-peaked cap with extra protection – a prototype of the first cricket helmet. Neville Cardus wrote: 'What is sanctioned by Lord's and thought good enough to beat Australia is legal and presumably desirable in this country, yet I have met no cricketer this summer who wants bodyline.' Opinion was coming round to the mainstream Australian view. Fourteen of the 17 county captains resolved not to pack the legside field: only Jardine (Surrey), Carr (Nottinghamshire) and Vallance Jupp (Northamptonshire) demurred. It is one of cricket's great ironies that, by the end of 1933, MCC had cabled the Australian board effectively to agree to most of their original demands. 'We agree, and have always agreed, that a form of bowling which is obviously a direct attack on the batsman would be an offence against the spirit of the game.'

After the West Indies series, Warner wrote in *The Cricketer*:

[Bodyline's] exploitation at Old Trafford will serve a useful purpose in giving Englishmen some idea of what this bowling is like, though it is well known that Constantine is at least two yards slower than Larwood, and also lacks his control of the ball.

A bowler must be fast to carry out this plan of attack, but it requires not only speed, but accuracy of direction and control of length. No batsman objects to fast half-volleys on his legs, however many fieldsmen may be placed on the legside. What is objected to is when the ball is pitched short. It is the length of the ball, not so much the pace of it, to which exception has been taken.

Short-pitched very fast deliveries on hard wickets on the line of the batsman's body look – even if the bowler is acquitted of all intention to hurt the batsman – as if the bowler was 'bowling at the batsman', in the sense in which that expression has hitherto been understood by cricketers.

It is akin to intimidation. At the end of the last century, and at the beginning of this, English cricket boasted many fast bowlers. Some hard blows were received at times. Sir Stanley Jackson, for example, had a rib broken by E Jones, the Australian, but these bowlers did not give the impression of bowling at the batsmen.

At all events, fast bowling was very much in vogue at that time, and no cry was raised against it, whereas today we have practically every Australian cricketer of every generation definitely opposed to what they call bodyline bowling.

This vast mass of opinion deserves the deepest thought and consideration. To suggest that the Australians are 'squealers' is unfair to men with their record on the battlefield and on the cricket field. Rightly or wrongly they believe that such bowling is contrary to the spirit of the game. One of the strongest arguments against this bowling is that it has bred, and will continue to breed, anger, hatred, and malice, with their consequent reprisals.

Admitting it is within the law – there are many things in cricket which, by the laws of the game are right, but which are 'not done'. Is it worthwhile if, as a result of bodyline, England and her greatest cricketing dominion are to 'fight' each other?

Some would urge that the Laws should be altered. I do not agree. This is a case where one should rely on the spirit, kindliness, and a good will which should be inherent to cricket.

Always have I been opposed to this bowling which has aroused so much controversy, and, right or wrong, I am only pleading for what I honestly believe is best for the great, glorious, and incomparable game of cricket. I am not the least of the lovers of cricket.

By November 1933, MCC had still not adopted the Australian board's suggested Law changes. Under pressure from Westminster and Canberra, however, the board resolved to send a team for the 1934 Ashes. During that season Larwood and Voce bowled fast leg-theory and hit several Lancashire batsmen during a Championship match, prompting a complaint from the Lancashire chairman TA Higson, also a Test selector. Larwood pointed out MCC's inconsistencies in the matter in print, and was never picked in Test cricket again.

Voce bowled two overs of bodyline in the short passage of play at the end of the second day of Nottinghamshire's tour match against the Australians. Woodfull threatened to put his team on the train for London if Voce was not stood down. He was attributed with sore shins and did not take the field next day, infuriating the Nottingham crowd. Of this day, Fingleton wrote poignantly: 'One who was there told me that he has seen nothing braver than the action of a diminutive parson who tucked his hat under his arm, walked along with the Australians through the hooting crowd and clapped them right to the middle of the pitch.'

Draggers and chuckers

England and Australia are today such pillars of orthodoxy that it is unthinkable that one of their bowlers could arrive in the cauldron of an Ashes Test with an action considered a little kinky. Witness the recent travails of left-arm spinner Jack Leach, a revelation with Somerset during their tilt at a maiden County Championship title in 2016. He was called into the winter England Lions squads, and seemingly poised to play a Test in India, only to be pulled up by officials at Loughborough because of concerns over his action; no one who had been watching Somerset with the naked eye had reported anything untoward. And, just in case a bowler does fall into bad habits, there is now an ICC panel which roots out illegal bowling actions.

In years gone by, coaching was not quite so formalised or uniform; HS Altham did not write the first *MCC Cricket Coaching Book* until 1952. Until television coverage, there was no lengthy footage for aspiring bowlers to imitate. Still, in England, no bowler was called for throwing in first-class cricket between the two world wars. Then, interestingly, three were called in 1952 – Essex's Doug Insole, Tony Lock of Surrey and Cuan McCarthy at Cambridge University. Insole's case was a red herring: 'I was fed up at Freddie Brown for not declaring at Northampton, so I chucked one at him.' But the cases of Lock, a left-arm spinner whose yorker was regularly under suspicion, and McCarthy, a South African fast bowler, were more serious. Neither was dropped after being called on the field, which suggests a certain reticence to turn up the carpet and reveal all the horrors. However, when English bowlers went abroad, they were subject to slightly different interpretations of the Law. Lock was twice no-balled on England's controversial tour of the West Indies in 1953–4.

It wasn't just bent arms that caused the problem. Until 1963, the Law governing no-balls concerned the position of a bowler's back foot: they had to keep part of it behind the bowling crease on landing. Inevitably, many quick bowlers became skilled at dragging their back foot while in their delivery stride, so they were letting go of the ball way in front of the popping crease. Frank Tyson was accused of this during his stunning performances in the 1954–5 Ashes.

Four years on, the England batsmen felt several Australian bowlers were flagrantly getting away with both dragging and throwing. Trevor Bailey said that Ian Meckiff, the left-arm quick, 'dragged, right through the bowling crease. It was fairly obvious.' England thought he chucked it, too: batting against Meckiff and the jerky off-spinner Jim Burke in the first Test at Brisbane, Jim Laker turned around to slip fielder Neil Harvey, and said: 'It's like standing in the middle of a darts match.' Harvey doubled up with laughter. Ian Peebles likened Burke's action to a policeman hitting a short offender over the head with his baton. EW Swanton wrote: 'I never saw anything so blatant as Meckiff's action that afternoon.' Bailey went to the length of taking films of Meckiff's bowling, and was convinced something had to be done. England also felt the seamer Gordon Rorke was frequently able to get away with dragging so far that he was actually delivering the ball from a distance of just 18 or 19 yards from the batsman. And two South Australia bowlers, Peter Trethewey and Alan Hitchcox, were nicknamed 'Trethrewey' and 'Pitchcox' by an unkind wag.

Freddie Brown, by now England's tour manager, wanted to lodge an official complaint about Meckiff's bowling with the Australian board, but the captain Peter May demurred. The England party instead made a private approach to Don Bradman, an influential figure on the board. 'And what of Lock and [Peter] Loader?' snapped Bradman, who advised England to get their own house in order first. There was little hunger to deal with the issue until the Ashes had been settled.

The opening Test at Brisbane was the first broadcast live on Australian TV, which put the bowlers under greater scrutiny than before. Not that the match was much of a spectacle: Swanton called it 'one of the dullest imaginable'. 'Barnacle' Bailey scored 27 in two hours in the first innings, then was promoted to No.3 and reeled off what is still the slowest Test fifty – from 350 balls. Australia won by eight wickets, and the next Test, at Melbourne, by the same margin – and the Ashes were as good as gone.

The former England bowler Bill Bowes, reviewing the tour in the 1959 *Spring Annual* of *The Cricketer*, was not impressed:

> Rorke, a big 6ft 4in fast bowler, not only had a very jerky action but had such a long drag in his delivery stride that his front foot came down a yard beyond the batting crease. It must have

been most disconcerting to the batsmen, and so far as spectators were concerned the cricket when he was bowling seemed
drab. Five times in the over he bowled so wide that the batsmen
attempted no stroke and then one had to wait for his leisured
return to the bowling mark.

Australia had regained the Ashes, and by playing a fast-
bowling battery of Davidson, Lindwall, Meckiff and Rorke in
the final Test they won the series 4-0. Cowdrey, a victim of the
first bad umpiring decision at Brisbane, was again unlucky to
be given run out when batting well.

These umpiring incidents were given much publicity, but,
let it be understood, there was no suggestion of cheating. It is
very difficult for batsmen to play a normal game if they have
not complete faith in the man giving decisions at the other end.
They tend to keep pads further away from the ball. For this
reason, it was unfortunate the Australian authorities did not
agree to change when change was suggested.

So far as 'jerking or throwing' is concerned I need only say
that on one occasion I was walking on the beach and passed
some youngsters playing cricket. I heard one say, 'I'm Jimmy
Burke.' He ran up to the bowling mark and deliberately threw
to the other end. I chuckled rather sadly. There was a fear for
the future of cricket besides humour in my mind. Apart from
Queensland every state side in Australia has a fast bowler of
doubtful action. When I greeted Ray Lindwall on his selection
for the fourth Test and congratulated him he said, with a grin:
'Yes. I'm the last one of the straight-arm bowlers.'

I shall never believe Sir Donald Bradman and his co-selectors
had no doubts about the action of Meckiff, Rorke, Slater or
Burke. I do not believe they were right to hide behind the fact
that 'no umpire had ever no-balled them'. Time will prove
whether the best interests of cricket were served.

In the same edition, Ray Robinson captured the complexities of the issue ahead of the next Ashes:

> If Test cricket really would be better for becoming less controversial, a lot of spring-cleaning will be needed before the Australians arrive in England in 1961.
>
> England mostly fell below 12 eight-ball overs an hour and averaged only 474 balls a day in the Tests … English batsmen received an average of 101 balls an hour throughout the Tests compared with 95 balls bowled to the Australians hourly. Every aspect of this problem of diminishing play calls for attention by the best brains in cricket.
>
> From the striking batsman's position the peculiar arm actions of fast left-hander Ian Meckiff and right-hander Gordon Rorke looked highly suspicious, but this was not borne out by scrutiny from side-on. Though cameras have been clicking like knitting needles at Meckiff and Rorke I am still waiting to see a film or photograph from side-on revealing an illegal thrust of either's elbow ahead of his wrist.

When the tour moved on to sleepier New Zealand, the England team sat down to watch a film of Lock's bowling. His teammates laughed, but when the lights came back up Lock was ashen-faced with embarrassment. As the English team sailed home, an MCC subcommittee – headed by chairman of selectors Gubby Allen – recommended the first-class umpires draw up a list of doubtful bowlers for the 1959 season. Lock wisely changed his style to one embracing a smoother delivery at slower pace. However, he was no-balled in 1959, as were two bowlers from Worcestershire, Derek Pearson and John Aldridge. First the Australian board, then MCC, made revisions to the Law, but they disagreed on the precise wording, which did not help.

The crisis rumbled on into 1960. Harold Rhodes of Derbyshire was called six times by umpire Paul Gibb in the match against the touring South Africans, and sadly became accustomed to cameras following him around in search of an incriminating still. South Africa's fast bowler Geoff Griffin was called in the same match by Gibb for dragging. Griffin had suffered an accident in his youth that left him unable to properly straighten his arm. But that would not save him. MJK Smith, who played for England in that series, recently told *The Cricketer* that it was common knowledge that Syd Buller, regarded as the best umpire in the world at the time, was going to call Griffin should he get the chance. Sure enough, Griffin was no-balled 11 times in his second Test at Lord's in June 1960, for throwing and dragging, and was even mercilessly called during a 20-over exhibition match when the game finished early. He had to finish the over underarm. Griffin never played another Test. Don Bradman went in to the South African dressing room to commiserate with Griffin, telling him that Buller was acting under instructions from on high. Bradman claimed to have overheard none other than Allen instructing Buller to call Griffin.

Bradman was in England at the suggestion of Richie Benaud, the Australia captain, who thought The Don's clout might help resolve the chucking crisis in time for the following summer's Ashes. Bradman was due to take over as the Australian board chairman, and was to speak at the Imperial Cricket Conference's annual meeting at Lord's. Benaud reckoned this the most significant ICC meeting in its history, as it passed resolutions to clamp down on time-wasting, throwing, dragging and running through the crease on to the danger area, and began to look at changing the lbw Law to take in balls pitching outside off-stump where a batsman was not offering a stroke. England and Australia also decided that during the first five weeks of the 1961 Ashes tour, when all the top bowlers in the country were expected to be playing, umpires would not call suspect actions on the field, but submit a detailed report to the authorities.

It all came too late for Meckiff. When coaching, he had to stomach youngsters shouting 'no-ball' as he sent a delivery down. His son was nicknamed 'Chucker' at school. Meckiff never pretended to have a flawless action, but for him, like Muttiah Muralitharan, the issue was congenital. 'I have a permanently bent elbow ... Being slightly double jointed in the shoulders, this gives me added strength and bowling power.' In the first Test against South Africa at Brisbane in 1963–4, umpire Col Egar no-balled Meckiff four times, and Benaud did not trust to bowl him again. Meckiff was carried off the field shoulder-high by a section of the crowd, and he immediately gave up cricket, aged 28. It would take another 30 years for the authorities to settle on a more sensitive solution to reporting suspect actions – one which might have spared the likes of Meckiff, Lock and Griffin such public humiliation.

The D'Oliveira Affair

Ted Dexter, the former England captain, said at the time: 'I come down on the side of honesty, a good honest piece of bungling by honest men.' Billy Griffith, the MCC secretary whose health suffered during the affair, maintained: 'The selectors have been desperately honest all along the line.' But the fullness of time has not been so kind to the 10 members of the MCC committee who initially left Basil D'Oliveira out of the England squad to tour South Africa in their meeting of August 27 1968.

One of the 10 men, Donald Carr, captured the grisliness of the affair. 'I would say the original decision was made on the basis of cricketing ability but it all looked so awful,' he told *The Wisden Cricketer.* 'I think I believed, or was talked into believing, that it was all on cricketing grounds. There had been so much chatter about it. I think there were people high up in the cricketing hierarchy in England who were talking a lot about it and knew what the possibilities could be. I felt it had not been very well handled.' Carr died in 2016 and Doug Insole, then the chairman of selectors and the last survivor of the 10, in 2017. The minutes of the selection meeting are not in the MCC archives, if they were taken at all.

In 1948, the Afrikaner-dominated National Party won the South African general election, and began to move towards implementing strict policies of apartheid. In cricket, the increasing segregation between white and non-white cricketers led D'Oliveira, from the Cape Malay community, to emigrate to England in 1960; other non-whites, like Cec Abrahams (father of John) followed. The England team who played South Africa in 1964–5 did so in front of segregated stadiums. Opposition to the regime grew, and campaigners worldwide began to advocate South Africa's isolation from the sporting world.

The warning signs were clear for MCC by February 1966, when New Zealand's rugby board cancelled their impending tour of South Africa over the home authority's refusal to allow three Maori players into the country. England's cricketers happened to be touring New Zealand at the time, with Griffith as manager. He was asked what he would have done in similar circumstances, and replied that MCC would have had little option but to cancel the tour. Later that year, D'Oliveira made his Test debut, against West Indies.

MCC were desperate to maintain friendly relations with

the South African Cricket Association, who they considered honest lovers of the game. Griffith flew out to South Africa at the start of 1967 for discussions, but achieved little progress on the D'Oliveira issue. It also became a matter for the British ambassador in Pretoria, Sir John Nicholls, in meetings with the South African prime minister John Vorster. MCC wrote to SACA on January 5 1968, stressing that the following winter's tour could not go ahead without assurances that there would be 'no preconditions' about selection of the England team. In March, SACA responded with a carefully worded reply – 'The SACA would never presume to interfere with the manner in which you choose your side to tour South Africa' – though MCC treasurer Gubby Allen later claimed that the MCC's letter had gone unanswered.

Viscount Cobham, an aristocrat who had played for Worcestershire and had business interests in the Republic, also met with Vorster, who told him bluntly that the tour would be off if D'Oliveira were in the England team. Cobham dashed off a letter, marked 'Private and Confidential', to a senior member of the committee, who passed it on to Griffith, and informed Allen. But, as the letter was private, Griffith was under no compunction to reveal the letter to the wider committee, and did not do so.

Meanwhile, a weaker than usual Australia team arrived in England for the 1968 Ashes. D'Oliveira, despite a poor series in the West Indies that had endangered his place in the England side, sneaked into the XI for the first Test. He made 87 at Old Trafford on a very difficult pitch against John Gleeson, Graham McKenzie, and with even Bob Cowper turning it square. D'Oliveira himself sent down 32 overs for 45 runs and 2 wickets.

But Australia took an early 1-0 lead, as John Woodcock reported in *The Cricketer*:

England were rescued from heavier defeat by a fine innings on the last morning by D'Oliveira, the first batsman, since Snow in England's first innings, to decide that Cowper could be driven. Except in West Indies last winter, D'Oliveira has shown a knack of making runs for England when others have failed. But on his recent record he can hardly be rated as a full bowler.

On the eve of the second Test at Lord's, at a celebratory dinner to mark the 200th Test between England and Australia, Griffith suggested to D'Oliveira that he declare himself unavailable for England, but available for South Africa. That, in his mind, was the only way the South Africa tour could be saved. It summed up the attitude of Griffith and other traditionalists: well-meaning, sympathetic to the plight of the non-white South African cricketer, but ultimately more concerned with the preservation of diplomatic ties between English and South African cricket. Indeed, SACA officials were guests of honour during the match, as is traditional in the first Lord's Test of the summer. 'Either you respect me as an England player, or you don't,' replied D'Oliveira.

The next day, EW Swanton, now editorial director of *The Cricketer*, approached him and suggested the very same thing. 'Swanton moved on equal terms with the establishment,' wrote Peter Oborne, in his acclaimed biography of D'Oliveira, 'so much so that he could not be distinguished from it.' Next morning, D'Oliveira was left out of the side for Barry Knight, the Leicestershire allrounder. England captain Colin Cowdrey explained this as a case of needing a seamer like Knight, rather than a medium-paced swinger such as D'Oliveira. Knight was not surprised to have been picked, having always bowled well at Lord's, and with England needing a win. But some have wondered whether this call was made in order to make it easier to leave out D'Oliveira later. Bob Simpson and several other

Australians were perplexed that England had left out a batsman of such quality.

D'Oliveira, demoralised by his omission, suffered a slump in form after Lord's. He was not even in the longlist of 30 players sent a letter to enquire about their availability for the tour of South Africa. Nor was Knight, though, who thinks it may have been assumed as professionals that they would definitely go. (However, the Gentleman–Players distinction had been abolished in 1962.)

Then, in late July, D'Oliveira received a mysterious phone call from Tienie Oosthuizen, a South African businessman who was a senior executive at a tobacco company connected to Rothmans. The Rothmans tag carried a lot of weight in cricketing circles: D'Oliveira had played in Rothmans Cavaliers matches sponsored by the firm in the past decade. Indeed, the inside cover of *The Cricketer* in 1968 was routinely taken out for advertising by Rothmans, outlining their upcoming fixture list of exhibition games screened on BBC2.

Oosthuizen summoned D'Oliveira to an office in Baker Street, where he offered him a contract to coach in South Africa for £4,000 a year, plus expenses, a weighty sum at the time. The catch was that he had to accept by August 14, a fortnight before MCC picked the touring party. Oosthuizen said he had contacts in South Africa who assured him that D'Oliveira would not be picked. He claims to have been acting on his own initiative, but the hand of Vorster must be suspected. D'Oliveira held out and declined the offer, encouraged by news from a source high up in English cricket – thought to be Cowdrey – that his place would be decided on merit.

The fourth Test, at Headingley, was the third successive draw of the series, meaning Australia retained the Ashes, as Woodcock reported in *The Cricketer*:

Had [England] held their catches, or at least a reasonable share of them, Australia would not now be rejoicing, as they are, in their retention of the Ashes for the sixth successive time …

The second day's play was all England's until the last 70 minutes when they lost three good wickets after a grand opening partnership between Edrich and Prideaux. Though he failed in the second innings Prideaux's first innings of 62 was much the most significant he had ever played. No one can have watched without thinking that Prideaux has 'got it'. He has served a long apprenticeship, having been 10 years in the game, but the time has not been wasted.

Fate then moved in D'Oliveira's favour. Concurrent to the fourth Test, D'Oliveira took 11 for 68 in a Championship match against Hampshire. England could at least rescue a series draw by winning the final Test at The Oval. Tom Cartwright and Barry Knight were each identified as the medium-pacer needed to complement the three quicks … until both stood down with fitness doubts. Even then D'Oliveira would have been 12th man. But, at lunchtime the day before the game, opener Roger Prideaux withdrew, citing a bronchial ailment. Prideaux admitted to Oborne years later that he could have played, but did not want a failure at The Oval to have endangered his selection on the South Africa tour. D'Oliveira was back in the team.

The high drama of the 1968 Oval Test has gone down in folklore. Following a stoic century from John Edrich, England were 238 for 4 when D'Oliveira came to the crease. He was skittish to start with, surviving a few half-chances to get to the close. Early next day he was dropped by wicketkeeper Barry Jarman off Ian Chappell on 31. Swanton called this 'the most fateful drop in cricket history'. Oborne wrote: 'This very hard chance was later to be used very effectively by D'Oliveira's critics as a way of diminishing his achievement.' As D'Oliveira approached his 50, umpire Charlie Elliott said to him: 'Well played. Oh Christ ... you've put the cat amongst the pigeons now.' He eventually made a brilliant 158. 'It was by no means the most technically difficult innings D'Oliveira ever constructed,' Oborne acknowledged. 'The conditions at The Oval were easy, and the Australia bowling attack was modest.' But, given the political tumult, Oborne still considered it the greatest innings in Test history.

Oosthuizen, betraying his proximity to Vorster's government, phoned Geoffrey Howard, the Surrey secretary, in his office, in the hope of getting through to Griffith. 'I can't get hold of the MCC secretary,' he said, 'so will let you take a message to the selectors. Tell them that if today's centurion is picked, the tour will be off.' In a quiet moment alone together in the dressing room, Cowdrey congratulated D'Oliveira, but was edgy about the political fallout. 'Can we get away with this without getting too involved in politics?' he asked. He quizzed D'Oliveira about the various scenarios that could occur on the South African tour – in Oborne's words, 'the handling of media interviews, the danger of breaking the law, the hazards at whites-only hotels and at formal receptions, the dangers from trouble-makers who would try to turn D'Oliveira into a political issue'. Then Cowdrey made him a promise: 'I want you in South Africa. If anyone at the tour selection meeting asks me if I am prepared to accept responsibility for anything that might happen on tour should you be selected, I shall say I am prepared to do so.'

There was a massive downpour on the final day, when Australia were 85 for 5. It was not until 2.15pm that the sun reappeared, and hundreds of spectators mucked in to help Ted Warn and his staff mop up the ground for play to resume at

4.45pm. England had an hour and 15 minutes to claim the last five wickets. D'Oliveira begged Cowdrey to bring him on, and he took the first wicket, bowling Jarman, shouldering arms, with one that cut back to clip off-stump. Derek Underwood, a specialist on drying pitches, did the rest. With all 10 fielders round the bat, David Brown took two sprawling catches at short-leg, before John Inverarity tried to leave one and was lbw, handing England an unforgettable win with minutes to spare.

Woodcock captured the drama of the last day in his report for *The Cricketer*:

England's victory in the last Test match at The Oval reduced men to boys. When, afterwards, I went back to my club, one of the staff said he had known nothing like it since the war. Upon the fall of the last wicket, with only five minutes left for play, the cheer from the members rang through the building.

In an incredible climax England took the last five wickets in 35 minutes after two-and-a-quarter-hours on the last after-noon had been wiped out by a storm which seemed certain to have saved Australia from defeat.

The match contained three centuries. Lawry's gave Australia their chance of seeing the game through; Edrich's was the cul-mination of his best series, which brought him an aggregate only seven fewer than Denis Compton's in 1948, the highest against Australia in England; D'Oliveira's raised strong politi-cal echoes, qua the tour of South Africa, and was proof of his temperament. D'Oliveira's outstanding innings took England near to their first-innings target of 500.

When the celebrations died down, Cowdrey set out across London in his Jaguar for the most contentious selection meeting in cricket's history. 'That meeting, the most controversial by far in the MCC's 200-year history, remains one of the best-kept secrets in the 20th century,' wrote Oborne. 'Far more is known about the cabinet meetings of the Harold Wilson government, the activities of the secret service in Moscow, or the details of the Poseidon nuclear missile programme, than what the England selectors said and did that night.' The meeting is said to have gone on for six hours. Insole has said that before they sat down he asked the selectors to banish all considerations other than cricket. It appears that three of the 10 present – Allen, Griffith and one other – knew from the Cobham letter that the tour would be off if D'Oliveira was selected; the others must have suspected the problems it would cause. Despite what Cowdrey promised, apparently no one, even Don Kenyon, D'Oliveira's captain at Worcestershire, spoke up for his inclusion. There was no vote. The selectors apparently decided that D'Oliveira's bowling – despite success in damp English conditions – was not strong enough in South Africa to classify him as an allrounder, and chose Cartwright instead as a bowler who could bat. The middle-order batsmen who beat D'Oliveira to a spot were Surrey's Ken Barrington, aged 37, and 24-year-old Keith Fletcher of Essex. D'Oliveira was named as a reserve in case of injury.

D'Oliveira heard of his omission when the Test squad was announced on the radio, in the dressing room at New Road, after scoring a century against Sussex. Graveney, Cowdrey's vice-captain, no less, was incandescent at the decision, and took D'Oliveira off into the physio's room, where he broke down in tears.

The media response was mixed. The more left-leaning newspapers did not buy the cricketing reasons. Alan Ross in the *Observer* contended that D'Oliveira's omission 'makes no sense at all in cricketing terms, and the reasons given to defend it can hardly be taken seriously'. John Arlott, the man who had brought D'Oliveira over to play for Middleton in 1960, was seething in the *Guardian*. 'MCC have never made a sadder, more dramatic, or potentially more damaging selection ... There is no case for leaving D'Oliveira out on cricketing grounds. Since the last MCC tour, South African pitches have become grassy, ideal for seam bowlers, of which South Africa deploy five. So England's tactical need is for a Test-class batsman who is a reliable bowler at medium-pace; only D'Oliveira meets that demand.'

But plenty of others accepted the selectors' logic, including Michael Melford in *The Cricketer*:

> D'Oliveira, like Milburn, is desperately unlucky and there will doubtless be those who will never allow themselves to believe that he was omitted for cricketing reasons. But if the selectors had the courage to call him back for the fifth Test, they can surely also be given credit for courage in leaving him out, knowing full well the inference certain to be drawn.
>
> Should he have been included – presumably in place of Graveney or Fletcher – purely to avoid the hullabaloo which would arise if he were left out? What sort of 'moral courage' would there be in that, if one may borrow one of the glib phrases of the moment?
>
> D'Oliveira was, Mr Insole said, regarded by the selectors for the purposes of an overseas tour purely as a batsman, as distinct from an allrounder, which put him in competition with Milburn and the others named. The two left out, Milburn and D'Oliveira, had modest tours of West Indies. Since Milburn was also a possible reserve bowler, the omission of both presumably follows the accepted doctrine that a true allrounder, especially on good pitches overseas, should be either a first

choice batsman or bowler and not just someone who will help out in either department.

'Felix', however, thought that MCC might have allowed The Oval dust to settle before choosing the touring side:

Hard on the result [of The Oval Test] – too hard, surely, after so emotional and taxing a day – the Test selectors plus the president, treasurer and secretary of MCC and the England captain and tour manager got down to choosing the team for South Africa, finishing their deliberations by all accounts in the early hours.

Other individual decisions however were small things compared with the passing over of D'Oliveira, following his unexpected and triumphant recall to the England team at The Oval. Views to this are apt to be both divergent and violent, and we would say here that while in no way questioning the objective motives of the selectors, D'Oliveira, after his success in both the Tests he was called to play against Australia, has been desperately unfortunate.

Elsewhere in *The Cricketer*'s November 1968 edition, Bill Deedes, a former Conservative minister for information in Douglas-Home's cabinet, wrote on the role of politics in sport:

When politics embroil cricket it is invariably the politicians and not the cricketers who are made to look foolish. The axiom was first established more than 30 years ago when Mr JH Thomas, then Dominions Secretary, farcically involved himself in the bodyline bowling controversy. It has held good ever since ...

The truth is that men who embark on intransigent policies will sooner or later find themselves in indefensible situations.

When you forsake government, when you coerce, then you are compelled to hold a rigid and unbroken front. That is why the Russians are in Prague. That is why South Africa dreads the smallest relaxation of apartheid and why they are unwilling to see D'Oliveira on the Durban cricket ground.

My concern here, however, is not what our moral judgement or physical reaction should be to South Africa's strange domestic policy; but how, when occasion arises, cricket should reach to what at root is an issue threatening to cleave the world. It seems to me that in a number of respects cricket has something to offer by way of guidance and example here, helpful to its own cause and that of humanity.

Robin Marlar, in his monthly press review, had lost faith in MCC's decision-making:

The MCC, aided by the cricket writers in no small measure, also got the message across that only cricketing reasons could stop D'Oliveira being chosen for the tour – come what may in the form of pressures from governments, hotel-keepers or who you like.

And, having achieved this, the selectors ignore the evidence of The Oval and leave him out – on the grounds expressed by Trevor Bailey on the radio – that he is a better player on English wickets than overseas. In West Indies – possibly. In South Africa, unproven. And so all his consistency here, documented by Ian Wooldridge on the Monday of the last Test, has availed him on naught.

Wooldridge feels that D'Oliveira is a political issue, Swanton that people will be wrong to assume ulterior motives. 'Considerations unconnected with cricket' will not have had an influence. For those like myself who have been slowly winning the battle to convince people that *this* is the truth, his omission on cricketing grounds which must be specious after his Oval performance is a terrible blow indeed. Winning that fifth Test was everything for the summer. D'Oliveira helped more than a little. Cricket is temperament and team as well as skill. On human relations grounds, on cricketing grounds his omission is deplorable. Bay on, you wolves of Fleet Street – alas you have cause.

However, John Woodcock was not convinced that D'Oliveira had made a watertight case:

Whereas Australia could be delighted with the performances of Chappell, Connolly and Redpath, and, to a lesser extent, Mallett, England made no discoveries in the Test series. Having appeared to establish himself as an indispensable link in the Test XI by his thrilling innings at Lord's, Milburn fell ill and ended the season by being left out of the team to South Africa. Disregarding the political ramifications of D'Oliveira's original omission, I thought from a cricketing standpoint that it was less of a mistake than discarding Milburn.

There was one more twist. On September 14, Cartwright bowled for Warwickshire, the Gillette Cup champions, against a Gillette Invitational XI captained by Cowdrey. Then, overnight, he pulled out of the South Africa tour, claiming to be unfit. Cowdrey tried to persuade him to start the tour, but Cartwright was adamant. He maintained in later years that his withdrawal was down to fitness, but also admitted to having qualms about going. 'A part of me wanted to be shot of it. Did I really wish to be part of these things?' Cartwright had been on England's previous tour to South Africa in 1964–5, and was appalled at what he had witnessed.

D'Oliveira was duly added to the squad, and three days later, addressing the Orange Free State National Party congress at Bloemfontein, Vorster decried the England side as 'not the team of the MCC but of the anti-apartheid movement'. Jack Cheetham, a vice-president of SACA and a former South Africa captain, and his SACA colleague, Arthur Coy, flew to London to try to break the impasse, but to no avail. MCC called off the tour.

As the full implications of the cancellation sunk in, John Arlott, the man who had done more than anything to bring D'Oliveira to England in 1960, made clear his upset in *The Cricketer*'s 1968 Winter Annual:

The omission of D'Oliveira aroused violent controversy. Mr SC Griffith, secretary of MCC, announced that there had been no question of political pressure or even of consultation with the South African Cricket Association. The selection had been made solely on cricket grounds. There is no reason to doubt his word: the selectors are honourable men. Their naivety, however, is staggering. What was the rest of the world to think when a man who on Tuesday, as one of England's best 11, scored 158 and took the crucial wicket in the only Test of the series which England won, was not included in their best 16 a day later?

It is difficult to think of any step ever taken by the cricket 'establishment' more calculated to mar its image. If it were a political move it was a stupid one. If it is argued that 'politics should be kept out of cricket' the only possible reply is that every international relationship, whether in sport or any other field, is part of a pattern of the way people live and behave, which is politics. D'Oliveira's Test record – an overall average of fifty; top of England's batting and second in the bowling this year – and his capacity for rising to the occasion were cited in criticism of his omission. This, however, is not the point of the discussion which is that, though it may have been a cricketing decision, its repercussions will be political.

An end to deference

It is hard to believe any Ashes series has been 'a fucking tea-party', as Allan Border feared it might be when Robin Smith dared to ask for a glass of water during a century at Trent Bridge in 1989. But a switch did seem to be flicked sometime in the 1970s. According to Kerry O'Keeffe, one Australian team meeting overseen by Ian Chappell went roughly as follows: 'Boycott? Bounce the cunt. Edrich? Bounce the cunt. Willis? Slog the cunt. Underwood? Bloody tight. Hard to get away. Slog the cunt.'

In Britain, the big social change was supposed to have taken place in 1962, when the old amateur–professional distinction was formally abolished. Still, after Len Hutton led England to victory in Australia in 1954–5 as their first professional captain, over the next three Ashes tours MCC appointed a privately educated former amateur to lead the side to Australia.

Peter May angered some of the 1958–9 touring party by taking his fiancée, Virginia Gilligan, with him; newspaper intrigue inevitably followed. 'Peter was a great friend and a good captain, but there was no doubt the whole business was a distraction,' Tom Graveney told Huw Turbervill in *The Toughest Tour* years later. 'Desmond Eagar and Freddie Brown were joint managers and they showed poor leadership. Let's just say Freddie was a better cricketer than a manager.'

This was the golden age of air travel – at least for those who could afford it. The 1962–3 tourists had taken the first part of the journey, from London to Aden, by air; and three years later they flew the whole way – via Ceylon – for the first time. Graveney dubbed the 1962–3 expedition 'the Sussex tour', on account of it being headed by Ted Dexter, with Bernard Fitzalan-Howard, the Duke of Norfolk (whose seat was Arundel Castle, in Sussex), as tour manager. The Duke apparently left most of the donkey work to his assistant Alec Bedser, while MCC secretary Billy Griffith – another former Sussex player – flew out to cover the Duke when he went home for Christmas. 'Dukie deserts his men' screamed one headline in Australia, but it turned out he had gone home partly to assist in a rehearsal for Winston Churchill's funeral.

To complicate matters further, Susan Dexter arrived to do some modelling, sometimes with her husband in tow. Fred Trueman quipped: 'All that the newspapers and television pro-grammes were full of was where the Duke's horses were running, where [Revd] David Sheppard was preaching and what Mrs Dexter was wearing.' Some of Trueman's other quips landed him in hot water. After Sheppard put down a couple of chances at slip, he advised the reverend to 'Kid yourself it's a Sunday, and put your hands together.' Cowdrey let one through, too: 'Sorry, Fred, I should have crossed my legs.' Trueman replied: 'Yes, and so should your mother.' (Trueman had £50 deducted from his good-conduct bonus.) His Yorkshire teammate Ray Illingworth was furious at being asked to do 12th-man duties one evening so that Cowdrey could take his wife to the cinema. The former amateur MJK Smith presided over a drawn series in Australia three years later, and was one of the most popular of all touring captains, but there was still some friction when he brought his family out for Christmas.

Cowdrey had led England to a 1-1 draw at home in 1968, and remained a saintly figure in the eyes of many, despite his foggy role in the D'Oliveira Affair. But when Cowdrey went down with injury, Illingworth stepped in to lead the side with great acumen. It apparently took Cowdrey three weeks to accept Illingworth's offer of the vice-captaincy for the 1970–71 Ashes. The patrician tour manager, David Clark, would doubtless have found it easier to work with his fellow Kentish Man. However, EM Wellings, reviewing the tour for *Wisden*, was sharply critical of Cowdrey's 'inability to come to terms with his position as vice-captain. He had long hesitated before accepting the appointment, and his cricket might not have been such a disappointment, if he had allowed himself to be absorbed into the body of the team. As it was, his slip catching went to pieces and with the bat he played only one worthy innings before the final stages in New Zealand.'

'The one sadness among the players concerned Colin Cowdrey,' wrote John Snow, England's cantankerous but lethal fast bowler. 'Not getting the captaincy was a terrible disappointment to him. Ray and he just didn't hit it off, and he didn't agree with the attitudes of the majority of us … he was a self-created exile. The waste of his great ability was a big loss to the side.' Snow was irked by a relentless schedule of cocktail parties, and Clark's insistence that the touring party wear blazers and ties in searing heat. And the players were less than impressed when Clark criticised the style of both Illingworth and Australia captain Bill Lawry in the first two drawn Test matches, suggesting he would rather both teams go for the win and risk losing.

The prospect of bouncing a tailender had once been summed up by Ray Lindwall's quip to Alan Davidson, after the left-arm quick had just sent a short one down at a No.8 in a Sheffield Shield match. 'You've just insulted all fast bowlers,' said Lindwall. 'You've admitted that No.8 can bat better than you can bowl.' But to win in Australia, England had always needed top-drawer fast bowling, and Illingworth had little squeamishness in testing the Australians with persistent short stuff in their own conditions. His trump card was Snow.

As early as the first innings of the first Test at Brisbane, Snow was warned by umpire Lou Rowan for bowling three successive short balls at Doug Walters. The essence of the problem was a fundamental disagreement over what constituted a bouncer. Snow generally aimed his short balls at the rib cage, rather than the head, and grew exasperated at Rowan's unwillingness (or inability) to draw a distinction. Snow wrote: 'I can safely say I have never come across another umpire so full of his own importance, so stubborn, lacking in humour, unreasonable and unable to distinguish between a delivery short of a length which rises around the height of the rib cage and a genuine bouncer which goes through head high.' At Brisbane, England were incensed when Keith Stackpole was given the benefit of the doubt when he appeared to have been run out by Geoff Boycott on 18. Stackpole was shown to be well short in photos published in the newspapers that evening. He went on to score 207.

There were six Tests in the series, so as to accommodate Perth's debut. There, Rowan refused to let England have use of the roller, in contravention of the regulations. And he warned Snow again for bowling short at Ian Redpath. Next ball, Snow ran in, shot one past Redpath's head, turned on his heel and said to Rowan: 'Now that's a bouncer for you.'

The next Test, at Melbourne, was abandoned due to heavy rain. The groundstaff worked furiously to make the ground fit, and each day it was announced that play would start 'as soon as the rain stopped'. But it never did. Snow felt that because so many Victorians had travelled from up-country to attend, the authorities felt duty-bound to provide them with some cricket. As it happened, MCC had flown its president, Sir Cyril Hawker, and treasurer, Gubby Allen, out for the match, and they agreed with Clark and the Australian board to replace the abandoned Test with a one-day international, which has since gone down as the first on record. There was a wider audience to satisfy, too: the advent of satellite television meant the 1970–71 series was the first Ashes screened across the length and breadth of Australia.

The administrators also agreed to scrap the second tour match against Victoria to squeeze in a seventh Test. In the England players' eyes, this merely gave Australia one more chance to regain the Ashes. The Australian authorities were to take £70,000 at the gate. The first Illingworth or his players heard about the extra Test was when Don Bradman popped down to the dressing room to thank them for their flexibility. Illingworth had to repeatedly pester Clark before the players were eventually awarded an extra £100 each. Nor was Snow impressed with the behaviour of the Melbourne public and their stewards. 'Despite the happenings in Sydney during the final Test, I placed Melbourne top of the nastiness league. "Have a go, yer mug" ceased to have any meaning when you'd heard it for the 300th time in a day. They had been raised on Australian Rules. They reminded me of the bloodthirsty crowds depicted in Hollywood biblical epics, calling for more when the Christians were thrown to the lions.'

The players' stance did not impress EW Swanton, writing his Australia tour diary:

Monday January 2: Hooray! Approval of this imaginative move [organising a seventh Test] proved universal in Australia and all but so among English critics: not however among the

England team, who forthwith decided first that their chances of getting back the Ashes had been scuppered and simultaneously that, for the added strain, they deserved more money. This they asked for with precipitate haste. Let me not condemn the whole team or even the majority for their short-sighted reaction to the situation. Even their militants might, however, have given authority credit for not having overlooked their interests.

Snow's list of scrapes with the umpires was racking up. In a state game, he was no-balled 17 times by umpire Ron Joseph – all, apparently, for overstepping. 'I just asked Joseph if he had brought his coat of many colours with him,' wrote Snow. In the fourth Test at Sydney, Snow delivered the decisive spell of the series, taking 7 for 40 to bundle out Australia for 116 and open a 1-0 lead. Unfortunately, in the midst of it Snow felled Australia's fast bowler Graham McKenzie with a short ball to the mouth, sending him into an early retirement.

Rowan then warned Snow in the fifth Test at Melbourne for intimidatory bowling, although Snow maintains Australia's Alan 'Froggy' Thomson had bowled six bouncers in an over (they were eight-ball overs) at Illingworth without censure. The umpires began to feel the pressure, too. Max O'Connell called 'over' as Snow had just let go of the eighth delivery, moments before Stackpole nicked it behind to Alan Knott. On this occasion, Snow felt clemency. 'I could quite understand his actions which illustrate the pressure umpires are also under in a Test.'

England did not feel the same about Rowan, as excerpts from Swanton's tour diary during the fifth Test show:

Tuesday January 26: A day to forget with both sides accepting the stalemate and [Geoff] Boycott and Edrich sealing the door without the slightest trouble against this weak Australian attack

… With only three frontline batsmen fit, Illingworth was justi-fied I think in not going for the win. Whether he was wise to say what he did to the press after the game is another matter entirely. It was a poor game and, though the major part of the blame for this lay at Australia's door, it was adding insult to injury to choose this moment to criticise the umpires.

Wednesday January 27: The Australian press today report that Illingworth described the umpires' action in warning Snow for intimidation and allowing Thomson to bowl short unchecked as 'unfair'. They quote him also as saying that some of the English players were 'dubious' about the validity of the off-break, which young O'Keeffe, the wrist-spinner, uses as an occasional variant. Apart from the principle of a captain criticising umpires both specifically and by implication, as Illingworth has done, one's view on this particular outburst is that it was ill-timed, injudicious, undignified and unjustified … The umpires have performed quietly and efficiently. I wish the same might be said of all the players.

With the Ashes still very much up for grabs, tempers rose during the sixth Test at Adelaide. Swanton recorded:

Friday January 29: The day had a large, ugly blot … On being given run out – a narrow decision, but probably a right one since his bat had not yet been grounded – Boycott hurled the bat several yards in front of him. That was not even the only thing he hurled as strong words were passed, and he ultimately made off with the boos of the crowd in his ears. Where, today one asks oneself, are the courtesies of combat, which the old professionals were zealous in preserving as any amateur? Boycott, we were later informed, had expressed regret (though not to the umpire) for 'a degree of displeasure' over what he thought was a poor decision. Not an honours degree anyway.

Saturday January 30: On the diplomatic front, David Clark apologises to the Australian board for the Boycott affray, Ray Illingworth to the umpire. Boycott regrets apparently only by proxy.

Bryon Butler, for *The Cricketer*, perceived a changing atmosphere among Australian crowds:

The biggest disappointment for me has been the attitude of the crowds. I was brought up to regard the Australian cricket fan as bluff, leather-lunged, drily-humoured, knowledgeable and, above all, fair. Things have apparently changed. Players react in different ways to a hostile crowd. Noise will cut like a pneumatic drill into the concentration of some players. Others react [like] John Snow. 'Snow thrives on public abuse and individual fear,' wrote Clive Taylor in the *Sun*. 'The crowds admire him but loathe him. They jeer and hoot every move he makes. He stalks through it all with an icy, menacing detachment that turns to laughter when he is back in his hotel.'

Matters came to a head in the final Test, at Sydney. England needed a draw to win back the Ashes. Rowan returned as one of the two umpires, meaning he and Tom Brooks – noticeably less hostile to short bowling – had stood in five of the six Tests to see play. England managed just 184 batting first, but then hit back. Knott made what England considered a cast-iron stumping against Walters, but Rowan did not give it out.

Then, later on the second day, with Australia 178 for 7, Snow struck Australia's No.9 Terry Jenner in the face with a short ball. Video footage shows the delivery was just short of a length, and would have hit Jenner's chest had he not ducked into it. He had to retire hurt. 'Just a minute, John,' said Rowan. 'I am not impressed by your performance and I am giving you a first warning.' Snow protested that the Australians had been bowling multiple short balls without warning. Illingworth joined his fast bowler to take up the issue. Rowan claimed both Englishmen swore at him, which they denied. As Snow headed down to fine leg, he began faux-conducting the crowd. Down by the boundary he was manhandled by a spectator – 'He was stoned,' said Snow – who had to be pulled away. Beer cans filled with urine and half-eaten pies rained down onto the out-field. Illingworth sat his team down in the middle in protest, before leading them from the field without the umpires' permis-sion – thought to be an unprecedented move in Test history.

The batsmen, Greg Chappell and Dennis Lillee, remained out in the middle. Rowan entered the England dressing room and threatened to award Australia the match by forfeit, which would have meant them retaining the Ashes. Clark and Alan Barnes of the ACB agreed with Rowan, which – after a long, disputatious tour – made Illingworth even angrier. After seven minutes off the field, the prospect of losing the Ashes after all their hard work prompted Illingworth to go back out on the field. England batted much better second time around to make 302, and Australia failed in their chase of 223, despite another contentious decision by Rowan, with Stackpole again reprieved. Across his five Tests, Rowan was involved in five dubious not-out decisions appealed for by England, four involv-ing Stackpole, who ended up leading Australia's run charts with 627.

Swanton was on hand to watch the end of this grisly mara-thon:

Saturday February 13: A day of shame wherein a finely contested match is interrupted by Ray Illingworth removing his side from the field without reference to umpires or batsmen following an accident to Jenner, who is felled by Snow with a bouncer, an angry altercation with umpire Rowan on the part of the captain and Snow and a demonstration by the crowd.

Rowan's warning to Snow for intimidation follows much short fast stuff by him in the morning, but this is only his second bouncer of the second over with the new ball. Illingworth is evidently furious and voluble, likewise Snow whose action in going right up to the pickets at long leg apparently prepared to continue the argument is too much for some who have seen their men under pretty contentious fire all the series. One grasps Snow's shirt and cans begin to be tossed on to the field, which is the immediate signal for Illingworth's action. The ground is quickly cleared by police and staff and England return to a hail of boos, having been warned by the umpires that if they remain in the pavilion they will lose the match by default. The crowd's misbehaviour is deplorable clearly – but they are reacting to a still more reprehensible situation in the middle.

Wednesday February 17: The England side chair their captain home and the Ashes are deservedly back at the sixth attempt and after 12 years. It remains only to count the cost.

England had edged the series, but their bowlers had not won a single lbw appeal across any of the seven Tests; Australia's had won five. Since 1969–70 a tweaked lbw Law had been adopted, meaning that a batsman could not be out if the ball pitched outside off-stump and he was attempting a stroke. It was not until 1972 that MCC – on the Australian board's suggestion – relaxed the Law to permit umpires to give players out if, in the aforementioned circumstances, they thought the ball was going on to hit the stumps. Neutral umpires were a whole generation away.

Still, Bill O'Reilly, the great Australian leg-spinner, had little sympathy for Snow or Illingworth in his review for *The Cricketer*'s Jubilee edition:

Snow ran foul of the umpires right round our cricket map. The first time I saw him he was involved in a no-ball display at Adelaide where a new umpire named Joseph called him so often that the early embarrassment was too much for South Australian officials, who have not invited that umpire to stand since. The pugnacious fast bowler was a difficult man to handle on the field – not only for batsmen, but for Australian Test umpire Lou Rowan and the English captain, Ray Illingworth.

Rowan, in my opinion, did a wonderfully contained job. There were countless times when a flare of temper from him could have aroused comprehensive embarrassments. He came out of the series with unrestricted respect. Illingworth, at times, seemed to be completely overawed with his own inadequacy in handling Snow's impetuosity – a feature which was given full throttle in the incredible 'walkoff' scene in Sydney.

Michael Melford felt Illingworth had overstepped the mark by taking his side off the field:

There were incidents and trends on the tour which made it overall a pretty sombre expedition on which to look back.

The increase in bumpers was one disturbing development which could occupy a treatise elsewhere. There were also events which, with the colourless cricket played, must have been responsible for the sad sound of an England captain more than once being booed to the wicket.

A lot has been made of Illingworth's walk-off at Sydney. Whether he was right to leave over the action of an odd drunk and a throwing of a few beer cans is not particularly important. It was regrettable that he should have gone off palpably in a huff without having had the courtesy to notify the umpires who control the game and the batsmen. He lost his temper with umpire Lou Rowan in a manner described by Richie Benaud as being more that of a South American footballer than an England captain. That he allowed a private letter to the Australian board to be leaked during the final Test before it reached its destination, that he did not make Boycott apologise for his behaviour in Adelaide, and that so eminent a player as Boycott should have set such a dreadful example, especially, though this is irrelevant, over a decision which the camera suggests was close and possibly correct.

Every allowance has to be made for the tension and the moment, but other players, past and present, have been under the tension and have taken what many think are monstrous decisions without loss of dignity. In the flush of victory excuses were made as usual in a string of predictable platitudes – modern sport is a business, you have to play it hard, winning is what matters and so on plus references to the old-fashioned ideals about sportsmanship held by ageing aristocrats at Lord's.

The Bodyline tour is still, after nearly 40 years, bitterly regretted on both sides and that whenever anyone misbehaves on the field, as did Boycott, it is still greeted by uproar. It is not taken for granted by the public whatever the modern and often distant commentator may think.

Snow was dropped the following summer, after a collision with India's Sunil Gavaskar in the Lord's Test, and left out of the tours to West Indies in 1973–4 and Australia in 1974–5, on account of being deemed a disruptive influence. It robbed England of their best fast bowler.

Australia, lesson learnt, hit back in the 1974–5 Ashes with two tearaways, Lillee and Jeff Thomson. Thomson riled traditionalists by saying on the eve of the series: 'I enjoy hitting a batsman more than getting him out. It doesn't worry me in the least to see the batsman hurt, rolling around screaming and blood on the pitch.' The going-over England's openers received in the early stages of the tour led to Cowdrey, now aged 41, being flown out for the second Test. He was still just about good enough to cope with the bombardment, but Cowdrey must have reflected that his kind of cricketer was on the way out. Thomson, who liked to surf in his spare time, saw Cowdrey getting out of a taxi in downtown Perth dressed up in a pinstripe suit. He entered the Waca at 44 for 1, to a standing ovation, and sidled up to Thomson at the bowler's end. 'How do you do, Mr Thomson I believe? I'm Colin Cowdrey.' Thomson replied, 'Fat lot of good that will do you, fatso.'

Rebel rebel

Packer is cricket's line in the sand. Forty years since it was sprung on a complacent establishment, so many arguments over cricket's future have been debated on a similar question – does maximising income from the game mean selling its soul?

To the generation administering cricket at the time, and those who reported it, the game was the thing. *The Cricketer*, under the aegis of EW Swanton, neatly captured the traditional stance in a short italicised note in its September 1977 edition, at the height of the Packer crisis. '*The Cricketer* will continue to monitor this tangled saga, hoping, as will our readers, that matters are resolved with a minimum of delay and with cricket harmed as little as necessary. We look forward to a time when events on the field of play are once again the major concern for us all.' But, Jim, what about paying the players what they were worth? 'It's the easiest sport in the world to take over,' Kerry Packer said soon after, 'because nobody bothered to pay the players what they were worth.'

The main charge that traditionalists like Swanton had against Packer was his own self-interest. The existing system may have been imperfect, but at least it was run by volunteers who did not seek to skim off huge personal fortunes, and who put the profits – such as they were – back into the game. Packer, when asked in June 1977 if his interest in cricket was half-philanthropic, replied: 'Hmm ... that makes me sound more generous than I am.'

In April 1976, Packer, the controller of Australian Consolidated Press and the Nine Network, offered the Australian Cricket Board A$1.5m for exclusive three-year rights to televise home Tests on Channel 9 – a figure roughly eight times what the Australian Broadcasting Commission had been paying. The ABC could never hope to match Packer's offer, but the ACB felt loyalty to the national public broadcaster. When offered the sop of exclusive commercial rights, Packer replied: 'That's no good to me. Come on now, we're all harlots. What's your price?' When the ABC's deal was renewed for just $210,000, Packer was incensed. And when he tendered a bid of £75,000 to show BBC coverage of Australia's 1977 Ashes series in England, he learnt that ACB chairman Bob Parish had endorsed the ABC's £53,000. Packer doubled his offer, and won – but it was hard to deny his accusation of an old boys' network at play.

So the Australian players – exciting, marketable and more restless than the previous generation – would have to be his route in. Packer had his way in through John Cornell, known to the Australian public as 'Strop', the sidekick on Channel 9's *The Paul Hogan Show*, and Austin Robertson, a former AFL player who was now Dennis Lillee's agent. Lillee had been suffering from spinal problems diagnosed on the 1973–4 West Indies tour, and the moment he went over on his shoulder in a Perth grade match back home, the ACB ceased paying his medical bills; he vented his anger in print.

The Australians' home Test fees had gone up from $20 in 1970 to $200 in 1975, but that was still small beer. 'We were so stupid,' said Ian Chappell. 'During the England series in '74/75 I was in the dressing room at the MCG and they announced the gate money was $250,000. I thought "We're getting $200 each, so that's $2,200. Where the hell is the rest of it going?"' One clue was that, Sheffield Shield attendances plummeting, the ACB needed to find something else to make up the shortfall. During one pay dispute, ACB secretary Alan Barnes declared in print that there were 500,000 men out in the country who would play for Australia for nothing. Chappell was about to give Barnes a piece of his mind, to see him already pinned up against a wall by Ian Redpath. 'Now bear in mind Redders was one of the milder-mannered blokes in the team,' said Chappell. '"You bloody idiot", he was saying. "Of course there's 500,000 blokes who would play for Australia for nothing. But how bloody good would the Australian team be?"'

The ACB were, unwittingly, about to lay on the best possible recruitment fair. In March 1977 Australia and England played the Centenary Test at the MCG, a gala celebrating 100 years of

Test cricket. Packer and his emissaries, Ian Chappell and Tony Greig, were busy signing up interested players for a planned breakaway series, dubbed World Series Cricket. Robertson started hanging around the dressing room, distributing envelopes containing $75,000 to Packer signees – their 'theatre tickets'. Somehow they managed to keep it all under wraps.

The authorities were blasé, and a little blindsided. Greg Chappell, the Australia captain, had written just before the Centenary Test that 'Australia leads the way in providing a far better deal for cricketers'. And two days out, an ACB subcommittee had met, including state captains, to discuss revenue arising from new Benson & Hedges sponsorship. Unbeknown to the board, four of the six captains had already signed for Packer. Hints had been dropped around the Centenary Test, with Greig telling Christopher Martin-Jenkins that more money would soon be coming into the game. But CMJ admitted his 'antennae weren't sharp enough' to read more into Greig's statement. In April, the Johannesburg *Sunday Times* reported that four South Africans had signed for an overseas league – but that in itself was nothing new in their years of isolation.

The story broke on the first weekend of May, with the Australians now in England for their 1977 Ashes tour. Rain had curtailed the first day of their tour game against Sussex at Hove and, with the rest day to follow, Greig was hosting a Saturday evening garden party for both sides at his house not far from the ground. John Snow tapped him on the shoulder to let him know that two Australian reporters, Peter McFarline of the *Age* and Alan Shiell of the *Australian*, had been asking players what they knew about a planned breakaway series. Greg Chappell denied all knowledge. But Greig was advised by his agent, the journalist Reg Hayter, to issue a statement: 'There is a massive cricket project involving most of the world's top players due to commence in Australia this winter. I am part of it, along with a number of English players.' The following day, the *Bulletin*, the Nine Network's official magazine, announced that 35 players had signed a three-year contract with JP Sport and Television Corporation Ltd (chaired by Packer) to take part in a series of six Test matches, six one-day games, and six three-day round-robin tournaments in Australia, beginning in 1977–8. The players included 13 of Australia's 17-man Ashes party, and four of the current England crop – Greig and the Kent trio of Alan Knott, Derek Underwood and Bob Woolmer.

Freddie Brown, the chairman of the Cricket Council, promptly removed Greig from the England captaincy for the upcoming Ashes series. 'The captaincy of the England team requires close liaison with the selectors,' declared Brown, 'and clearly Greig is unable to do this as his stated intention is to be contracted elsewhere during the next three winters.' He was replaced by Mike Brearley, although the Packer signees were not barred from selection.

During an emergency meeting at Lord's on June 14, the member boards of the ICC agreed to meet Packer. The Lord's Test itself ended in a draw, with Packerites Woolmer (120) and Greig (91) thriving. The showdown came on June 23. The ICC set Packer five demands: WSC must not exceed six weeks; it must obey the Laws of Cricket; the series must fall under the auspices of the home board, who would approve venues and officials; Tests and other official matches would take precedence over WSC games; and none of the Packer sides should represent national teams. Packer was ready to accept all that, so long as he could be guaranteed exclusive TV rights once the existing ABC deal expired in 1981. Richie Benaud took him for a 40-minute wander around Lord's while the ICC deliberated. They did not like the idea of being held to ransom, and eventually informed Packer that he would have to line up to bid with everybody else.

The matter had begun as an Australian dispute, and it was their team who was worst affected. Craig Serjeant and Gary Cosier realised while netting at Lord's that they had been overlooked by Packer and hidden from the negotiations. Len Maddocks, the put-upon tour manager, said: 'I do not envisage the present development having a detrimental effect on the tour.' Geoff Boycott, to make his 100th first-class hundred in the Headingley Test, reckoned them the most focused Australia team he came up against, even though England won 3-0. Cosier was not so sure. 'An awful, awful tour,' he said. 'There were arguments all the time.' Two days after the Ashes were surrendered at Headingley, Cosier turned up for a team meeting at the Waldorf Hotel in London to find the WSC 13 had left for the Dorchester to meet Packer, who was imploring them not to lose their nerve; a threat of a ban had led Jeff Thomson and the West Indian Alvin Kallicharran to withdraw under legal advice from their agent, David Lord.

Things had changed for the English, too. When the TCCB promised the England players a £9,000 bonus for winning the Ashes, Brearley ensured it was shared equally among all the players, including the Packerites. And the threat of Packer defections prompted a businessman, David Evans, to put in more money for the players: the England's Test match fee immediately rose from £210 in the 1977 series to four figures.

The Cricketer editor David Frith wrote of the enveloping crisis:

'Have you no morals?' Colonel Pickering, in company with Professor Higgins, asked Alfred Doolittle. 'No, I can't afford 'em,' Eliza's father replied. 'And neither could you if you was as poor as me.'

In the eyes of many a cricket follower Doolittle represents the Test cricketer tempted to sign a contract with Australian media baron Kerry Packer. Test match fees are inadequate when set against the takings at the gate, and perhaps a cricketer whose exhilaration at playing for his country has dulled may be forgiven for going where the money is. John Snow, on the assumption that he has played his last game for England, has escaped criticism in this matter. Greig, Knott and Underwood have not. Since none of them is a poor Doolittle by any stretch of the imagination they are less easily forgiven. Clive Lloyd was one to speak with admirable candour when, without attempting to claim that cricketers everywhere would benefit, he said it was an offer he simply could not afford to ignore. Every man has his price, be he sportsman, commentator, or street hawker.

The irreconcilable aspect of the two forces – established Test cricket and a threatening commercial takeover – would appear to be the matter of timetables. There is no scope for such a series as Mr Packer plans. If the compromise which he is said to be prepared to welcome is at all possible, it would surely mean restricting his programme and even those of the Test-playing countries. Does Test cricket have to give way? When it is in danger, as it now undoubtedly is, it has to work for preservation. Should the Packer Plan be short-lived, Test cricket will have been diminished only temporarily. Should it prosper, Test cricket will be poorer, with one anomaly being that it is hard to see from where the commercial organisation will draw its future 'stars' if the major countries are reduced to fielding second elevens with much-lessened public appeal.

It is a thorny one for the International Cricket Conference to deal with, and the delegates will need to examine closely the benefits promised by Mr Packer, ie greater incentives for players everywhere, large sums to be spent on coaching schemes, and greater investment in Australian TV contracts not concerning Australian sides. The ICC would seem to have the power only to bar certain players from Test cricket: a threat likely to be effective only upon the younger players. Not all the 35 signed up have received advances on their fees, and presumably by withdrawing they would risk only a breach of contract action which probably would have less than a 50-50 chance of success.

Deceptions are not easy to forgive, but Tony Greig has been punished by the loss, thus far, of the England captaincy. It is to be hoped that there will be no further deception, and that good sense will prevail on both sides. Something good can yet come out of it, but the potential danger remains like a black cloud over the pavilion as the 1977 Test series is played out.

As the matter rolled on through the Ashes summer, Swanton made clear his disapproval:

A preliminary ICC meeting on June 14 decided to invite Packer to discuss his plans with them prior to the full annual ICC meeting, which takes place at Lord's on July 26–27. When he did so the ICC went further to accommodate the situation Packer had created than most lovers of cricket can have anticipated. They were willing to accept the intrusion of a six-week programme into the Australian summer and take responsibility for its control: in fact to legitimise the bastard child despite the sordid circumstances of its conception.

Faced with this united front of utter reasonableness Packer then emerged in his true colours by demanding that on expiry of the Australian Cricket Board's present contract for the televising of Test cricket with the ABC in 1978/79 his companies should be accorded the exclusive rights. Granted these, Packer was apparently prepared either to stage a short face-saving programme or to settle with his performers and call the thing off.

So much for the protestations that he had come into cricket to improve the lot of the downtrodden first-class cricketer! His players, one and all, and not least his truculent spokesman, Tony Greig, were seen to be mere pawns in a local commercial dogfight. On this account Packer was happy to threaten the financial structure of international cricket on which the game at large depends. When he was given the only answer he could possibly have been given – that he could compete for the next TV contract with any other interested parties – amiability turned to threats: 'I will now take no steps at all to help anyone. It's every man for himself and the devil take the hindmost.' To which the world of cricket will be inclined to remark with a concerted voice, '… And the devil take K Packer!'

Who but a ruthless tycoon could have supposed that a body of sportsmen would have sold down the river organisations such as the Australian Broadcasting Commission to whom they have been contracted since the dawn of broadcasting? Obviously such a proposition was unacceptable.

We may be hopeful in the end that this piratical promoter will be seen to have bitten off more than he can chew. Certainly in Melbourne, and probably in Sydney also, the recognised cricket grounds can be legitimately barred to him. I expect there may be some blood-and-thunder cricket which will have a curiosity value to some. (The spirit of the enterprise may be gauged from the announcement already made that tailenders will be given no immunity from bouncers.) That the Australian sporting public in any significant numbers will prefer exhibition games with no official status to the real thing, from my knowledge of them, seems unlikely.

As regards those who have 'gone over', individual circumstances differ too much to incline one to any universal condemnation. It is too much maybe in these days to expect those greater cricketers in their midst, suddenly offered an unexpected and substantial windfall, to take due account of their responsibility to the system which has, at considerable cost, produced them, and to which they owe all they have achieved. One cannot imagine the generations before them, though they were in relative terms far worse off, defecting in such numbers from Test cricket – and certainly not in such secrecy. It is the deception of men already making a handsome living out of the game and who were closely involved with the authorities, especially in Australia, in a scheme to make more, that has caused bitterness among those who put so much effort into running the game. Yet I am prepared to believe that some of the younger signatories may not have fully realised the implications of their contracts, and are known now to be harbouring doubts. How excellent if all such had the moral courage to pull back!

Frith's diary of 'The Packer Affair' demonstrated the impact on the 1977 Ashes:

July 14: *Melbourne Age* writer Peter McFarline attributes Australia's defeat in the second Test [at Old Trafford] to loss of spirit, especially among the younger players, some of whom fear they may have destroyed their careers by signing for Packer.

July 28: On the morning of the Trent Bridge Test match Jeff Thomson announces his withdrawal from the Packer camp. His letter refers to his obligation to Radio 4IP Brisbane, with whom he is under a 10-year contract, and to his desire to play for Queensland and Australia. Thomson's manager, David Lord, seeing it as a 'major breakthrough', says: 'It took a lot of guts for Thommo to do what he has done. I shall be seeing as many players as I can in an attempt to persuade them to follow Jeff's example.

As the Trent Bridge Test gets under way a representative of Packer's Channel 9 group lodges a protest that an advertising hoarding for Channel 10 network near the long-off boundary is occasionally seen on the television screen. The protest is rejected.

August 14: Kerry Packer, receiving a hostile reception from some of the 400 spectators, plays for an Australian Press XI against an English Press XI at Harrogate on the rest day of the fourth Test match. He makes two not out, and holds a slip catch (off David Lord's bowling) and another as wicketkeeper.

With lines being drawn in the sand, Swanton felt the need to stress that *The Cricketer* was not a lapdog of the cricketing establishment:

We continue in this issue the full factual chronicle of 'The Packer Affair'. Depressing though the whole matter is, this is the game's authentic journal of record. It has been so for 56 years and no doubt it will remain long beyond our Diamond Jubilee in 1981, by which time, if the world's cricketing authorities continue to deal with the evolving situation as they have started, the present commotion may be remembered just as a temporary dislocation similar to other severe but transient palavers in the past.

Readers of *The Cricketer* – all but the very young – will know that we are far from being blind supporters of authority and the status quo. We have opposed many edicts that have emanated from Lord's, especially those ordained by the counties and the ICC. In this case however it seems to us – and to the cricket world surely almost to a man – that each move by the TCCB, by the Cricket Council, and by the ICC has been reasonable, logical and best calculated to serve the interests of cricket as a whole and Tests and other first-class cricket in particular.

And Jack Fingleton, a former Test cricketer and revered journalist, showed that not all Australian ex-cricketers sided with Packer:

Whatever the upshot of Kerry Packer's onslaught on the citadels of cricket, Test cricket seemingly will never be the same. England and Australia will build up their Test teams to their previous strength, of that I have no doubt, but the dominant pull of money has come into the game to stay. I have my reservations about sponsorship.

I hope sponsoring firms will not demand over-much for the support they give the game. One rather fancies that Mr Packer got his grand illusions about running the international game from the success of the Centenary Test in Melbourne in March 1977.

It is not my intention here, however, to discuss the very grievous wrongs of Mr Packer, as I see them, in his attempt to take over big cricket, for such it is. I see no need to alter my first impression of his move, written for the London *Sunday Times* as far back as May, when the story first broke, that I could see no future for the Packer scheme beyond, say, a year or so. I cannot see that cricket played on makeshift pitches will appeal either to players or the public.

Nor, ignoring for the nonce the legal niceties of the affair, do I conceive that constituted cricket authority, as we know it, can be expected to ripen future plums through its many processes for Mr Packer to plunder for his factory. Much is in the offing as I write this, the day after the final Test at The Oval. Our Australian board has to meet in Sydney and decide what it will do about our defectors. It could be that the board will hit back hard in the control it still thinks it holds over those players who toured under Greg Chappell in 1977 but the uncertainty of their actions and what would come out of it must have made for an unpleasant atmosphere for the tour.

Thus I am pleased to have made my tours when I did. It would be easy to make too much of Mr Packer's raid upon international cricket but any cricketer who has toured abroad in his country's colours can appreciate the atmosphere that surely must have existed in the Australian camp. Most of the team were admitted Packer men. Those who were not were Serjeant, Cosier, Hughes and Dymock. There was a cleavage for a start, the wanted and the unwanted. Manager Len Maddocks saw fit to issue a statement well into the tour that there was no division in his team, that they were actuated in doing their principal job, holding the Ashes. That there was a necessity to issue such a statement made the real position apparent.

Warwickshire and Kent were probably the counties affected most by the Packer crisis, as was clear from the reaction of Brian Johnston, the *Test Match Special* commentator, writing in *The Cricketer*:

I have recently had to make a personal decision. I have reluctantly resigned my membership of Kent, due to their committee's decision to offer new contracts to their Packer players.

I am not vindictive nor do I bear any malice or ill-feeling to the players concerned. They have all been – and I hope still are – my friends. I do not begrudge them their understandable desire to ensure their financial future, if that is what they think they have done. But I do not approve of the way they did, though I appreciate that it was largely forced on them. Apart from the financial side I also cannot help wondering if they have done the right thing by themselves. What satisfaction can great cricketers like Alan Knott and Derek Underwood get from playing limited-over cricket on football fields under floodlights with a hefty ration of 'Blood and Bouncers'? But all that is their affair and not mine …

The defections to Packer should have given [other] cricketers their opportunity to try to become England cricketers and so increase their earnings. Because remember that, by committing themselves to Packer during the winter months, those England players who signed for him voluntarily opted out of any future tours abroad for England for at least three years.

That is my chief quarrel with them and it's not just because I am an old square. Look at the voting of the Cricketers' Association and see what their fellow players think about it. Neither they nor I see why Packer players should come back in the summer and expect to play for their counties, thereby denying young players qualified for England a chance to gain experience and prove their worth.

The 1978–9 Ashes series went ahead, played out alongside the second season of WSC. England were missing Greig, Knott, Underwood and Woolmer to Packer; Australia were without all their senior players. Bob Simpson, 41, had answered the call to captain an inexperienced side against West Indies and India in 1977–8, but then headed back into retirement, leaving 26-year-old Yallop in charge for the Ashes. 'I remember bumping into some of the Aussie guys involved in the Packer series at the airport,' said Ian Botham. 'They actually wished us well, and I thought, "my goodness, there must be some friction over here".' Bob Willis reckoned Yallop a pawn in a wider game. 'He wasn't the usual forceful Aussie captain we were used to coming up against, and you felt at times the strings were being pulled by Bob Parish and Ray Steele [ACB officials]. I got the feeling they thought the public face of official cricket had to be a kindly one, and they chose Graham to provide that face.' Yallop, a mild-mannered Melburnian, admitted the pressure on him, from friends, the media and the officials, was at times 'unbearable'. Left without a tour manager, and players who barely knew each other, he had to organise tickets, taxis, laundry for the players and more.

The cricket wasn't all bad: the tearaway Hogg caused havoc among the England batsmen. But Brearley was bemused by Yallop's captaincy: 'At Perth they took Hogg off when he'd taken two wickets for no runs on a green wicket. It was an extraordinary decision. He wanted short spells but I'd have thought any bowler in the world would have wanted to bowl a side out there.' Ian Chappell, watching from afar, was not impressed either. 'He said they would win 6-0. Then they lost the first Test and he said they could still win 5-1. It was fanciful stuff. It didn't help having someone as astute as Brearley, against someone who was ill-equipped to captain not just a Test side, but probably any side.' Australia lost 5-1. No wonder Yallop called his autobiography *Lambs to the Slaughter*.

There was another show in town – by now setting the agenda with day/night cricket, white balls, drop-in pitches and bouncers permitted to the tailenders, all tub-thumped by the catchy advertising jingle 'C'mon, Aussie, c'mon' that has become a touchstone of Australian sporting culture. The first season of WSC had generally played out in moderately populated show-grounds away from the traditional venues. But when the New South Wales Cricket Association was stripped of its domi-nant rights to the Sydney Cricket Ground, Packer had lights installed, opened the gates, and 44,377 people flooded in to watch WSC Australia play WSC West Indies. Ian Chappell reckoned: 'That night at the SCG was the moment we were accepted as the Australian cricket team.' The Channel 9 cover-age set the pace with more camera angles – no more 'staring at the batsman's butt for half of the match', as Packer put it, which was the view the audience had when Bob Massie was taking his 16 wickets at Lord's in 1972, meaning they could not see the extent to which he swung the ball.

Packer even had the gall to have a handwritten note deliv-ered to Brearley, challenging England to a Test against Ian Chappell's WSC Australians – with $50,000 at stake for the winners – an eerie forerunner of the Stanford 20/20 for 20 between England and the Stanford Super Stars in Antigua 30 years later. Brearley refused. The establishment tried some accoutrements of their own in the Ashes: skydivers arriving with the match ball and coin, marching displays and athletics events during intervals. 'But the essential factor of a winning Australian team was missing,' wrote Alex Bannister in *Wisden*, 'and attendances dropped to alarming levels by the final Test.'

Swanton was similarly downcast in *The Cricketer*:

True enough, England at home in 1977 beat Australia's full available strength 3-0. But Packer had already scrawled his writing on the wall. Australia's forces, the futures of so many of them signed away, were rather less of a match for Mike Brearley's well-co-ordinated side than has been the team taken over – and who can have had a more difficult inheritance? – by young Graham Yallop.

Yet the new Australia will not win the confidence of its own critical public unless and until it can soon begin to deliver the goods. The danger is that, with this welter of cricket going on and so-called Australia XI's under the Packer banner playing here, there and everywhere, supporters of the game are becoming both bored and confused. They want to identify with one Australian team, and that the best available.

As for the World Series circus, despite wholesale publicity and brilliant TV camera work, it is being rumbled for what it is, a programme of exhibitions performed by mercenaries who alone, for good commercial motives, are interested in the result. In the long run it is the number of paying spectators which will determine the future of WSC, for advertisers will not support games played in almost empty arenas.

The reality was that both sides were losing money. The 1978–9 series had suffered losses of £445,000 – thought to be the first time the Ashes had failed to break even – and the ACB's overall deficit was $35,000. In April 1979, news emerged that the ACB had granted Packer exclusive 10-year TV and commercial rights to Australian cricket, in exchange for winding up WSC. Packer seemed to have got more than he ever wanted; the new settlement seemed to resemble more his vision of cricket than the traditional one. The ICC, apparently keen to avoid any disharmony before the 1979 World Cup in England later in the summer, rushed the deal through, though Australia still turned up for the tournament with a second-string side. Trevor McDonald wrote: 'It had always been agreed among ICC members that no individual country would contract a unilateral agreement with WSC. Yet the Australian board's agreement was reached with the utmost haste and to the embarrassment of some member countries. The sight of Mr Packer and Bob Parish cooing delightedly in accord was not one for weak stomachs.'

It demonstrates how much world cricket has changed that India were asked to postpone their visit in 1979–80, to accommodate England and West Indies, the two biggest bankers of the time. Australia were to play three Tests each against the two visiting sides, plus a surfeit of Benson & Hedges-sponsored one-day matches with a final, which would be the best of five. The pattern of the triangular one-day series, a fixture for another 30 years, was born in the Packer settlement – and this in a country where the establishment board had not organised any ODIs between December 1975 and January 1979.

Brearley didn't like it much. 'It was a very ill-thought-out tour,' he said. 'Most of the regulations for the one-day internationals, of which Packer had wanted to stage about fifteen, had not been decided by the time we got to Australia. The result was that I became the one responsible for standing up for our point of view. That should have been the job of the administrators. It was all the most voracious aspects of Packer.' Brearley did manage to resist certain Packer demands: England stayed in traditional white kit in the ODIs, compared to the outfits trimmed with stripes worn by Australia and West Indies, though they did agree to coloured pads and gloves to help the umpires make decisions. England also refused to play with a white ball except in day/night games, and rejected the use of a white ball at each end. The advent of night cricket, and the lax attitude towards bumpers in WSC, made helmets almost universal.

Packer claimed to have brought a fresh young audience to cricket, but others were wary about newcomers failing to observe the courtesies and rhythms of the game. Brearley arrived in Australia sporting a bushy greying beard. A sharp Australian wit dubbed him 'the Ayatollah'. But, once he started grumbling about the tour arrangements, he became fair game. One banner at the MCG read: 'Gold Medallion Award For Greatest Whinger Would Have To Be Won By J. M. Brearley, Classical Music Lover'. Brearley's players had plenty of coarser language, plus cans of urine, lobbed in their direction. At the end of England's first one-day match, with West Indies' last man Colin Croft needing to score three off the last ball, Brearley stationed all his fielders, including wicketkeeper David Bairstow, on the boundary. When Croft was bowled by Botham, Bairstow was struck by a piece of metal thrown from the crowd.

It did not help Brearley's cause that, two weeks out from the tour, the TCCB had declared the Ashes would not be up for grabs in the three-Test series. Ian Chappell was predictably narked: 'It shouldn't be up to one country to say, "we think on this occasion we won't be playing for any trophies, so bad luck if you win."' When they did, 3-0, the Australians went out and bought a run-of-the-mill trophy from a sports shop and christened it 'Ernie'. West Indies, on the other hand, decided to put the Frank Worrell Trophy at stake, and pulled off their first Test series win in Australia.

Reg Hayter, now editor of *The Cricketer*, commissioned Tony Lewis to report on the post-Packer peace settlement:

It was exciting in Australia watching the multi-coloured road-show leap into action. It was tiring, too, and quite infuriating to be hopping from airport to airport without the usual relaxation of a game of golf with Australian friends. If the Australian board has a mind to continue at this speed, and indeed next year they are repeating the triangular experiment with India and New Zealand, and the year after with Pakistan and West Indies, then there will never again be a chance to make any friends.

The Australian board has linked its national cricket to television and, through television, to a wider marketing field. The financial implications, though not revealed, are extremely beneficial to the game out there and, perhaps more importantly, the Australian board has finally killed off the devil on its own doorstep – World Series Cricket.

It was easy to see the likelihood of cricket being launched into a cheap entertainment jungle when they wheeled on the pop group at the Melbourne Cricket Ground during the lunch interval. Six young men in a variety of scruffy attire were driven over the outfield on top of a lorry to save the popular side and proceeded to deafen everyone for 40 minutes.

Suggestion: abandon the television advertising campaign which is currently depicting aggression. They show Lillee bowling a bouncer which knocks a batsman's helmet off. They say the Aussies are going to take the hide of the Poms.

Ultimate lesson: it is realistic to put the promotion and marketing of cricket into the hands of a professional agency. It is equally sensible, as Bob Parish, chairman of the Australian board, told me, not to tie the hands of that agency behind its back. However, every answer that agency comes up with, every major campaign or each tiny gimmick should always be measured against the time-honoured guideline – is it in the best interest of cricket and cricketers?

My history master used to award penalty kicks for dull play on the rugby field. If a boy ever risked a punch or a tantrum, he would expect to be sent to 'the cooler', which really meant standing still on the touchline until recalled to play. The schoolmaster's name is worth recalling because it came to my mind in Australia a short while ago as I sat watching first Ian Chappell's bat-throwing argument with the umpire at Brisbane, then Dennis Lillee's aluminium equivalent at Perth. Sam Evans would have had them both on the sidelines.

The post-war generation did their pads up with buckles on the outside because Denis Compton was said to do it that way. I have seen a schoolboy off-spinner kiss his cap because Tayfield used to do it; young West Indies fast bowlers wear their shirts open and carry a medallion of sorts on a neck-chain because Wes Hall blasted them out that way. What Lillee and Chappell demonstrated was an example which might make schoolmasters tear out their hair and youths throw beer cans on the Sydney Hill.

Someone wrote to me shortly after Lillee had thrown his bat, and accused me of bias. Why was I suggesting a ban on Lillee but not on Geoff Boycott who, the year before in Perth, was said to have tossed his bat to the ground and called umpire Don Weser a cheat? I must plead, first, that I did not see the Boycott incident and, if that is not an acceptable get-out, I must confess my own confusion.

It is obvious that the Packer Revolt was all about cricketers fighting for the status of their profession and for money which was a fair compensation for being among the best players in the world. Finally, Mr Justice Slade undid the cage which had trapped their aspirations.

The Australian board gave them their wings by setting up the triangular commercial experiment, and many sponsors came up with the hard cash. Most players, I know, understand that with their new incomes from commerce comes a widening of their responsibilities. No longer does their involvement begin and end on the field. There are receptions to honour, prize-givings to attend, and many miles of video-taped promotion to act out.

On [one] occasion, Clive Lloyd, so disgusted with the closing actions of one match, did not even appear for the presentation. Deryck Murray deputised. David Hookes threw his bat, causing £25 worth of damage to a dressing room. Viv Richard's [sic] bat bounced off a seat through a window.

I am certainly not the judge of any of these reported happenings, but it is worth the new regime of international cricketers standing up, while the guns are cooling, to consider the style, indeed the image, of their profession as a whole. Surely the right sponsors will only stay with a game of honourable behaviour?

On balance, however, traditionalists were just relieved to see the fences mended. John Woodcock wrote:

> However distasteful in some respects and unsettling in others the England tour to Australia was, at least it was better than the alternative would have been, namely another winter of bitter strife between the traditional game and Mr Packer's well-organised and highly paid mercenary force ... No side can expect to beat Australia with a middle order that supplies virtually no runs. These, reputedly, are the best batsmen in England we are talking about, and they are being paid big money. However ghastly an itinerary they were subjected to in Australia, there can be no excuse for such impoverishment as this.

The establishment had barely come up for air before they were hit with an even more serious issue. Some of the more traditionally minded cricket journalists were upset that South Africa had been banned from international cricket in 1970 – as they drew a distinction between the hard-line policies of the apartheid regime and the attitude of their cricketers and their board. But then, in June 1977, came the Gleneagles Agreement – when the heads of Commonwealth governments agreed to discourage their sporting organisations from contact with South Africa.

Many of the leading South African players were said to be opposed to apartheid, and wanted to help the new unified body, the South African Cricket Union, bring about multiracial cricket. But by 1981 they had gone 11 years without any international competition, and were getting desperate. Packer had brought unprecedented wealth into the game, and South Africa were not seeing the benefits of it. And so Ali Bacher, who had captained South Africa in their farewell 1969–70 series against Australia, began planning for an unofficial tour by a group of English professional cricketers. SACU worked closely with the apartheid government to prepare the ground for these rebel tours, and private sponsors would fund it.

In between county seasons and England tours, most English professionals were still free agents, making them ripe for plucking. Boycott, coming to the end of his international career, was approached by a local music executive while on holiday in South Africa in 1980–81, and began putting the word about. On the West Indies tour in early 1981, Boycott, Botham, Gower, Graham Gooch and John Emburey agreed in principle to take part in a private tour of South Africa. Then, in summer 1981, came Botham's Ashes – which made his legend and revived cricket in the eyes of the British public.

The following winter, though, England went through an interminably dull Test series in India. England fell behind early on, then came up against a succession of dead pitches, negative Indian tactics and unyielding home umpiring. Gooch said all these were factors in his decision to defect. Emburey and Alan Knott would ring each other's hotel rooms to talk about the tour, communicating through the code of chess moves. Botham was said to have been offered £50,000, but turned it down because he could not have looked his old friend Viv Richards in the eye. Boycott called Botham's statement 'unnecessary and pukemaking'. Years later, Bacher showed the journalist Jack Bannister a copy of the letter Botham had put his name to in the Caribbean. The England captain, Keith Fletcher, rejected a reported £45,000 but, after overseeing a 1-0 defeat in India, was replaced as captain by Willis.

Wayne Larkins thought the rebels might get a three-month ban for going to South Africa; they were slapped with three years. So a Willis-led England went to Australia in 1982–3 without Boycott, Gooch, Emburey, Peter Willey and others – and lost 2-1.

For the 1985 Ashes in England, it was Australia who faced disruption from the South African issue. Before the tour, it emerged that Kim Hughes, who had resigned as captain after losing at home to West Indies in 1984–5, would be leading a team of Australians to South Africa over the next two seasons. Seven of them, Terry Alderman, Dirk Wellham, Graeme Wood, Rod McCurdy, Wayne Phillips, Murray Bennett and Steve Rixon, had been named in the Ashes squad. The great irony was that Packer, who now owned the Australian TV rights, offered financial inducements to Wellham, Phillips and Wood, persuading them to renege on an offer of A$200,000 from South Africa. Australia's young captain Allan Border was furious, and initially refused to tour with them, but backed down after talks with them and the board. Carl Rackemann and John Maguire were among those initially called up to replace the rebels – until both revealed they too had signed to go to South Africa. Those Australians who did go to South Africa found themselves banned for two years by the ACB, ruling them out of the 1986–7 Ashes.

CMJ, now editor of *The Cricketer* and previewing the 1985 series, was yet to be convinced that South Africa's isolation was the right move:

Australia's touring team in England is neither weaker nor stronger as a result of the three late changes which the ACB made to the original selection because some players refused to sign a contract restraining them from playing in South Africa. Now the Australians have managed to get a representative side into the field, the issue is not how strong that side will be, but what can be done, or whether anything should be done, to ensure that countries in Test cricket are represented by their available players.

But it is nevertheless true that the South African Cricket Union is as guilty of plundering the resources of other countries as Kerry Packer was in 1977. The established authorities have every right to feel incensed when someone comes along and fleeces all the wool. Yet they have, to some extent, brought the present troubles on themselves.

None of this need have happened if the advice of the ICC party who went to South Africa in 1979 had been taken. Reporting that 'there is ample evidence that entirely integrated cricket does exist and is played on a regular basis at club and provincial level', the fact-finding commission recommended that a 'strong team representative of as many countries as possible from the ICC be sent to play a series of matches at the highest representative level'.

Even the most bitter opponents of the South African government recognise the distinction between the blunt and heartless racialist policies of the hard-line Afrikaner and those of sportsmen and administrators who wish to encourage sport for all colours and to use it as a means of achieving gradual social integration between the races in South Africa. Had cricket administrators recognised that the tour recommended by the working party would have rewarded the SACU for its reforms in the 1970s, they would have forestalled the desperate remedies to which they have since resorted. There need have been no 'rebel' tours. Given reason to hope for an eventual return to the international cricket fold, the South Africans would have continued their efforts to resolve their political differences with Hassan Howa and others. Instead we see the South Africans putting into practice Kerry Packer's law: 'there is something of the whore in all of us; every man has his price.'

News of Mike Gatting's second proposed English tour broke midway through the 1989 Ashes. The series was a disaster for England, who selected 29 different players to Australia's 12, and were trampled all over by Border's hungry young team. England manager Micky Stewart let slip that Kent's Alan Igglesden, chosen for the sixth Test at The Oval, was 'the 17th-choice seamer'. Not many were enamoured with David Gower's captaincy. Devon Malcolm said he felt Derbyshire prepared better for games, while the *Sun* declared Gower England's worst leader since Ethelred the Unready. But most pointed the finger at the selection panel chaired in recent years by Peter May and Ted Dexter.

CMJ, reporting on the fourth Test at Old Trafford for *The Cricketer*, was dejected:

It was cruel luck for Russell, and for all the Australian opponents, not least the 'man of the match' Geoff Lawson, that the breaking of the South Africa story on the morning of the fifth day should so have stolen the thunder.

No one will know how much an unsettled subconscious affected the performances of the nine England players who at some stage during the first four Tests had either decided or were wondering whether to go to South Africa. So momentous a career decision must play on the mind. England were preoccupied much of the time, however much they must have tried to concentrate on the job in hand. It had been the same for Australia in England in 1977.

CMJ's report from The Oval captured the full extent of England's chaotic selection:

The chief interest in the match lay in the performance of the younger members of the England team. The selectors also had included Nasser Hussain and Eddie Hemmings in their party of 13 but the youngest and oldest members were omitted, leaving Atherton, Stephenson and Igglesden to represent, perhaps, the England of tomorrow. Stephenson had been chosen partly on the strength of an impressive hundred against Holland in a one-day match the previous week when the side representing England had lost the first and won the second of two limited-overs matches under the captaincy of Peter Roebuck. Igglesden, however, had been called up only the day before the match. Fraser, the original choice, had to withdraw with a knee strain. DeFreitas, tactlessly chosen in his place ahead of Thomas, the 12th man at Trent Bridge, after Malcolm had pulled out because of back spasms, promptly strained a hamstring. When Thomas was approached again he politely declined. He had been asked by the South Africans to replace DeFreitas in England's mercenary team and he was going to take the instant security offered thereby in place of the uncertain future with 'official' England. Inquiries were then made about the fitness of several bowlers, Watkin and Cowans included. Gower was in favour of Agnew, but his fellow selectors settled for the youth of Igglesden, who had laboured hard all season for Kent having himself spent the winter in South Africa, mainly in recuperation after a knee operation.

People must judge for themselves whether all this amounts to sheer bad luck or muddled management on the part of the England committee. There was an element, I think, of both. It did not end with the uncertainty of who would play. During the match Mike Gatting confirmed, but a TCCB spokesman denied, that an approach had been made to him to return to the England fold. Then the name of Ian Greig came up as a possible alternative captain to Gower and the others in the West Indies. 'What makes you think he is still eligible for England?' was the response of a senior member of the TCCB. The impression being given, as the cycle of failure continued to evolve, was of too many chiefs acting independently of one another, each as anxious as each other to avoid any blame for the hand-to-mouth governance of the first-class game. The relentless media exploited every indiscretion like so many Terry Aldermans, apparently delighting in the general malaise.

Meanwhile, in his journal of the 1989 season for *The Cricketer*, Leicestershire seamer Jonathan Agnew gave insight into the whispers on the county circuit:

Week ending August 5: With the exception of Old Trafford, where the Ashes were finally surrendered, events on the pitches everywhere paled into insignificance alongside the announcement that 16 English players – two of them black – will undertake a 'rebel tour' of South Africa.

'London's Own' cartoon of Jack Hobbs from the second edition of The Cricketer, in May 1921. Hobbs' return to Ashes cricket in summer 1921 did not go to plan.

'A Team of Demons' – the all-conquering 1921 Australia team illustrated in The Cricketer, with captain Warwick Armstrong in the centre.

Cartoon from June 1921 depicting England's defeat in the first Test at the hands of Jack Gregory and Ted McDonald.

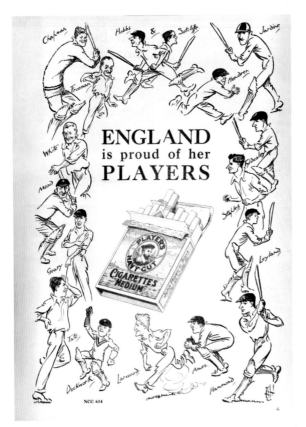

A cigarette company congratulates England on their 4–1 victory in the 1928–9 Ashes, under Percy Chapman, appearing in the 1929 Spring Annual.

An advert for Sykes bats that appeared in The Cricketer *during Bradman's unbelievable Ashes summer in 1930.*

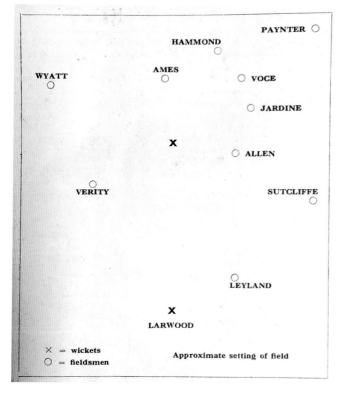

Illustration of Bodyline field placings from 1933.

Roy of the Rovers-style cartoons from August 1977, revisiting Bodyline.

'Laker's Match', from a series of comic strips entitled The Fight for the Ashes,
published in June 1977.

A star-studded advert for Slazenger bats on the cover of the 1949 Spring Annual.

The excited Oval crowd part ways to allow victorious England batsmen Denis Compton and Bill Edrich to leave the field in the 1953 series.

Australia's Gordon Rorke bowling during the 1958–9 series, highlighting the dragging of his right foot across the popping crease with the ball still in his hand.

Cricketers at Sea

1959 English team embarking at Tilbury

Travel the Test-Team way to and from Australia with P & O

Follow the example of so many English and Australian Test teams and make your way to Australia in a P & O liner.

Aboard a modern liner you enjoy unsurpassed comfort in an unforgettable atmosphere. Fine food prepared by experts. Service that satisfies your every need. Surroundings and entertainments

designed to delight. And the glories and benefits of sun and sea air. You arrive relaxed, refreshed, ready to go.

For full details see your local travel agent—or contact:

14/16 COCKSPUR STREET, LONDON, S.W.1. WHItehall 4444 122 LEADENHALL STREET, LONDON, E.C.3. AVEnue 8000

An advert for P&O ferries from The Cricketer *in August 1959, showing the winter Ashes party. The 1965–6 side were the first to make the entire trip to Australia by air.*

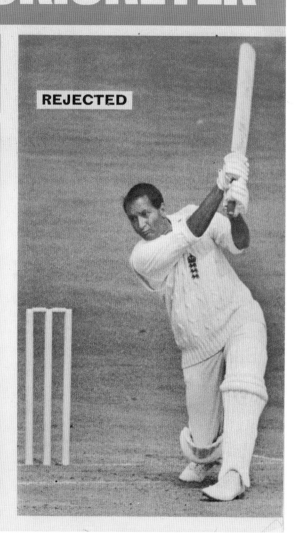

TWO SHILLINGS & SIXPENCE   SEPTEMBER 6 1968

THE CRICKETER

**BIG NAMES;
BIG ISSUES**

REJECTED

FINGLETON
Tribute to
McCabe

COMPTON
Save the
Cavaliers

SWANTON
Answer to
LBW Problem

W. F. DEEDES, MP
Politics
& Sport

MELFORD
Our Men in
S. Africa

Cover of The Cricketer *from September 1968, after Basil D'Oliveira's omission from England's party to tour South Africa. EW Swanton, the editorial director, disapproved of the 'Rejected' headline chosen by the assistant editor, Christopher Martin-Jenkins.*

A young Dennis Lillee bowls during the 1972 Ashes series. He took 31 wickets – a big factor in a thrilling 2–2 draw.

In 1974–5, Colin Cowdrey (the non-striker) was flown out to reinforce an England line-up terrorised by Lillee and Jeff Thomson, seen here bowling to David Lloyd in the second Test at Perth.

'Ashes to ashes, dust to dust—if Thomson don't get ya, Lillee must . . .'

Sunday Telegraph, Sydney

An illustration which originally featured in the Sunday Telegraph, Sydney, *after Australia regained the Ashes in 1974–5.*

Derek Randall pulls Lillee during his legendary performance in the Centenary Test at Melbourne in March 1977. Kerry Packer was busy recruiting for World Series Cricket behind the scenes.

The 1981–2 Winter Annual cover, showing a rejuvenated Ian Botham taking the final wicket, of Terry Alderman, in the fourth Test at Edgbaston in 1981.

An illustration celebrating Ian Botham's performance in the 1981 Ashes.

The scorecard from Headingley 1981, highlighting the performances of Ian Botham and Bob Willis.

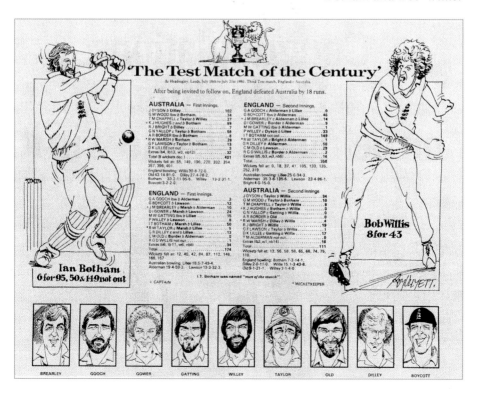

The October 1985 edition of The Cricketer, *marking England's regaining of the Ashes in 1985.*

The January 1995 cover of The Cricketer *featuring Shane Warne and reports on England's poor start to the 1994–5 series.*

Steve Waugh's twin hundreds in the third Test at Old Trafford are lauded, as he pulls Australia back into the 1997 series. Waugh did not lose an Ashes series after 1986–7.

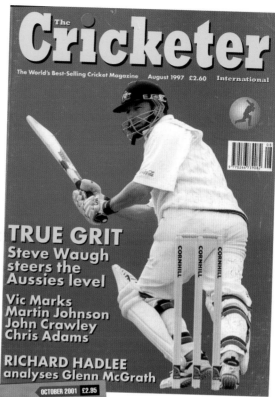

The Cricketer's October 2001 cover featured Mike Atherton on his retirement. He won just six of his 33 Tests against Australia.

Andrew Flintoff pleads for an lbw decision against Shane Warne during the unforgettable finale to the Edgbaston Test of 2005.

An image from the fifth day at The Oval in 2005 demonstrating the hysteria which surrounded the series. Not since 1981 had cricket been more popular among the British public and The Oval could have sold out many times over as fans clambered to watch England attempt to regain the Ashes for the first time in 18 years.

Captain Andrew Flintoff looks on pensively as England are whitewashed in the 2006–7 series.

Happier times for Flintoff. The September 2009 issue celebrates England's first win over Australia at Lord's since 1934.

CHRIS ROGERS • JAMES ANDERSON • JASON ROY • MARK RAMPRAKASH • MIKE SELVEY • NASSER HUSSAIN

THE WORLD'S NUMBER ONE CRICKET MAGAZINE   SEPT 2015 VOL. 12 NO. 13 **£4.50**

the cricketer

HOW ENGLAND WON BACK THE ASHES IN 18 CRAZY DAYS

THE AVENGERS

INTERVIEWS
ANALYSIS
REPORTS
OUR BEST XI
BEHIND THE SCENES

DOMESTIC T20 SPECIAL INVESTIGATION IS THE SHORT FORM OF THE GAME IN NEED OF INTENSIVE CARE?

The Cricketer *channels a 1960s TV series to mark England's regaining of the Ashes after a topsy-turvy 2015 series.*

The generally angry reaction, particularly at Phil DeFreitas and Roland Butcher, must be more intense than any of the rebels could have thought possible when they signed their two-year contracts, rumoured to be worth at least £85,000 tax free. Reaction, that is, by everyone except those on the professional cricket circuit who viewed the tour as inevitable.

Week ending August 12: Further developments on the 'rebel' front: Roland Butcher and Phillip DeFreitas have now pulled out. The reasons for their doing so being because of threats against themselves and their families. Butcher's benefit was also being hit with some members of the committee resigning in protest. The South Africans must have been delighted to have recruited two blacks, and their change of mind will be seen as a triumph for the anti-tour lobbyists who are campaigning vigorously.

Gooch, who had captained the 1981–2 rebel tour, did not sign up for the Gatting trip, as he did not want to put his family through the mill again. He sued the *Daily Mirror* for libel when they incorrectly reported him as having signed, and settled out of court for £18,000. Gooch led England, missing the second batch of rebels, into the next Ashes in 1990–91, and Border's side thrashed them again.

It was not until the apartheid system was dismantled that South Africa returned to international cricket, and the spectre of rebel tours went away. From the Centenary Test of March 1977 to the 1993 series in England, virtually every Ashes Test had been affected one way or another by Packer or South Africa.

15 Minutes of Fame

Huw Turbervill

I**T IS HORRIBLE** when cricket is kept a secret. It is such a wonderful game, the entire nation should share in it. It has happened. The Ashes triumph in coronation year, 1953. Jim Laker's 19 wickets in 1956. Ian Botham's glory in 1981, Andrew Flintoff and co. in 2005. Cricket's 'watercooler' moments.

Earlier in this book Simon Hughes has chosen his greatest Ashes XI, and Gideon Haigh his five best series. I want to write about some of the fabulous cricketers not included in those sections. Like Richard Ellison, who provided me with a particularly vivid memory of my teenage years, when he sliced through the Australians at Edgbaston in 1985. BBC1 had switched to the six o'clock news so I had to listen in on a radio at my grandmother's house in Wales. Up and down the stairs I ran to delightedly report the fall of another wicket. There are 23 players in this section – wonderful cricketers who owned a particular Ashes moment – a match or series, maybe ... even if they did not dominate for years like some of the players you have already read about. It might have been their one summer in the sun ... or, as Andy Warhol said, their 15 minutes of fame ...

Captains' knocks

David Gower 1985

We tend to have mixed feelings about Gower now. There was the 1989 Ashes hammering, the difference of opinion with Graham Gooch that led to the premature curtailing of his career; the oh-so-funny mirth on programmes like *They Think It's All Over* ... unfunny comedians daring to poke fun at a genius of his trade for 'flashing at one outside off-stump' a few too many times. With one notable exception, Gower was undamaged goods in 1985, though. He had survived the humiliation of West Indies' 'Blackwash' in 1984 to lead England to a laudable series win in India. His batting was also much loved. No one back then was doubting his batting brilliance. 'Well, my captaincy was a mixed bag,' Gower told *The Cricketer* in 2015.

> Some might remember those two series wins (India 1984/85, Australia) – others might remember the defeats to West Indies! 1985 was not as dramatic as '81, with the same headline stories. It did not have those close games, or the drama. 1986/87 was also important because winning in Australia seems to count for more for us. But I have never forgotten 1985 – blow the rest!

Gower has extra reason to recall it, as he was the leading run-scorer in the series by some margin, with 732 at an average of 81.33, ahead of Allan Border (597 at 66.33) and Mike Gatting (527 at 87.83). Presented with the series' six scorecards, Gower savours the chance to reflect languidly; as if he is enjoying one of his fine wines, or building one of the three graceful Test centuries he made that summer.

It seems to be a given before any Ashes that the visitors are decried as being useless. It even pre-dates Glenn McGrath! So the Aussies who arrived in '85 were told they were not very good by their press, and by ours, and we had to make sure they did not turn out to be too good – or better than people thought. I think we were nicely set up, after winning in India; it is very different out there, so that was a proud moment, representing four months' hard work. But the Ashes remains a fresh start whatever happens beforehand. If you win in India and lose the Ashes it all turns quickly the other way.

England won at Headingley, only for Australia to hit back at Lord's. Gower then made 166 in the draw at Trent Bridge, while the Old Trafford Test also ended in stalemate. Edgbaston was next up in the penultimate Test.

We were at the Plough and Harrow in Birmingham for the team dinner. I got up to say, 'We are looking good still, it's 1-1 with two to play and we need to win one soon, what do we need to do differently?' There were bread rolls flying at me from various elements. Probably Allan Lamb. Probably Ian Botham. In fact, almost certainly Lamb and Botham. Which might have been slightly disconcerting for the more conservative of our number. But it was enough for me to think – because it was not Ed Miliband being thrown off the hustings – that everyone was still confident. Spirits were high, it did not need a long rousing talk to get them going, and none of the bread rolls actually hit me! In fact that was the only worry, it would have been nice if some had been on target. So off we went.

Richard Ellison then helped bowl Australia out for that precious win.

'More often than not one can tell whether David Gower is going to play a big innings,' wrote Christopher Martin-Jenkins in *The Cricketer*.

As he has so often since the early weeks of this miserable summer, he immediately played in to the 'v' from the middle and soon after the first of a crystal river of boundaries began flowing from his blade. (Such a favourite blade that when it began to crack along the bottom inside edge he sent for binding rather than a new bat.) The Australian over-rate was sluggish all day, except when Bob Holland was rolling up his accurate but gentle leg-breaks, and it was in the last session, in which Australia had left themselves 38 overs to bowl, that the stand (with Tim Robinson who made 148) took on the appearance of a raping of innocents (they put on 331 for the second wicket).

Another epic second-wicket stand – this time 351 with Graham Gooch, who made 196 – set up the series-clinching innings win at The Oval. 'It was always one of my favourite grounds,' Gower told *The Cricketer*. 'It was an easy "win the toss and bat" job, and what a day, 376 for 3 – one of my best days ever. I played as well as I could do; I love the pitch there, it comes on the bat, has true pace and bounce, and Graham played a brilliant knock.'

'The final Cornhill Test at The Oval was only 50 overs old when the Australian team knew, in their honest moments, that the Ashes had gone for at least 18 months,' wrote CMJ.

England, having won the toss on a beautiful day and thus gained the valuable first use of a hard, true, relatively pacey pitch, had recovered formidably from the early loss of Robinson. 200 had just come up on the board below the gasholder, the sun was beating down out of a sky which would not have looked out of place over the Nullarbor Plain, a tightly packed crowd was full of London humour enhanced by the pleasure of beautiful strokeplay and of seeing the Aussies on the run, and Gooch and Gower were in their heaven.

Steve Waugh 2001 and 2002–3

It is difficult to think of someone with a greater aura of Ashes invincibility than Steve Waugh. Yes, and that includes Sir Donald Bradman. While Bradman famously averaged 99.94 in Tests, of course, that dropped to 'only' 89.74 against England, and 56.57 in the Bodyline series of 1932–3. Of his eight Ashes series, two were lost (1928–9 and 1932–3, with one drawn, 1938 – the second of his four as captain). Compare to Waugh. After his debut series in 1986–7, he was on the winning side in his other eight Ashes series, the latter two as captain. He averaged 58.18 against England, compared to 51.06 overall.

He had a poker-playing air of supremacy about him. There is an interesting story about a 'meeting' he had with his England counterpart Nasser Hussain ahead of the 2001 Ashes. Both writing for the *Sunday Telegraph* that summer, a photoshoot was set up. They did not speak to each other. Hussain probably did not know how to break the ice with the 'Iceman', and Waugh would have been absolutely determined to give nothing away. He knew England saw him as some kind of Yul Brynner gunslinger figure from *Westworld*: implacable, merciless, unrelenting. Steely determination. Mentally impregnable. Behind a cold façade.

Two Ashes innings encapsulate that image: the first – as it is widely recalled, 'on one leg' – at The Oval in 2001; the second at the Sydney Cricket Ground in 2002–3, when he was fighting for his Test career. Such was his mastery as he defied the odds to make centuries, you feel he could even have shown King Cnut how it was done.

During the third Test of 2001 at Trent Bridge he tore a muscle and had to be carried off on a stretcher; he felt humiliated and frustrated as Australia were about to retain the Ashes. Scans showed he had a five-centimetre tear in his lower left calf and another 'breaking point' higher up, of two centimetres. As he sat in a wheelchair he was told that he faced a 'three- to six-month layoff'. His first thought was 'Bullshit – that can't be right', although he could barely wiggle his toes. Most people would have taken the next plane home, but Waugh was indomitable and, with his wife's blessing, he vowed to be back for the fifth Test at The Oval, to lift the replica trophy. He embarked on a 19-day recovery programme that involved up to 10 hours a day of physio with Erroll Alcott, and exercises. The first 15 days consisted of hands-on treatment, and only by the 16th did he start running. The 'magic hands' [of Alcott] realigned the fibres and kneaded away the scar tissue four to five hours a day.

Somehow he made it on to the field, but he must have still been full of self-doubt. In some ways it was a selfish, risky decision. What if the injury recurred and he made few runs in the match? He began well enough, but 30 runs in he twinged a muscle, and then a buttock strain soon followed. He was creaking like a rusty gate. He told his brother and batting partner Mark to cut out the quick singles, but was grateful that Hussain had set in/out fields 'that made for long, easy singles'. Moving stiffly, he somehow made it to 99, then took off for a quick single, running as if wearing lead boots. He dived in, and the image of him lying on the dirt with his bat raised is one of the Ashes' most memorable. That Australia were 501 for 3 suggests they could have won the game without him, but how much more satisfying for the tourists it was that their commander was there to apply the finishing touches to a demoralised England.

In *The Cricketer*, Peter Perchard wrote:

Who writes Steve Waugh's scripts? Well, he does, of course. Against medical logic and all odds he took part in his farewell Test in England, won the toss on a batsman's dream strip, saw his brother to a 20th Test hundred then, after a cautious few overs in the 90s, completed his 27th Test hundred and his ninth against England. Barely able to walk, he brought up the century with a dramatic scrambled single, throwing himself over the crease in a cloud of dust. For a moment he lay still, face down, until up came the bat, raised like a periscope, followed by the gritted smile: Clint Eastwood had won another shoot-out.

Later in the same issue, Jason Gillespie wrote:

What a fantastic finish to our tour, the fifth Test at The Oval was a great cricket spectacle with some excellent, individual performances from both sides. Steve Waugh's unbeaten 157 was truly a gutsy performance. Having severely injured his calf in the Trent Bridge match, to come back into the side just 19 days later and play an innings like that was inspiring. He was hurting, everyone could see that. But he played through it and produced another amazing performance. The captain really showed what we Aussies are made of!

While physically not incapacitated in the next Ashes series, in 2002–3, the pressure Waugh was under this time was enormous. Going – again – into the final Test, at the Sydney Cricket

Ground, he was 37 and had been having a moderate series, with 197 runs in six innings – poor by his standards. Australia were winning the series emphatically, but the Australian selectors could be ruthless. They had such an unenviable conveyor belt of talent, they did not want to seem to be bed-blocking. The chairman of selectors, Trevor Hohns, publicly gave Waugh his backing only up until this Test. Waugh says he had not decided his future either way. The good news was that the qualities that had taken him to the brink of 10,000 Test runs appeared to be returning in the fourth Test in Melbourne: tremendous hand-eye co-ordination and fast hands. Hussain knew Waugh was at his most dangerous when confronted by a challenge, but had not helped his own cause by riling him in that fourth Test. Australia's captain had come in at 265 for 3 in the first innings and Hussain gave Justin Langer an easy single to get him on strike. Waugh called it 'under-10 stuff' and went on to make 77.

Waugh still needed a century at Sydney, however, and the stage was set: the second-biggest crowd in Sydney history, plus one in nine Australians watching on television. Waugh came in 56 for 3, a situation Hussain realised was 'dangerous'. Everything clicked for Waugh. 'I was loving batting,' he wrote, feeling the same joy he had when he was a seven-year-old. He passed 10,000, cover-driving emphatically and carving boundaries over the slips. Hussain admitted: 'Whatever I did, I couldn't seem to stop him.' The final over of the second evening arrived with Waugh five short of three figures. Hussain opted for rookie off-spinner Richard Dawson to bowl it. The first three balls were dead-batted, before Waugh square drove the fourth for three. Adam Gilchrist then pushed a single. Waugh felt that Hussain had deliberately given it to him, playing his part in the theatre, trying to add to Waugh's pressure, although

Gilchrist apparently thought it was the last ball. Predictably Hussain interrupted Waugh's concentration by going to talk to Dawson. Hussain admitted he had 'no cunning plan but [wanted] to stall things, get Waugh nervous and hope he made a mistake'. Waugh said in many ways Hussain's hands-on style was what England needed, but admitted: 'At times he went over the top with his badgering of bowlers, appearing to be more of a nuisance than a help.' Waugh wiped the sweat with his beloved red rag. Alec Stewart asked him, 'Do you write your own scripts these days?' Hussain takes up the story: 'Dawson bowled a perfectly good ball and those Waugh hands just flicked it away through the covers with complete disdain. It was pretty much the ideal ball. He only gave Steve about two inches of width outside off-stump.' His 29th Test century – equalling Bradman's total, in his 156th Test – was his. He admitted it was 'a Cinderella story'. Was it the loudest roar at a cricket ground ever? And, as *Wisden* argued, the 'greatest century in Ashes folklore'? Despite Australia losing the match, he had earned the right to decide when he should go, and played another 12 Tests.

'When Waugh reached his 29th Test hundred with the last ball of the second day to draw level with Sir Donald Bradman, a nation went into raptures,' wrote Stephen Brenkley in *The Cricketer*.

They say that the Melbourne Cup horse race brings Australia to a stop each November but as Waugh edged nearer the epic landmark, the enthralment could not have been less. More than 2.1 million people tuned in to the last hour of the innings on television, a huge audience in Australia. A full house at the SCG held its collective breath at one moment and exhaled with relief the next. Waugh brought more to the occasion than the consummate professionalism which has marked his batting life. Everybody knew that he was playing for his career. For weeks the country had talked about little else other than whether he should continue or quit. Waugh kept on insisting that it was in his hands, but only a big innings would ensure that. A charging rhino with the scent of blood may be easier to placate than an Australian Test selector smelling a lack of runs. With two overs to go on the second day, Waugh had reached 88. He decided to go for the landmark there and then. A four to third man and a gambler's two against the throw helped him to 98 with one ball left. It took an age before Richard Dawson bowled it. Waugh simply stroked it through the covers for four, as though it was destiny.

Ricky Ponting 2006–7

Ricky Ponting had taken the loss of the Ashes in 2005 very personally. Australia captains had become unaccustomed to losing to England since Mike Gatting's men swept all before them in 1986–7. It would have been a jolt to anyone's pride to be the Australian who was responsible for the sequence ending. Ponting could have quit the captaincy after that series in England. After all, his tactical acumen had been called into question. Only he can explain why he put England in at Edgbaston after Glenn McGrath had withdrawn through injury. He was determined to put things right, though, and that took courage. 'They are out on loan, the Ashes,' he said. 'It's less than eighteen months away, and then we'll have them back.' He did win them back, thanks to a 5-0 annihilation, and, in making big centuries in the first two Tests, he could not have made a more impressive, personal statement.

It had not helped that Michael Vaughan was injured, and Andrew Flintoff had to take over the England captaincy. He was chosen ahead of Andrew Strauss, even though coach Duncan Fletcher had doubts about Flintoff's 'tactical nous, man-management skills under pressure and his self-discipline'. Flintoff's task was also made harder by the absence through injury of Simon Jones, who took 18 wickets in the first four Ashes Tests of 2005 before damaging his ankle, and the decision by Marcus Trescothick to fly home for personal reasons.

England started badly at Brisbane. This was personified by Steve Harmison spearing the first delivery of the match to Flintoff at second slip. Lazy thinking suggests the writing was on the wall at this very moment. Surely that is hokum. One ball is one ball. Harmison could have laughed it off and struck with a wicket in that first over. A dropped catch would have been more significant. Harmison did not recover, though, and his first two overs cost 17. Australia racked up 602 for 9 declared, of which Ponting made 196. He was in the form of his life; that was his ninth century in 12 Tests, equalling Steve Waugh's national record of 32. He then added an unbeaten 60 second time around, passing 9,000 Test runs in the process. He juggled his bowling and fielding resources successfully enough as well to secure a 277-run win.

The pivotal match of the series followed in Adelaide, however, with England losing, despite posting 551 for 6 in the first innings. 'Still to this day I do not understand what happened,' wrote Fletcher. 'I do know, however, that the result of the [second] Test changed the lives and careers of quite a few people, especially me.' A rabbit caught in the headlights is such a cliché, but how else can you describe England's performance against Shane Warne on that final day?

Ponting hit 142 in Australia's reply, and was crucially dropped by Ashley Giles at deep square leg off Matthew Hoggard when 35. Warne, with 4 for 48, then hustled England out for 129 in

73 cathartic overs, and Ponting, with 49, helped his side over the line in rapid fashion. 'To turn a Test around like that, it doesn't happen,' he said. 'Our cricket over the last three days has been as good as you'll ever see from any team.' While Ponting did not make another century in the series, he led the Australians to a 5-0 win, their first Ashes whitewash since 1920–21. John Townsend, in *The Wisden Cricketer*, wrote:

As the prominent Aussie rules coach Mick Malthouse is fond of saying, the Chinese characters for crisis and opportunity are identical. Ponting took the loss of the 2005 series personally and, instructed by a blunt directive from his board to take charge of the team, he set about a ruthless campaign to recover reputation, honour and the Ashes. The ferocity of this desire may not be recognised in England. There is a compulsion in Australia, a relic of colonial intransigence perhaps, to hold the Ashes. We are obsessed by cricket – and also by winning. The prominence of sportsmen is solely predicated on team success. Losing is for wimps – just look at Prime Minister John Howard, who shuffles further than any premier to avoid being pictured with a team that came second or worse. Personnel were swiftly changed. Sentimental ties to Jason Gillespie were cut. Stuart Clark, called up as cover in 2005, completed the fourth-best debut year in Test history. Mike Hussey was installed and ran up a century average. But above all Ponting destroyed attacks with a clinical savagery rarely seen since Viv Richards' prime.

Gideon Haigh, later in the issue, went further:

The sentiment is best summed up by the broadcaster Alan McGilvray. 'Nobody will ever touch Bradman. He was a man apart.' The temptation is to nod in agreement but it is actually a big call. To say a man's records will never be surpassed is one thing; that they will never be touched is only slightly less emphatic a generalisation than that they will never be approached. And, as it happens, Bradman's records are being approached right now: Ricky Ponting's runs go on increasing like inflation in Weimar Germany. If there was a turning point, Ponting thinks it was at Cape Town in March 2002, where he scored his first second-innings hundred, piloting Australia to a four-wicket victory which he clinched with a six. Since then he has averaged a tick over 72, buttressed by no fewer than 23 hundreds. It is not Bradman but it is, as the Australian cricket media is inclined to remind readers, 'Bradmanesque'. The 'esque' is an important qualifier, for the comparison of Ponting with Bradman is that of 21st-century Tasmanian apples with 20th-century Bowral oranges. Ponting has already played more than twice as many Tests as Bradman in barely half the span of years. About 20 years ago Bob Simpson roughed a précis of 'the Australian Way' of batsmanship: 'Batsmen were basically back-foot players, most of them hooked, and were strong cutters and on-side players.' The identikit is not a total match, partly because Bradman and Ponting are great players and thus more complete. But there is no doubting the enterprise and confidence that pervaded Bradman's batting and now animates Ponting's. Born of hard pitches with true bounce, not giving much encouragement to the seam bowler, and fast outfields. Repaying the boldness and also hitting the ball along the ground. In the time-honoured fashion Bradman and Ponting also worked towards the No.3 slot that is customarily occupied by the most complete batsman in the team.

The series of 2006–7 is probably Ponting's finest Ashes hour. His own personal performances, the whitewash, the vanquishing of his old enemy Fletcher – how much more satisfying could it have been? The fact is that he still ended up becoming the only Australia captain to lose three Ashes series, magnificent batsman that he was.

Comeback kings

Geoffrey Boycott 1977

Romance and Geoffrey Boycott do not always go together. He is a cricketer more associated with cussedness, determination, dour defence and – alas, in the eyes of his critics – self-centredness. August 11 1977 really was the most romantic of days for him, however, as he made his 100th first-class hundred on his home ground in Leeds.

Boycott had been in self-imposed exile, missing more than three years and 30 Tests. A cocktail of reasons have been cited, but one was his annoyance that Mike Denness, and not him, had succeeded Ray Illingworth as captain. He had been heavily criticised for rejecting national duty, especially when England were being tenderised in Australia in 1974–5. He might not even have been recalled, in fact, if Dennis Amiss had not failed twice for Warwickshire in the match against the tourists before the Trent Bridge Test. So Boycott returned for Nottingham, and it did not start well, running out local hero Derek Randall. He made amends by scoring his 98th first-class hundred (107). England only needed 189 to win that match; in theory he could have reached his 99th, but his 80 not out instead contributed to a seven-wicket win, putting England 2-0 up in the five-match series with two to play. The 99th then duly arrived for Yorkshire against Warwickshire at Edgbaston in the Championship.

With No.100 looming, the media were most excited, of course, and the pressure got to someone even as stubbornly determined as Boycott. 'I avoided all their attentions as best I could,' he said, 'but the pressure mounted steadily.' He felt forced to take sleeping pills the night before. He woke late, and felt 'tired and listless', so he hoped England would field; instead Mike Brearley won the toss, and batted. Boycott lost his captain to the third ball of the match, but saw Bob Woolmer, Randall and Tony Greig offer solid support at the other end. He was dropped by Rod Marsh, low to his right, on 22, and by lunch had reached 36. Then, at tea, he had moved on to 79. Just after the break Marsh thought he had caught him, but Bill Alley rejected the vociferous appeal. 'He got a big nick on one just before I went in,' said Graham Roope. 'Ray Bright was bowling and the whole ground heard it.' Boycott said it had hit his wristband: 'They thought they had me, but then the Aussies thought they had me many times over the years and they didn't. I didn't worry about it. I just knuckled down and got on with it.' He was becalmed for a 45-minute spell, scoring only five, but just before 6pm his moment came, as he punched his 14th four from his 232nd ball straight to the Football Stand, off Greg Chappell. He had become the 18th cricketer to reach 100 hundreds. 'I saw it then with something approaching elation,' said Boycott. 'As soon as it left his hand I knew I was going to hit it and I knew where I was going to hit it. Long before it pitched I knew what I was going to do, as though I was standing outside myself. It was all just noise. It was the most magical moment of my life.' An invasion of boys held play up for about eight minutes, and Boycott refused to continue until his cap was returned, much to the bemusement of the distinctly unim-pressed Australians. Yorkshire secretary Joe Lister had to make a public announcement and it was eventually returned to a policeman.

In *The Cricketer*, John Woodcock wrote:

Boycott's return to Test cricket, after three years in his northern fastness, was pure theatre. How the Australians must be wishing that they had not got Amiss out so cheaply in his two innings for Warwickshire against them just before the England team was chosen! Had they not done so Amiss and not Boycott would probably have played at Trent Bridge, and on his record against them the Australian bowlers would have had less trouble from Amiss. For Boycott the match [at Headingley] was a personal triumph of the sort very few sportsmen ever enjoy. His 191, made before his own kith and kin, was his 100th first-class hundred. The cheers that greeted it on the first evening, after more than five hours of single-minded accumulation, must have echoed across the Pennines. Boycott's return to the side gave the batting at Headingley, as it had at Trent Bridge, the stability which it has too often lacked in recent years. The fact that he was slow to make his runs, and was only passively in command, never mattered. Already two matches up in the series, England could afford to take their time. When eventually Boycott was last out for 191, after tea on the second day, he had made England more or less safe from defeat. He could hardly have come nearer than he did to becoming the first Englishman ever to carry his bat against Australia in England.

Jack Fingleton opined in *The Cricketer*:

Geoff Boycott had informed Alec Bedser that he was available again for England and the second Test but, undoubtedly resenting the fact that Boycott was not available for England when they wanted him, the selectors passed him by. The writing was on the dressing-room door, however, that Boycott would return from his self-imposed exile and those who knew the man and his methods knew that when he did he would monopolise the Test batting stage. The Australian attack seemed moderate at Old Trafford and Boycott returned to plague it. He had decided somebody would pay for his long absence from Test cricket and they would be the Australians, and, if need be, the spectators into the bargain. I don't think I have seen anybody more certain of hitting a four than Boycott when he sets his mind to it. He is a great plunderer of the loose ball and he brings the bowler to that pitch by his rocklike defence, mainly forward. With his bat alongside pad, Boycott has the best defence in modern cricket. He props forward in the belief that umpires won't give him out lbw with his front foot down the pitch and such tactics are the despair of the bowler.

Terry Alderman 1989 and Mitchell Johnson 2013–14

Being mastered by English batsmen is one thing for Australian bowlers to stomach, but being stymied by their fans is something else. In differing ways, Terry Alderman and Mitchell Johnson came to curse backpacking tourists. The former because he rather foolishly tackled a marauding fan at Perth during the 1982–3 series, the latter because he was given a verbal battering by the Barmy Army in 2010–11; they both took their revenge on the English, in 1989 and 2013–14 respectively, however.

In 1982 Alderman was hot and bothered at the Waca after spending five sessions in the field. The last thing the Australians wanted to see was a pitch invasion by a dozen young Brits.

Alderman gave one of them a shove, but decided to do something a bit more dramatic to a repeat offender, a 19-year-old unemployed English migrant named Gary Donnison, who had just thumped him on the head. Alderman ran 20 yards, floored him with a rugby tackle, but landed badly on his right shoulder. He had dislocated it, and did not bowl in a competitive match again for a year. 'I have heard that he got his act together and is a reborn Christian with a wife and three kids,' Alderman said, 'so some good came out of it, I suppose.' He then missed the 1985 and 1986–7 Ashes after receiving a three-year ban for going on the rebel tours to South Africa in 1985–6 and the year after. Unfortunately for England – and Graham Gooch – he was back four years later, though.

It was not the first time that Alderman had shone in England, of course. Ian Botham may have stolen all the headlines in 1981, but Alderman was a constant thorn in England's side during that series, taking 42 wickets in the six Tests at 21.26 apiece. Although he had a reasonable time in the 1990–91 Ashes, taking 16 wickets at 26.75 each, it was playing in England that he loved: 83 at 19.33 in Tests on Albion soil, 87 at 34.62 elsewhere. He also took 75 first-class wickets at 22.81 for Gloucestershire, and 174 at 20.72 for Kent. If only he had been English!

He was not a menacing bowler, in the sense that he did not have an inventory of insults up his sleeve, or a predilection for hurting batsmen, as one or two of his compatriots had. He kept things pretty simple. Usually with a smile on his face, he would approach silently with a bit of a mincing run, then – with all shoulder – send down a steady diet of awayswingers interspersed with off-cutters. To somebody like Graham Gooch, who was brave and brilliant against the quicks, it was lethal. So used to planting his front leg on the line of middle stump and drilling through mid-on and midwicket, he was trapped in a nightmare from which he could not wake up. 'Alderman was a good bowler,' he admitted. 'Smooth, accurate and thoughtful. Everyone knew by now I was one of the famous "right-arm" batsmen who liked to hit the straight ball through mid-on or wider.'

Alderman started how he meant to go on. David Gower famously put the Australians in at Headingley, of course, and they racked up 601 for 7. When England replied, it was Gooch lbw b Alderman 13. Although he was lbw to somebody different in the second innings (Merv Hughes), a pattern was emerging.

In *The Cricketer*, Christopher Martin-Jenkins wrote:

Terry Alderman, with 10 for 151 in the match, was the eventual matchwinner in a performance which underlined the intense commitment and unity, as well as the batting ability of the Australian team. Alderman is a bowling craftsman and a character admired and respected by all: he was a most appropriate 'man of the match'. Alderman, nipping the ball either way off the seam and delivering from wicket to wicket, had Gooch lbw playing across his front pad. He continued to trouble everyone by means of his consistently probing line and length.

Then, in the second innings:

Having taken the new ball soon after the start, Alderman took three of the last six wickets, the remaining two by winning two more of a total of four lbw appeals, all of them close. The reasons for so much leather on pad were partly the low bounce of the pitch, partly Alderman's ability to draw the batsman forward and partly his skill in swinging it late from leg to off, having delivered the ball close to the stumps. He exposed a clear weakness in most of England's batsmen who tend to plant the front foot down a moment before the bat and to play across their front pad. It is just the sort of thing which, if they are to earn their corn, Ted Dexter and Micky Stewart must work to improve.

Gooch was out lbw Alderman in the second innings at Lord's, with the bowler recording match figures of 9 for 188, and CMJ wrote:

Alderman learned his craft in Australia and polished it in England. He keeps the game essentially simple. He knows that the best right-handed cricketers look at each other from 22 yards over their left shoulders. In Alderman's case, the virtue of being 'sideways on' in the stride before he delivers is enhanced by the fact that he bowls from so close to the stumps, delivering the ball from wicket to wicket. This, plus his ability to move the ball late off the seam either way, is why 10 of his 19 wickets in the first two Tests were gained leg before wicket. He reserved the best ball of all, however, for Robin Smith and it cut away late to hit the off-stump at a time when Smith, playing brilliantly, was a shot away from a maiden Test hundred.

Match hauls of 3 for 61, 5 for 115, 7 for 101 and 7 for 96 followed for Alderman at Edgbaston, Old Trafford, Trent Bridge and The Oval respectively. Gooch had asked to be withdrawn from the line of fire in Nottingham to work on his technique, but was restored for the final. The result: lbw b Alderman 0, and c&b Alderman 10. Goodness knows what Gary Donnison made of it all.

Johnson had not just one or even a dozen Poms to curse, but a singing army of them. He arrived in England in 2009 with great expectations on his shoulders, and took 20 wickets in the five Tests, but they were a little on the expensive side, at 32.55 apiece. The home series in 2010–11 was worse, however, with 15 at 36.93. He had endured a shocking opening Test in that series, taking 0 for 170 in Brisbane. 'He bowls to the left, he bowls to the right, that Mitchell Johnson, his bowling is shite,' sang the Barmy Army. Johnson fought back that series to take 9 for 82 in the Perth Test, but it was a disappointing time for him overall, and Australia lost. Injury then kept him out of the 2013 series, but he did play in the one-dayers afterwards and was quick, seriously quick. It was a taster of the shock and awe to come. He knew the 2013–14 Ashes was his chance to silence his critics, and help Australia avenge the 3-0 defeat in the English summer just gone. 'I was judged by my failure in England in 2009 and my struggles in the year after that,' he wrote. 'But redemption is possible and now was my moment to prove it.'

Johnson was incredible in that series. Like a cross between a medieval catapult and a raging bull; at his best, a left-arm hybrid of Dennis Lillee and Jeff Thomson. Brisbane: 9 for 103. Adelaide: 8 for 113. Perth: 6 for 140. Melbourne: 8 for 88. Sydney: 6 for 73. Incredible stuff. 'This new Mitchell Johnson was nasty and very aggressive. He had found himself, he had found an inner peace, and he knew that he had control,' wrote Kevin Pietersen. 'He knew the power of his aggression. He knew we feared him being nasty. He was bowling hostile, bowling fast and aggressively, and he was bowling in really good areas. In previous Ashes he wasn't doing that: he was always giving you a release ball where you could score.' Australia whitewashed England, and it was mission accomplished for Johnson. 'The Barmy Army had been getting a bit chatty before I started to take wickets,' he wrote, 'so when

I did I celebrated one by advising them to shoosh up a bit. I made sure they knew when I took a five-wicket haul by giving them a special wave.'

In *The Cricketer*, Andrew Miller wrote:

It's turning out to be the ultimate tale of redemption. As Mitchell Johnson admitted in these pages last month, there were times in his last Ashes campaign, three years and a lifetime ago, when he longed for an injury to spare him from his plight. Somehow, with (quite literally) a favourable wind blowing in off the Swan River, he had bowled Australia to victory in a sizzling Perth Test only to revert to type at Melbourne and Sydney. He's still not sure how he got it so right on that day at the Waca but crucially he's given up caring about the nuances of his art and reverted to what he's always done best – bowling as fast as the wind and putting the fear of God into opponents. Johnson's recent displays were a throwback to his breakthrough series in 2008/09, when he smashed Graeme Smith's finger with a 95mph lifter and threw a maiden Test century into the mix as well. Woe betide any team allowing Johnson to score runs against them. His first-innings 64 at the Gabba not only hauled his side out of a considerable hole; it provided early evidence of the confidence coursing through his veins. One show-stopping day later Johnson's shocking speed and aggression had changed the series beyond measure.

Andrew Flintoff 2009

Andrew Flintoff had been famously legless a few times, but his bowling display in the second Test at Lord's had nothing to do with booze, and everything to do with sheer bloody-mindedness and courage. It was clear that captain Andrew Strauss and his teammates had tired somewhat of the circus that surrounded him. He had a busy management team in Chubby Chandler's ISM, keen that he maximised his commercial worth. That centred around his 'laddio' image. Stories like the drinking exploits after the 2005 Ashes series ended were pivotal to that. Most recently there had been a rumpus in the preceding spring when he had overslept and missed a trip to the First World War trenches in Ypres, Belgium. There was also the nagging question, after so many injuries, about when he was going to retire, the latest being a sore knee that he had said had swollen to the 'size of a beach-ball'; there was a tear in the ligament, and he faced a six-month lay-off after surgery. So it was probably a relief when the announcement came ahead of the Test that he would quit at the end of the summer. To a man no one could have failed to admire his courage that morning, though. You could almost sense the surgeons in the background, itching to see him clamber onto the operating table so that they could pore over his knee with their needles and scalpels. They had to wait, however. For now, he had three jabs, two in the back of the knee and one in front, and cortisone injections around the joint.

The first three innings of the match had gone to plan for England. Strauss had made 161, forming the basis of his side's 425; then James Anderson had taken four wickets as Australia struggled to 215. Opting not to enforce the follow-on, the hosts' top seven all chipped in with scores ranging from 27 to 61, Flintoff himself enjoying a flighty, unbeaten 30. The tourists, despite needing a seemingly impossible 522 to win, were not out of it at stumps on day four, however. Flintoff had removed openers Phil Hughes and Simon Katich, both with well-executed plans conceived with bowling coach Ottis

Gibson, but Michael Clarke was on 125 not out, and had put on 185 with Brad Haddin, who was unbeaten on 80. And so we came to the final act of the match. Flintoff felt like he had 'broken his leg', but took some more anti-inflammatory injections and painkillers. He bowled 10 overs unchanged from the Pavilion End, hobbling back to his mark each time, valiantly charging in with 25,000 spectators urging him on, to take three more wickets. In his book, *Ashes to Ashes*, he wrote: 'I told Straussy that I'd be bowling until Australia were all out. He asked me if he had much choice and I told him he hadn't and started running in from the Pavilion End.' His first of the day arrived with his fourth ball, Haddin's edge flying to Paul Collingwood at second slip. Flintoff assumed one of his famous poses, likened to Nelson's in Trafalgar Square. He could have had Mitchell Johnson lbw with a full toss, but overstepped. Graeme Swann took the key wicket, Clarke being deceived by a slow, loopy ball. Nathan Hauritz was then bowled, shouldering arms to Flintoff, before he bowled Peter Siddle. It was only his third five-wicket haul in Tests, a strange statistic, especially considering his imperiousness in the 2005 Ashes. In that series, like many others, Flintoff was just too good at times for batsmen to lay a bat on him. While his line was nearly always immaculate, he also occasionally struggled to move the ball away from the right-hander. The only thing missing was the last wicket, Swann pegging back Mitchell Johnson's middle stump instead. It ended England's 75-year wait for a victory at Lord's over Australia, and was undoubtedly a fitting way to go.

'This is not the first time Andrew Flintoff has appeared on our cover and, despite his impending retirement from Test matches, it will probably not be the last,' said then *Wisden Cricketer* editor John Stern.

Flintoff does not have the stats to match Ian Botham but he does have the sense of occasion and indomitable will – particularly when the Aussies are in town. Writing in the *Guardian*, Duncan Fletcher's sour assessment of Flintoff's last-morning performance at Lord's was that he had 'chipped in with that long overdue five-wicket haul'. Cold-hearted analysis supports Fletcher's grudging view but since when were sports fans governed by logic? The contrary view is that of Simon Barnes, that Flintoff's capability to perform great deeds makes him a great player. I am not sure about that one either but I am more in that camp than Fletcher's. That Monday morning at Lord's was theatrical, visceral and devastating. The shrieks of relief and delight that greeted Brad Haddin's departure would have been replicated any-where people were permitted (or able) to follow the action at the start of a working week. Despite his obvious flaws, or maybe because of them, Flintoff inspires devotion. It is his humanity as much as his heroism that gets us going and makes grown men weak at the knees. Gideon Haigh com-mented after Lord's on the deference of the English press towards Flintoff. The winners in the deference stakes have surely been the Australian team. They have traditionally had a low opinion of most England players yet they speak of Flintoff with a reverence normally reserved for one of their own. Perhaps they are conditioned to be so shocked when any opponent lays them low that they believe there must be a higher power at work. We have always had reservations and frustrations about Flintoff but cool judgement can wait for another day. I cannot know how this series will turn out but for now, thanks Fred.

Owning the Ashes

Alec Bedser 1953

It is a source of regret that although I interviewed Alec Bedser about his Ashes away series, he died before I could quiz him about the home ones. I would have enquired as to whether he minded that, for all his brilliance in the first four Tests of the 1953 rubber, the Australians managed to slip off his hook in those matches, while it had been left to others to finish the tourists off in the finale at The Oval. We must look at it as though Bedser was a boxer, bloodying and beating his opponent through the early rounds, so much so that the last blow was not actually as monumental as it appeared.

Many have questioned the excellence of Bedser, and there were murmurings he was fading by 1953; and old footage confirms he was far from express-quick. He was well-built and athletic, however, and had a classic action, and he could bowl long spells. His stock ball was the inswinger, but he threw in fizzing leg-cutters to mix things up. And he was resourceful. He never gave up. When he was confronted by frustratingly flat Australian pitches, with balls that had tiny seams and became scuffed after only a handful of overs, he out-thought opponents by switching to cutters. 'Up he came, over after over, his head rocking as he swung his arm with all the power of the strongest pair of shoulders ever given to a cricketer,' wrote EW Swanton in the *Daily Telegraph*.

It was a good year to be English. It was coronation year, Everest was conquered by a British expedition, and at last the Ashes were recovered 19 years after England had relinquished them on home soil. Bedser was in his prime. The first Test was at Trent Bridge, where his wickets gave England a chance before they were denied by the weather. His match figures of 14 for 99 – a Trent Bridge

Test record – were the best by an Englishman since Hedley Verity's 15 for 104 against Australia at Lord's. Former England seam bowler Bill Bowes described the action in *The Cricketer*.

Bedser began well. He uprooted the middle stump of Graeme Hole with only two runs scored, but after that Arthur Morris and Lindsay Hassett dug in hard. They were still together when rain caused the players to leave the field a quarter of an hour before lunch. Morris and Hassett began steadily and increased in confidence. A few drops of rain began to fall and Len Hutton led his men to the pavilion. The two batsmen had their 'eye in', another ball was due, and a rest for his bowlers was desirable. It was a tactical opportunity not to be missed. There were 25 minutes plus a tea interval of rest for the bowlers and the value of the break was noticed when Bedser had Morris lbw. Four runs later Harvey was snapped for a duck by Compton in Bedser's leg trap. During the night there had been quite a lot of gentle rain and drizzle and at odd times during the morning there was moisture like a barber's spray in the air. The clouds were low and threatening and the atmosphere suggested it would be a good day for the swing bowlers. Beginning the afternoon session with a new ball, Bedser and Trevor Bailey began something which, since the famous Verity match at Lord's, had never been seen. At least, it was Godfrey Evans who started it, for he made one of the most spectacular catches in years down the leg side to dismiss Richie Benaud. He threw himself full length to catch the ball. Bedser swung into action, and using the heavy atmosphere to perfection, flattened the off stump of Hassett, who had now made 115 very valuable runs. Bedser then bowled Don Tallon. The Evans-Bailey partnership accounted for Ray Lindwall, and Bedser finished off with the wickets of Alan Davidson and Jack Hill. Six wickets fell for the addition of only six runs. Spectators cheered themselves hoarse and Australia were out for 249. Bedser had the magnificent analysis of 7 for 55 and interestingly enough, his spells with the three new balls of the innings had been 1 for 7, 2 for 5, and 4 for 2, respectively.

Then, describing the second innings, Bowes wrote:

Bedser bowled Hole with a very similar delivery to that of the first innings, a good-length ball moving in after pitching … In the next Bedser over Hassett got a really nasty one. The ball stood up from a good length, hit the bat handle and glove, and lobbed for an easy catch to Hutton in the leg trap. This was a real slice of luck for Bedser and England, but there was everything of a deep-laid plot in the next success. Another man was put into the leg trap, where Neil Harvey obligingly edged to Compton on the first day, and once again the batsman fell.

Hutton gathered all his fieldsmen around Keith Miller, who showed his disapproval by vigorously lashing at the ball. He succeeded in making the fieldsmen vacate the more dangerous holdings but to the astonishment of everyone, I think including Bedser, hit the worst ball bowled straight to mid-on. It was a full toss and it emphasised the truism, the better the bowler the better his bad ball. Benaud was bowled Bedser behind his legs, and at this stage Bedser had the magnificent return of all five wickets, taken in 11.1 overs at a cost of only 22 runs. His analysis of 14 wickets for 99 in the match, 7 for 44 in the second innings, was tribute to his magnificent bowling. Bailey said: 'It was the best fast-medium bowling I have ever seen for an entire match.'

The second Test at Lord's ebbed and flowed thrillingly, culminating in a gripping final day that saw England cling on for dear life thanks to Willie Watson and Bailey. The on-song Bedser this time took 5 for 105, becoming the first Englishman to 200 Test wickets. 'He was a tremendous bowler; he could bowl all day,' said Tom Graveney. England gave the tourists a big scare in the rain-decimated third Test at Old Trafford. Only 13 hours and 50 minutes were possible in Manchester, but there was still time for Australia to feel panic. Harvey scored 122 as the tourists made 318, Bedser taking 5 for 115. England replied with 276. Johnny Wardle gave Australia an anxious time on the fifth day, taking 4 for 7 as the tourists stumbled to 35 for 8, only 77 ahead. It was the ninth successive Ashes Test to be drawn or abandoned. Bailey proved to be England's saviour again in the fourth Test at Old Headingley, although this time some of his tactics proved more morally contentious. There was no problem with The Barnacle's stonewalling with the bat, but his leg-theory bowling ultimately cost Australia enough time to knock off the winning runs. At Old Trafford Bedser set a World Test record in the Australians' reply when he passed Clarence Grimmett's 216 wickets. Bailey once again stonewalled the Australians for 38 in 262 minutes. It was grim stuff, but how his country thanked him for it. Bailey then resorted to bowling leg-theory to help deny the Australians, who fell 30 runs short of victory. So the series rested on The Oval. A sixth day was allocated to try to ensure there was at last a result, although a draw would have been enough for the Australians, and an English record of 26,300 spectators flocked to witness the occasion. In the first innings of the match Bedser struck the first blow, dismissing Morris for the 18th time in 20 Tests. He then overtook Maurice Tate's Ashes series record of 38 wickets (1924–5) on his way to 39 in the rubber with the dismissals of Hassett and Ron Archer. For once he was outshone, though, by debutant Fred Trueman (4 for 86 in the first innings) and the spinners Tony Lock (5 for 45) and Jim Laker (4 for 75) in the second. Ever the patriot, Bedser would not have minded.

Chris Broad 1986–7

Chris Broad's Test career was like a sandwich containing exquisite meat, with stale, unworthy bread either side. Mike Gatting's squad shone in the 1986–7 Ashes series; nearly everyone playing their part, if not in the Tests then in the numerous one-dayers. Broad was the individual success story, however, and for one winter he was the best batsman in the world.

That he did not have a lengthy Test career, being confined to 25 Test caps, is an indictment on the failings of the English system and the impetuous nature of selection at that time.

If Broad grilled the Australians like a steak with his three centuries in the second, third and fourth Tests, Ian Botham was like the mallet that tenderised, with a brutal century in the series opener in Brisbane.

Famously the tour started dismally, with England losing to Queensland and Western Australia. 'There are only three things wrong with this England team – they can't bat, can't bowl and can't field,' wrote the *Independent*'s Martin Johnson. Broad had made a few scores early on the trip, and his last three campaigns for Nottinghamshire had been pretty decent. His first five Tests brought only moderate returns, albeit facing the rampant West Indians, however, and no one predicted he would go down in Ashes folklore like this.

'I had played for England in 1984, but not since, so I was excited – it is every English cricketer's dream to go to Australia and play in the Ashes,' he said. 'It was my first tour, but it became the high point of my career. The selectors would chop and change so much in those days – one bad Test at home and you could be dropped. So I liked being on tour. You knew you would be involved in up to five Tests, and then have time to rest and prepare, rather than having to shoot off to play a Benson & Hedges Cup game with your county the next day. I don't know how confident we were – we had confidence as individuals, but we didn't know how we would perform as a unit. There was not the professionalism that there is now. There was little planning and no analysis. There was no single plan as to how we were going to win the series, it was just a reliance on individuals to play as well as they could. [Team manager] Micky Stewart's role was to organise practice and pre-match preparation – he was also a shoulder to lean on for Gatting, but he was no strategist.'

After Botham's 138 had set up England's win at the Gabba, Broad then announced himself with 162 at Perth. Christopher Martin-Jenkins wrote in *The Cricketer*:

The combination of a superb pitch for batting and some wayward Australian bowling, especially but not exclusively in the crucial early stages, enabled Chris Broad and Bill Athey to put on 223 for the first wicket, the fourth largest opening stand by England against Australia. Broad's simple, straight-bat technique – no hooking and seldom even a square cut – and genuine hunger for runs makes it likely that though he will never make an easier Test hundred, he will surely add to the one reached with a sweetly timed stroke off Greg Matthews, his 17th four.

Broad then made 116 in the draw at Adelaide. 'We responded well to their big score, and I was delighted to score another century,' said Broad. 'I suppose Australia got themselves into the best position of the series so far, but it was always going to be a draw.' Of his three centuries, though, the one at Melbourne was probably the most pivotal, playing a key part in an English win. Australia actually lost the Test with their abject first-innings display, collapsing to 141 all out with Botham and Gladstone Small taking five wickets each. Steve Waugh called it an 'abysmal showing', and said: 'The worst part of our display was that Botham took five wickets on his reputation alone ... long hops were nicked to the keeper or chopped on to the stumps; it was the presence and aura of a great cricketer that had us spellbound.' Broad said: 'Australia threw it away, but we caught well all tour – Jack Richards, Botham, and led by the unsung hero Athey, at short-leg or short midwicket.' England were 95 for 1 at the end of the first day, with Broad on 56. 'I was standing in the old dressing rooms, and I told myself, "Right, Broady, we need to score a few more here." Other times I had just gone out and batted, but I knew we had to build a bigger lead. Unlike the other two centuries, I was nervous in the 90s. I'm sure the MCG had something to do with it. It was a fantastic atmosphere there, like a bullring.' Broad reached 112, his third hundred in successive Tests, in England's 349. Australia fared little better second time round, making only 194, to lose by an innings.

CMJ wrote:

England's first innings, which eventually gained them a lead of 208, owed an immense amount to Broad's third Test hundred in successive Ashes Tests. Herbert Sutcliffe made three hundreds in two matches at Sydney and Melbourne but only Jack

Hobbs, Walter Hammond and Bob Woolmer had previously scored three in three consecutive Ashes Tests for England. In Broad, England have a batsman who, rather like John Edrich, has absolutely no interest so recent as the last ball bowled. His concentration is applied to the ball which lies ahead and by keeping the bat rigidly straight and skilfully leaving anything lifting nastily around his off-stump, he slowly built another firm foundation for England.

Broad was named International Player of the Season after making 487 runs in the Tests at 69.57, and another 559 in 14 one-day internationals. 'John Edrich had said to me at The Oval at the end of the previous summer, "Enjoy yourself – the crowds will be hostile but they will appreciate good cricket,"' said Broad. 'I was hit on the neck by an apple in a one-day match at Perth. I turned around and all I could see was a huge sea of smiling faces. On the other hand, going out to the wicket, or acknowledging a big score, the crowds were very generous.' Broad's love affair with Australia was not over yet. England played a one-off Test at Sydney in early 1988 to celebrate the bicentenary of Australia as a nation. Broad scored another century, although his display was marred by controversy. After being bowled by Waugh for 138 he flattened his leg stump with a swing of his bat. It was a moment that has stuck to him – although it did not stop him becoming an international match referee. He was fined £500 by Peter Lush and issued with a stern warning. He made another century, his sixth, in his next Test in Christchurch, but that was to be his last. 'I'd like to think I would have had a longer international career these days,' said Broad. 'Those kind of selectorial issues were partly why a lot of players went on rebel tours to South Africa [Broad went in 1989–90]. That Ashes win should have a springboard for sustained success. On paper it was an incredibly strong side, but we should have had a lot more success in the Eighties with all those talents. Gatting did a fine job on that tour – he was a real players' leader – so why did England only win two Tests out of 23 under his leadership? You can't blame everything on facing a fantastic West Indies. It was appalling, a real mystery.'

Mark Taylor 1989

The closest England had come to facing Mark Taylor before was in the final Test of the 1986–7 tour, when there was speculation that the wrong player of that surname had been selected. As it happened, debutant Peter Taylor had rather a good match at the Sydney Cricket Ground, taking eight wickets with his off-breaks and scoring 53 runs. So Mark had to wait two and a half years for his chance to face them. In his first two Test appearances against West Indies, however, he had not given any great indication that England would be cursing the sight of him by the end of the summer of 1989.

'Taylor has been described more than once as the perfect team man, and so it proved in his two Tests against the West Indies,' wrote Bob Guntrip in *The Cricketer*.

It was hardly a fairy-tale Test debut. He compiled just 67 runs at 16.75 with a top score of 36 while pushing for quick runs in Australia's second innings at Adelaide. It was, perhaps, the right innings at the right time. It's that capacity to play the right knock that's the Taylor hallmark, and those fortunate enough to have witnessed his elegantly crafted 136 in the first Test at Headingley will agree that there is more to Mark Taylor than the succession of edges and dabs that characterised his batting in Adelaide. By the time he boarded Qantas flight QF1 for London Heathrow, the grinning Taylor had had his back well and truly slapped, not least by Ian Davis, who, as opener for Australia and New South Wales in the 1970s, understood only too well the task that lay before his youthful successor. 'I regard Mark very highly,' says Davis. 'He has the ability to pick up the line and length of the ball very quickly and hits very solidly down the ground and through the off-side. He's a very solid cricketer who plays within his limitations; his temperament is right to open as well, because he's not intimidated by the short stuff and can maintain his concentration to pick the right ball to hit – and he plays the cut and square drive very well indeed.' Davis believes Taylor's cool temperament outweighs any deficiencies in his strokeplay. 'I guess it's a bit surprising he's not as strong off his pads as most, maybe because he's a bit slow on his feet. But he gets his on-side ones and twos regularly. He's the right man for the job. No doubt about it.'

His scoring sequence in the 1989 Ashes was remarkable after that 136: 60 in the second innings; 62 and 27 at Lord's; 43 and 51 at Edgbaston; 85 and 37 not out at Old Trafford, and then ... Trent Bridge. The first day of the fifth Test was enough to break the heart of any English fan, myself included, as the tourists reached 301 for 0. 'The openers, Taylor and Geoff Marsh, by putting on 329 for the first wicket, left behind all previous opening stands in an Ashes Test match,' wrote CMJ:

It took England just over seven hours to part them ... this was a superb exhibition of controlled batting, perfectly attuned to the tempo of a five-day Test. The openers were never, in fact, negative; certainly not Taylor, who, no doubt to his surprise as well as his immense delight, has taken to Test cricket like a dog to meat. His technique is straight from the text book, head always over the line, footwork positive and precise, and his judgement of the ball to hit seems to be impeccable. It truly seems as though Australia has uncovered a second Arthur Morris. Indeed his aggregate in this series has surpassed the best that Morris ever mustered in five Tests against England and only Everest, in the person of Sir Donald Bradman, stands ahead of him in the way of aggregate records for Australia. His 219 was his first double-hundred in any class of cricket and I daresay part of him was mildly disappointed that England's batsmen could not manage to force him to have a second innings.

He added 71 and 48 in the final Test at The Oval, to give him an aggregate of 839 runs at 83.90. This time there was no doubt Australia had picked the right Taylor.

Michael Slater 1994–5

It was the equivalent of Sugar Ray Robinson skipping out of his corner and imposing himself on his opponent, raining down blows, catching them on the hop. England had travelled to Australia with a degree of expectation. Raymond Illingworth, that old sage who knew how to beat the Australians, had finally been installed as chairman of selectors. Mike Atherton had not been captain for long; he was not yet ground down by the shackles of the English county system. It did not take long for illness and injury to start picking off Atherton's men one by one, however. Just 48 hours before the first Test in Brisbane, Devon Malcolm contracted chicken-pox. His most recent Test had been at The Oval, when he had decimated the South Africans, taking 9 for 57. He had always been inconsistent, so England fans would not have put their mortgages on him giving their side a decent start at the Gabba, but it was still a bitter blow. At least they had a readymade replacement … or so they thought. Step forward Martin McCague. Born in Northern Ireland, raised in Australia, plucked by England for the raw pace he had shown for Kent. It later transpired that he had taken 'the David Boon Challenge' on the flight out, and was apparently ahead on Duckworth/Lewis when the management made him smell the coffee. Drinking too many beers 10,000 feet up? Never did Boon, Rod Marsh or Doug Walters too much harm, eh? He had also made a promising Test debut at Trent Bridge in 1993, dismissing Mark Taylor, Boon and Steve Waugh in the first innings. Alas the ordeal of returning to Australia but in the colours of England proved too much. Ridiculed as the 'rat who joined the sinking ship', and suffering from a stomach complaint, he and Phil DeFreitas were humbled by Slater's blade. DeFreitas' first ball of the series was woeful, in some ways worse than Steve Harmison's wide to second slip 12 years later. Short, wide and slow, it screamed 'cut me' more than any birthday cake ever has. 'After that first ball everybody looked at each other and said we've had it!' said Angus Fraser. 'It showed how fragile we were as a team.' DeFreitas and McCague conceded 26 in the first four overs, serving up a mixture of offside long-hops and leg-side dross.

Mark Nicholas wrote in *The Cricketer*:

Michael Slater, who had enchanted in England 18 months previously, cut the first ball of the match for four and continued to do much as he pleased up until tea when his partnership with the elegant Mark Waugh was in full bloom. The dashing Slater was a joy to watch. He is quicker on his feet than almost anyone in world cricket at present and punished anything short of a length with a Bradmanesque relish. His running between the wickets was a delight and the general joie de vivre of his play warmed the hearts of even the sternest pundits, who were enthralled by the enthusiasm and the confidence of the young New South Welshman.

Slater utterly imposed himself on England, finding the fence 25 times in an imperious 176, a brilliant basis for a 184-run win. He apparently modelled himself on Viv Richards as a youngster, chewing gum and practising his strokes in the back-yard of his Wagga Wagga home. When it came to his own Test career, he retained that swagger. Steve Waugh said he was an 'excitable, flighty dasher' and had 'lightning feet and a slash-ing blade'. His bat certainly seemed to scythe down much more quickly than other players'. Perhaps if he had been born in Revolutionary France he would have been much in demand. He brought a carefree, adventurous style to opening, long before the aggression of T20 had permeated the Test scene. He adored the Ashes. He made 58 in his maiden Test innings against England at Old Trafford in 1993. The following match at Lord's he made 152. The Brisbane century was his second against England, and he would go on to kiss his helmet in his trademark way five more times against them, including twice more in that series, 103 at Sydney and 124 at Perth as Australia won 3-1. On that Waca knock, Vic Marks wrote in *The Cricketer*:

Before scoring Slater edged to third slip where Graham Gooch, diving to his left, could not grab a hard chance. Slater went on to score his third hundred of the series. His innings of 124 was a frenetic, exhilarating affair. There were instinctive, lofted drives off the pace bowlers, some quicksilver running between the wickets as well as a few air shots.

Michael Vaughan 2002–3

Michael Vaughan's light as a cricketer shone too briefly for somebody of his talents, if the truth be told; injury and the pressures of leadership played their parts in that. But when it did shine, my goodness it could have guided ships into the port of Alexandria. There were two aspects to his cricket ability, of course. One was as the crafty, canny captain who won the Ashes in 2005, ending England's interminable, 18-year wait; the other was the wonderful batsman who lit up the English summer of 2002 and the subsequent winter.

He seems almost everywhere now. On television and radio, tweeting and opining in newspapers and anywhere that will have him. The image I like to hold of him, however, is as the graceful batsman stroking Glenn McGrath to the cover fence, or swivel-pulling Jason Gillespie. I have it in my head that he is wearing England's exquisite blue cloth cap, with three white lions on its front, though I expect he always wore a helmet ... I never saw Walter Hammond bat, but Neville Cardus wrote of him: 'One cover drive, off the backfoot, hit the palings under the grandstand so powerfully that the ball rebounded halfway back. His punches, levered by the right forearm, were strong, leonine and irresistible, yet there was no palpable effort, no undignified outbursts of violence.' The same description could be applied to Vaughan during the Ashes series of 2002–3 (he was a bit thinner than Hammond, mind). Like Chris Broad, Vaughan made three centuries in one series down under. Unlike

Broad, he was in a struggling England side, one that was beaten comfortably. 'He batted like the best player who had ever lived,' wrote Marcus Trescothick. 'He was as good as it gets,' added his captain, Nasser Hussain. 'He was the best English opener I played against ... and the only guy I've ever seen succeed after McGrath made his annual declaration of intent upon the opposition's key batsman,' wrote Australia captain Steve Waugh. 'It only served to give me a real confidence injection that McGrath rated me so highly,' said Vaughan. The problem for England was that Australia had big guns of their own, especially Matthew Hayden, a contrasting player to Vaughan: barrel-chested, tall, brutal.

Vaughan had given a taste of what was to come that winter, with 115 at home to Sri Lanka, then 100, 197 and 195 against India. 'He'd only had one problem the summer before – he kept getting out in the 190s!' said Mark Butcher. 'There was some talk about him not opening in Australia so that he was not exposed to McGrath, but he handled it.'

Vaughan scored centuries in Adelaide, Melbourne and Sydney to make it seven in 12 Tests, an amazing display against such a skilled attack: McGrath, who managed 19 wickets at an average of 20, Gillespie, 20 at 24, Shane Warne, 14 at 24 and Andy Bichel, 10 at 35.

Vaughan actually had a poor game in the series opener in Brisbane, making 33 and 0, and it was the belligerent Hayden who set the tone for the series. After Hussain had given Australia first use only to see Simon Jones twist his knee agonisingly on the sandy outfield, Hayden smashed 197 (although Waugh was critical of the tourists' lack of aggression and reluctance to bowl bouncers). Hayden – referred to as Buzz Lightyear by England – then followed that up with 103 in the second innings.

Vaughan had twisted his knee practising his fielding just before the start of the Adelaide Test, but was persuaded to play. Then Gillespie delivered a ball that fractured a bone in his shoulder. Vaughan still made 177, although there was a big row when Justin Langer believed he had caught him on 19. 'Vaughan batted as well as I've seen anybody,' said Butcher. 'It was absolutely beautiful, and was the making of him.' In the fourth Test at the Melbourne Cricket Ground he scored 145 to beat Dennis Amiss's England record of 1,379 runs in a calendar year. Then, at the Sydney Cricket Ground, he made 183, helping England to a consolation win. 'He had an utterly brilliant series that settled the issue of who should be England's next captain firmly in his favour,' wrote the other obvious candidate, Trescothick. 'Vaughany doesn't wait for opportunity to knock, he simply batters the door down with another breathtaking century,' wrote Butcher in *The Cricketer*. 'He really is the best in the business right now.' While Vaughan was playing like the No.1 batsman in the world, however, Australia had a batting unit that was firing on all cylinders. Ricky Ponting made centuries in Brisbane; numbers 1 to 10 made scores of between 19 and 71 in the only innings they needed in Perth; Justin Langer (250) and Hayden battered the tourists in Melbourne; and Waugh (102) and Adam Gilchrist (133) got in on the act at the SCG. England needed more than just one player to be producing great cricket consistently if they were to stop this amazing side.

Alastair Cook 2010–11

Reading cricketers' autobiographies, it is fair to say you will not find a multitude of lengthy passages describing an

Alastair Cook innings. Take the 2010–11 Ashes, for instance. Graeme Swann: 'Cook churned out another hundred at Adelaide.' Kevin Pietersen: 'When we bat at Adelaide Cook is at his best, dogging out 136 not out by the end of the second day.' Churning. Dogging. Oh dear. No one ever underestimates Cook's class or value to his side, but the clips and nudges off his legs, and the pulls and cuts do not make the writer reach for the adjectives. His 766 runs in that series at an incredible average of 127.66 were instrumental in England's triumph. At Brisbane, he started off with 67, then his unbeaten 235 in tandem with Jonathan Trott (135 not out) took England to safety. His 148 in the second Test prompted Andrew Strauss to string a few sentences together, though. 'He was extraordinary at Adelaide,' he wrote. 'He left the ball brilliantly and went along serenely to his century without ever looking as if he was going to get out. He was remarkable – his hunger, his desire, the way he recognised that the team needed him to keep playing well. He was very selective in the shots he played. He cut very well. He drove well through extra cover, though he didn't doubt very often – he just picked the right balls. He'd had a tough summer. Aesthetically you will not find a top three less pleasing on the eye than ours, in fact they would all have a decent claim to being the ugliest batsman in the world, but I wouldn't swap any of them.'

Cook had a moderate match at Perth, making 32 and 13, before finishing the series so strongly, with 82 at the Melbourne Cricket Ground and 189 at Sydney. 'Future generations may miss the overwhelming authority achieved by English individuals in this series; partly because the players themselves were apt to underplay them,' wrote Gideon Haigh in *The Wisden Cricketer*.

Alastair Cook's response to an interlocutor at Adelaide about the sweat of his long toil there was a kind of tour motif, 'I'm quite lucky – I don't really sweat that much.' Thanks for the readymade headline, Cooky: England retain the Ashes without breaking sweat. Before the tour Cook was an England player whose measure the Australians would have felt they had. In a gloating overview of the visiting team for the *Sydney Morning Herald* published on the eve of the Gabba Test, Stuart Clark dismissed him airily: 'Opponents around the world would have realised he is predominantly a square-of-the-wicket player, and now bowl full and outside off-stump as there is a question about his ability to leave the ball.' Question answered, methinks: Cook gave his bat-on-ball happy opponents a lesson this summer. That flowed, however, from a confidence in his ability to dispose of the bad ball. It is when you are worried where your next run will come from that you play strokes you should not. Cook should be Sir Leavealot because he had the swordplay to go with it.

Kings of collapses

Fred Spofforth 1882, Fred Trueman 1961, Richard Ellison 1985 and Stuart Broad 2015

There is nothing quite like those spells in Test cricket where everyone senses that a wicket could fall off any ball. The sight of a bowler running in, the crowd trying to blow on his back, a sense of disbelief in the air. A quartet of Ashes spells of seam, swing and speed spring to mind, delivered by Fred Spofforth, Fred Trueman, Richard Ellison and Stuart Broad.

If radio had been around in 1882, home fans would no doubt have gathered around it, tearing their hair out, biting their fingernails, cursing 'yet another' England batting collapse. Yet when Frederick Spofforth said about an unlikely Australian win, 'This thing can be done', not many believed him. Cricket matches between England and Australia had been taking place officially since 1877, but it was the ninth Test between them – a one-off match at The Oval in the late summer of 1882 – that led to the creation of the Ashes. A tense, closely fought match was dominated by Spofforth, the seam bowler known as The Demon, who took 7 for 46 and 7 for 44 (that 14 for 90 is still the second-best figures by an Australian in Tests). He is said to have been Australia's first true fast bowler, some of his pace achieved by a high leap just before he released the ball, perhaps a bit like Imran Khan. As England closed in on their target in the fourth innings of the Test, about the time he made his famous prediction, one spectator is reported to have dropped dead of heart failure in the excitement, another said to have gnawed through his umbrella handle. It was a strong Australia side, but England were not expected to lose the three-day affair, and had indeed looked in charge for most of the game.

Spofforth wrote about the match for *The Cricketer* in Volume I, number 5:

When Mr [Pelham] Warner asked me to write an article for him, he said he wanted something about the Test match at The Oval in 1882. It is a long time ago; yet I can recall almost every incident in that famous game as well as if it had been played last week. There were two splendid teams, and both thought they would win. Mr [Billy] Murdoch won the toss, and sent in HH [Hugh] Massie and AC [Alec] Bannerman, but we made a sorry show, being all out for 63, and were most disappointed. I might speak for myself, and say I was disgusted, and thought we should have made at least 250; but when England went in they did very little better, only making 101. Australia's second innings started well enough, Massie and Bannerman putting on 66 before the former was bowled by AG [Allan] Steel for 55. On returning to the pavilion Massie, disappointed, told me he was very sick, because he had no right to hit the ball; but he said Steel was commencing to bowl well, and he thought another four would cause him to be taken off. The second wicket fell at 70, and with the exception of our captain, run out 29, no one did anything and were all out for 122, leaving England 85 to win. An unfortunate incident occurred in this match, namely, the running out of SP [Sammy] Jones, but so much has been written on the event that I merely mention it. Anyway, it seemed to put fire into the Australians, and I do not suppose a team ever worked harder to win. With only 85 to make to win, WG Grace and AN [Albert] Hornby commenced England's second innings. I bowled Hornby at 15, and [Dick] Barlow at the same total, but then WG Grace, who had been missed by Bannerman, fielding very close in at silly mid-on, and [George] Ulyett made a stand, and reached 51 before another wicket fell, Ulyett being caught at the wicket by [Jack] Blackham. I had before asked Murdoch to let me change ends, as I was having no luck, and [Harry] Boyle then got WG caught by Bannerman. Then came the most exciting cricket I have ever witnessed. Four wickets were down, and only 32 runs required; but I must confess I never thought they would be got. [Hon] A Lyttleton and AP Lucas then came together, and at one time Boyle bowled no less than nine overs for one run, and I 10 overs for two runs. Then we agreed to let Lyttleton get a run, so as to change ends. Bannerman was to allow one to pass at mid-off, which he did, and Lyttleton faced me, when I bowled him. This was the real turning point, as Lucas, getting opposite to me again, turned the first ball into his wicket, and six wickets were down for 63, and we all felt we were on top. With seven more runs added, I bowled M [Maurice] Read and Boyle got [Billy] Barnes caught. AG [Allan] Steel then came in. I pitched a ball about four inches outside his off-stump, he started to play forward to it, before he had touched the ball I was off in the direction of silly mid-on, and Steel quietly played the ball right into my hands. CT [Charles] Studd and [Ted] Peate then came together, and Boyle bowled Peate for two, and Australia had won by seven runs.

The pressure had told on England – one of the earliest examples of choking in the Test game. The home batsmen's lips were said to be ashen-grey as they came out to join the run chase. In the August 31 edition of *Cricket – A Weekly Record of the Game*, editor Charles Alcock printed a notice saying: 'Sacred to the memory of England's supremacy in the cricket field which expired on the 29th day of August at The Oval. The end was Peate [after Ted Peate].' Two days later, much more famously, Reginald Shirley Brooks published a mock obituary in the *Sporting Times*, and the Ashes were born.

★

Trueman routing the Australians with a spell of 5 for 0 on his home patch at Headingley in 1961 must have been one of the most electrifying periods of play in Test cricket. Aesthetically pleasing as well – 'Nobody matched him for a side-on action,' wrote Scyld Berry. England, needing to win the series outright, required something special from Trueman after they had lost the second Test at Lord's to trail 1-0. On a testing surface, he had already taken 5 for 58 in the first innings, but the match was in the balance in the second innings at 98 for 2, a lead of

36. Neil Harvey had reached a half-century. 'At this decisive point, May brought Trueman back to bowl down the hill from the Kirkstall end,' wrote EW Swanton. 'The ball old and the wicket slow, Trueman decreased his run by half and his pace a couple of yards, aiming to cut the ball back from the off. He at once got Harvey with a stopper.' Former England seamer Bill Bowes was awestruck writing in *The Cricketer*.

Ball after ball, with unerring precision he dropped into the dusting bare patches. Bringing the ball back like a fast off-spinner he moved in to shatter the stumps of Bobby Simpson and so claimed three wickets in 15 balls at a cost of only one run. Richie Benaud was his next victim, bowled out for a duck – the first Australian captain since 1902 to be out for a pair. The irrepressible Trueman then had Ken Mackay caught at the wicket second ball in the last over before tea. Mackay had also failed to score. In 4.2 overs Trueman had taken the wickets of Harvey, Norman O'Neill, Simpson, Benaud and Mackay at a cost of only one run. Never can there have been such a devastating spell of fast bowling in Test cricket and by a Yorkshireman in front of a Yorkshire crowd the applause as success followed success was almost deafening. Never did any bowler have a greater reception than Trueman when the England captain and players stood on one side to let him be the first into the pavilion. From 99 for 2 Australia had gone to 109 for 8. It was almost unbelievable. It took England 22 minutes after the tea interval to complete the annihilation. Wally Grout scored seven before he pushed back a catch to Jackson. Alan Davidson was out to a spectacular diving catch by Colin Cowdrey at slip off Trueman to give the fast bowler his sixth victim at a full cost of 30 runs, and Australia were all out for 120 runs. Trueman was, indeed, the hero of the piece with 11 wickets for 88 runs in the match.

England's optimism was short-lived, though; they lost at Old Trafford, drew at The Oval, and the Ashes were gone again.

★

Richard Ellison's dramatic spell of 4 for 1 in 15 balls at Edgbaston in 1985 did prove decisive, however. He was far from first choice, with five other bowlers falling by the wayside. Even a heavy cold did not stop him, though, as he charged to the man-of-the-match award. It made for captivating television (that is until BBC1 cut to the six o'clock news – so I can only imagine how sensational being at the ground would have been). The strange thing was he had done little in four previous Test appearances to suggest how devastating he could be, and then little again after this series had concluded. He did not have the pace to be effective overseas on benign surfaces. Everything was aligned in Birmingham, however, like models of the sun, moon and earth choreographed so beautifully in Stanley Kubrick's masterpiece *2001: A Space Odyssey* (swapping the celestial bodies for the pitch, the weather, the occasion). England captain David Gower relived the spell in an interview with *The Cricketer*.

> We stuck them in, they got a few more than we wanted, but it was a pretty good pitch. I have no idea why I put them in – maybe there was something in the weather! We did OK and had them 218 for 7 but Henry [Geoff Lawson, with 53] could bat a bit. But when we replied with 595 for 5, we were not too fussed! I have very fond memories of that innings of mine [215] – it was my highest in Tests, and I only made two double-centuries. We lost a bit of time at the start and at the end of the match. Elli [Richard Ellison] had an outstanding game, taking

6 for 77 and 4 for 27. He did swing it, and the advantage was that Australia had not seen him before.

First to go was Kepler Wessels, caught by Paul Downton, then nightwatchman Bob Holland was swiftly despatched lbw first ball, and when Graeme Wood departed Australia had slipped to 35 for 4. Now was Ellison's prize moment. The masterpiece that he can proudly bequeath on the history of Test cricket. The absolutely decisive blow. 'Border going on the fourth evening was the key, Ellison bowling an absolute beauty,' said Gower. 'It swung back a bit, hovered, took another route, came down a bit, and clipped the top of off-stump! We thought we had a chance then at five down overnight. But it was persistent drizzle. I got to the ground and Border was giggling. Eventually we got a break from the weather … and Botham finished it off.'

Ellison took another seven wickets at The Oval, giving him 17 at 10.88 apiece in the series, and England won the series 3-1.

★

Broad's 8 for 15 at Trent Bridge in 2015 was perhaps the most stunning spell of the lot, though – not just for his brilliance, but for how inept Australia were against him (although it was a very green pitch). Many overseas batsmen cannot cope with English conditions, when the ball is swinging and seaming; and another widely accepted theory is that the irrepressible growth of T20 has damaged Test batsmen's techniques. The best argument for both would be simply to play footage of Broad putting Australia to the sword here. Broad has enjoyed many similar spells. Several quiet matches, a few whispers about his place, then an emphatic reminder of what makes him great. Being 'on a roll' could have been a phrase made for him.

England led 2-1 going into the match, but Australia's hopes of squaring the series ahead of an Oval finale were dead by the first morning as they subsided to 60 all out. 'Australia saved their worst performance in modern memory for their most important match in a generation, while England's perfect opening day secured what, just weeks ago, appeared unlikely Ashes glory,' wrote Adam Collins in *The Cricketer.*

From the moment Alastair Cook sent Australia in, piling on the pressure after their meek batting performance at Edgbaston, the purpose was clear: break the visitors and break them now. Enter Stuart Broad. Big Bad Broad; pantomime villain from central casting. He has bowled plenty of second overs of Tests, but very few first; it was only the fifth time in his career that Jimmy Anderson has not been there for the over-one honours. In a sign of what was to come, Broad's second ball to Chris Rogers was exquisite seam bowling, catching the edge to the cordon in a method that would be repeated seven further times before his morning was done (that was Broad's 300th Test wicket). Steve Smith arrived in England the world's top-ranked batsman. He left Trent Bridge in the first innings four balls after he arrived, squared up to a delivery he could have left if not for shuffling so far across his stumps. The manic tempo of this match was set and would not alter. David Warner's inside edge in the second over exposed a brittle-at-best middle order of Shaun Marsh, Michael Clarke and Adam Voges. They contributed 11 runs – falling to a trio of substandard drives, fends and pushes – as Broad raced to a five-wicket haul in world record time. Taking stock: six of Australia's wickets had fallen for 29 runs after just 37 balls – also the quickest on record – unprecedented chaos. Lower-order resistance extended the innings for another dozen overs, but no more;

111 balls were all it took. Australia's Ashes defence in barely an hour was utterly shot; the team completely humiliated. Broad's 8 for 15 was as close to cricket perfection as exists. Once in a lifetime, he said, you have a spell like that. His just happened to be in a Test where it could not have mattered more. In three consecutive Ashes-winning rubbers in England he has been the man of the match, speaking volumes of his big-game prowess.

The look on his face when Ben Stokes produced a stunning catch in the gully to remove Voges said it all. Broad could not believe it, both teams could not believe it, the crowd could not believe it. Even now the events seem unreal.

Fifteen Minutes of Fame

David Steele 1975

Only four cricketers have won the BBC's Sports Personality of the Year award in its 63-year history. The triumphs of Jim Laker, in 1956, Ian Botham, in 1981, and Andrew Flintoff, in 2005, do not need explaining; their brilliance during those years' Ashes series enthralled a nation. The fourth cricketer's win in 1975 was perhaps more surprising. His batting was superb, make no mistake about that, but it was his courage and the quirkiness of his appearance that captivated sports fans this time. 'A grey-haired middle-order batsman for Northants, he played in steel-rimmed spectacles and looked years older than his actual 33,' wrote John Thicknesse. Most famously he was described by the *Sun* newspaper's Clive Taylor as 'The bank clerk who went to war'.

Mike Denness lost the England captaincy after the first Test at Edgbaston in 1975, when he had given Australia first use of the uncovered pitch, only for weather to make life treacherous for the hosts. Tony Greig took over with his side trailing 1-0, and pushed for Steele's inclusion. His game was based on a solid defence and a fearless approach to playing fast bowling, although his record for Northamptonshire, an average of 31 over 12 seasons, had not made a compelling case for inclusion. Despite finding himself lost on his way to the Long Room (usually he would descend from the away dressing room) he scored 50 and 45 on his debut at Lord's against Dennis Lillee, Jeff Thomson, Max Walker and Ashley Mallett.

In *The Cricketer*, Tony Lewis wrote:

David Steele quickly proved why he was chosen. England were again heading for disaster, 49 for 4, Dennis Lillee taking the wickets of Amiss, Edrich, Wood and Gooch … Steele, however, marched in to lunch to a hero's reception, 36 not out. The one difference in his play from others is that he plunges forward on the front foot. Lillee, Thomson and Walker in Australia may sort him out, but on this wicket at Lord's which had no special bounce, he had the confidence to recognise that he could play forward to balls well up to him. Amiss, Edrich and Wood rather lingered on the back foot. Yet the balls dug in short Steele hooked downwards and, in fact, he was as quick as anyone to move onto the back foot. Why has he been in the background so long without being chosen for England? Is this one innings, which he extended after lunch to 50 exactly, a chance affair? I suppose he has never looked an outstanding player. His runs have often been grafted cheerlessly. Most seasons he averages just over 30. This one he is up to 45-plus. More than anything he is recognised by professional players as a man of heart and determination, the qualities which appeared to have gone from the England side at Edgbaston. For the moment all one can say is that he did every bit as well as everyone hoped for him.

He then made 73 and 92 at Headingley in an attack spectacularly augmented by Gary Gilmour, and 39 and 66 at The Oval: a total of 365 runs from 860 balls. It was not enough to tilt the Ashes England's way, with the last three matches drawn (the one in Leeds partially thanks to the 'George Davis is innocent' campaign, of course), but he had certainly tried his best. 'I don't think the Australians or the crowd could quite believe what was happening,' wrote Graham Gooch. 'Most of them hadn't seen him before, his prematurely white hair in direct contrast to the blue of his gleaming new England cap, Elastoplast round his bat, his "Groucho Marx" walk, and the wonky tilt of his cap-peak framing those peering, glinting spectacles.'

Alex Bannister wrote in *The Cricketer*:

Steele would be much less than human if he didn't enjoy his triumphs to the full. He has the satisfaction of those who have worked for a position and have earned the right to success, and he can inwardly chuckle at those who doubted his class at Test level. In a contradictory way he is a personality without a personality – a very ordinary bloke with rimless specs, prematurely grey hair, and a succinct wit. Yet those average qualities, the absence of tiresome gimmicks, and the sheer romance of an old pro cocking a snoot at the rampant Thomson, Lillee and Co, have combined to make Steele a folk hero. In appearance he is as unlikely a top sporting figure as could be imagined. Put him alongside Freddie Brown, Wally Hammond, Ted Dexter, and others with that magic ingredient called presence, and he would be out of place. But put him in a tight spot for England, as he was in his first Test at Lord's, and he lacks no comparison with any contemporary player.

Steele played only one further series, against the rampant West Indians the following summer. In five Tests he made 308 runs at 30.80 against a fierce attack led by Michael Holding and Wayne Daniel. It is difficult to think of an England player who made such an impact in such a short space of time, though, not just as a player, but in capturing the heart of the nation. Only one springs to mind: he played for Northants, too, and that was Colin Milburn.

Rodney Hogg 1978–9

If the winter of 1978–9 was like a mound of coal for the Australians, they found a diamond underneath it all: Rodney Hogg. Kerry Packer had taken Australia's best players for World Series Cricket, including Dennis Lillee, Jeff Thomson and Max Walker, but Hogg tried manfully to plug the gap. He took an Ashes record 41 wickets in the six matches, but that did not prevent England winning 5-1, with Brearley becoming the first captain to take a handful of Tests down under, and only the second England captain after Len Hutton to regain and defend the Ashes.

That winter World Series Cricket, after a limp first season, had really taken off. The Chappells, Lillee, Thomson and Rod Marsh were all performing under the wealthy businessman's banner, rather than against England. The tourists were also without Dennis Amiss, Derek Underwood, Tony Greig, Alan Knot and Bob Woolmer, but were still too strong.

England encountered Hogg for the first time when they suffered a surprise defeat to South Australia. 'We had never heard of this fella,' said Geoff Miller. 'He bowled quick and straight. Just ask Clive Radley what it was like to face him. He bowled a short ball at Clive that hit him straight on the head, splitting his forehead.' John Lever recalled: 'Clive laughed afterwards, and said, "If they all bowl like that I'm f—ed!"'

Australia won the toss in Brisbane, but soon regretted the decision, slumping to 26 for 6 in steamy conditions. They rallied to 116 all out, but England replied with 286, despite Hogg's 6 for 74. Australia fared better next time round, making 339, but still lost by seven wickets. Hogg was even better in the second Test at Perth, taking 5 for 65 and 5 for 57, but England again won comfortably. Gower, only 21, was the sole batsman on either team to make more than 400 runs in the series at an average of more than 40, but he found facing Hogg a challenge. 'He was as quick and mean a bowler as any I have faced, and he also had the temperament to match,' he wrote. 'When I was leaving the field with a century to my name in Perth, the fact that I had edged and missed a few against him early on had clearly been festering with him, and he came up and called me "an effin' imposter".'

'Of the Australian bowlers only Hogg could match [England's],' wrote John Woodcock in *The Cricketer.*

With 17 wickets in his first two Tests, this 27-year-old Victorian (though he plays for South Australia, he was born in Melbourne) was extending a remarkable start to his Test career. Even Thomson took fewer wickets in the first two Tests of 1974/75 than Hogg did in December, and Hogg had no Lillee to back him up from the other end.

There was another 10-wicket match for Hogg in the third Test at the MCG as Australia hit back, winning by 103 runs. It was Brearley's first defeat in 16 Tests. 'On a ground where he had never before enjoyed the smallest success, Hogg's figures for the match were 10 for 66 from 34 overs,' wrote Woodcock.

> Over the same five days Bob Willis, England's most successful bowler in the first two Tests and one of the game's great triers, took 0 for 68 and bowled only 20 overs. Hogg's continuing triumph (27 wickets in the first three Tests) could be accounted for partly by his speed (appreciable, without being quite 'like fire'); partly by his line, which was good enough to give the batsmen very little to punish; and partly by his length, which is seldom short. It could also have had something to do with a healthy disregard for 'Poms'.

England were in real danger of letting the series slip in the fourth Test at Sydney, only to stage one of the great comebacks to win by 93 runs and retain the Ashes. Australia captain Graham Yallop received the approval of his board to bring in a local football coach to motivate his side for the fifth Test at Adelaide, but England still won by 205 runs, and the tourists won the sixth Test at Sydney just as comfortably as they had the fourth there. Hogg had not lost his sense of humour, however, greeting Derek Randall by putting a fake snake on the pitch. Really Hogg himself had been responsible for Australia's only venom that winter.

Reviewing Hogg's series in *The Cricketer Spring Annual*, Brian Bearshaw wrote:

> For a man who, nine weeks earlier, had told me he was not thinking about Test cricket, he had suddenly become the

hottest property in the game. Hogg leans well forward in his run-up to the wicket, as if he cannot get there fast enough, and gets much of his pace at the delivery stride where he puts in so much effort that he occasionally falls flat on his face. His teammates are used to it. They ignore him and Hogg just grins – not a common sight on the field – and starts his walk back. There's something of the rough diamond about Hogg, but he has a pleasing way with it.

Bruce Reid 1990–91

England's expedition to Australia in the winter of 1990–91 was so troubled that the last thing they needed was such an awkward and skilled bowler to face as Bruce Reid. 'He was always a dangerous bowler with his great height, six foot eight inches, and his ability to mix the ball angled across the right-handers from over the wicket with an occasional in-swinger, but he has emerged from a long break from cricket because of a serious back injury to become a potential world beater,' wrote Christopher Martin-Jenkins in *The Cricketer*.

Several things blew up on this tour. One was the feud between captain Graham Gooch and David Gower. The other was Gooch's hand after he had cut it in fielding practice and it had become infected. No one doubted Gower's genius, but his sometimes cavalier approach irked Gooch, who was rightly trying to drag England out of the indulgent 1980s into a more professional era. Gower and Allan Lamb were criticised for visiting a casino during the first Test, although Gower had already been dismissed; Lamb was not out and fell quickly the next day. Then there was the Tiger Moth incident, with John Morris. Most significantly on the pitch, however, Gower was duped into giving his wicket away just before lunch on day two of the fourth Test at Perth, flicking a Craig McDermott half-volley down fine leg's throat, with Gooch looking on disbelievingly at the non-striker's end. 'I consider I might have got it wrong and that I should have accepted David for what he was – a big-match player of great natural ability, touched with genius – and simply regarded him as an automatic choice,' said Gooch. Certainly Gower did not have a bad series, scoring centuries at the MCG and SCG in the second and third Tests respectively. Gower had as much success as anybody against Reid, the player of the series, who took 27 wickets in the first four matches at 16 runs apiece.

In the first two Tests, England led on first innings, only to be blown away by, first, Terry Alderman at the Gabba, and then Reid at Melbourne, where he took 6 for 97 and 7 for 51. In that second innings, *Wisden* called it '50 minutes of madness' as England lost six wickets for three runs. Respectable draws were achieved in the third and fourth Tests, and it was only the fifth – once a series defeat was inevitable – that saw a gulf develop between the sides. 'The first two Tests after the first innings could have gone either way, but a star performer came through each innings,' said Angus Fraser. 'Reid bowled unbelievably well.' His match figures were 5 for 93, 13 for 148, 3 for 79 and 6 for 112. 'He has earned his success without recourse either to silly invective or bouncers at the batsman's head,' wrote CMJ.

This was a brilliant performance all the happier for the fact that he had looked unlikely to be able to make any sustained comeback to first-class cricket. Robin Marlar remarked once that Colin Milburn had struck a blow for fat men everywhere. Bruce Reid has done the same for thin ones.

For the greater part of 20 years England seem to have been more prone to batting collapses than any of the regular Test-playing countries. As recently as last season in England, against New Zealand at Edgbaston, in a match England actually won, if you please, they managed to lose their last seven wickets for 29 runs. Who bowled them out? Richard Hadlee five for 53 and a spell of five for 17 in eight overs and two balls. Who repeated the dose in Melbourne? A highly unusual and, in this form, high-class fast bowler: Reid 7 for 51 and a spell of 4 for 0 in six overs. Nine wickets fell for 47 runs, the last six for three runs in 12 overs in the pathetic dive by which England catapulted themselves towards defeat from the jaws of victory. One could go on. Reid's analysis was the best against England since ... some time ago? Actually, since April 1990, when Curtly Ambrose took 8 for 45, the last five of them for 18 runs in seven overs and four balls. It would be unwise for the TCCB to plan a match against the rest of the world: Ambrose at one end and Reid at the other would induce in an England batting team such a state of paranoia that they might not score at all.

Stuart MacGill 1998–9

Every time a *Batman* film series is launched, the producers have a sit-down and list potential villains. The Joker is always the obvious baddie to start things off. Then, if the film is a success and a sequel is given the green light, what about the Riddler? England's Ashes tour of 1998–9 seems a bit like this. The tourists had some uplifting news at the start of the series – their nemesis since 1993, Shane Warne, would be missing after failing to recover from a shoulder surgery. Yet his understudy, Stuart MacGill, proved more than an adequate replacement, taking 27 wickets at an average of 17.70 in four Tests, the same number Warne had taken four winters earlier in five at 20.33. If you will permit me to stretch the metaphor even further, in fact, MacGill – a tempestuous cricketer – combined the fieriness of the Joker with the mysteriousness of the Riddler. 'If you're facing Australia in Australia, then losing the No.1 bowler in the world has to be good news,' said Mark Butcher. 'History has shown, though, that MacGill had an even better strike-rate than Warne. The whole leg-spin thing was a bit confusing to us. We just never could get to grips with Muttiah Muralitharan, Warne or MacGill.'

Muralitharan had been England's tormentor in their final Test before the tour, at The Oval, a defeat that had taken some of the shine off an encouraging series win over South Africa. England coach David Lloyd cast aspersions about Murali's action, saying: 'I have my opinions that I have made known to the authorities.' It all added to the sense that his side had a major problem against spin and were fixated by it. They were lucky to escape with a draw in the opening Test at Brisbane, with MacGill heaping pressure on them on the last day before a violent storm saved them. MacGill was not needed at Perth, and still England lost inside two days and two sessions at Perth; and they were then steamed alive at Adelaide, MacGill taking 4 for 53 in the first innings. Already the Ashes had gone. The first day of the Melbourne Test was washed out, then MacGill took 4 for 61 and 3 for 81, hitting a career-best 43 in between. England actually won a fine victory, but MacGill was a man revelling in his chance finally to emerge from Warne's shadow. People were actually speculating that he was now a match for Warne, and the fifth Test at Sydney gave everyone the chance to compare them. It was unfair on Warne, who had recovered from his injury but looked ring-rusty. Although he removed Butcher with his fourth ball, he took only one more wicket; MacGill took 12 in total (5 for 57 and 7 for 50) as Australia won to secure the series 3-1. 'In his first over after a nine-month absence from Test cricket, Warne inevitably captured a wicket, that of Butcher, but MacGill was the chief tormentor,' wrote Vic Marks in *The Cricketer*. 'He spun his leg-breaks prodigiously and with venom; he offered more googlies than his senior partner, though he was less accurate. For much of the afternoon Taylor had Warne in reserve while MacGill and Colin Miller were doing the damage. Not a bad situation for a Test captain to be in.'

About the second innings, Marks wrote:

On the final day the Australians were unrelenting. Glenn McGrath made the initial breakthrough, Miller disposed of John Crawley, inadvisedly padding up, but the rest were undermined by MacGill. Graeme Hick and Alex Tudor were bowled around their legs sweeping; Nasser Hussain's valiant 54 ended when he presented a return catch, but the most freakish dismissal was the last. Peter Such was caught and bowled via the boot of Mark Waugh at silly point. MacGill immediately pocketed the ball, a treasured memento of a career-best performance which brought him 12 wickets in the match. He was in a day dream by the end after an astonishing first outing on his home ground during which he comprehensively outshone his senior partner. This time improved accuracy was combined with prodigious spin and indecipherable variations.

The Best of *The Cricketer*

Jamie Crawley

T HERE ARE FEW things in sport that get tongues wagging, teeth grinding, pens racing or keyboards clicking like an Ashes series. The full spectrum of scrutinising and castigating responses – disappointment, despair, anger, ecstasy – has been displayed in the pages of *The Cricketer* by its editors, contributors and readers for all but a century. Players, commentators and supporters have come and gone but the fervour which accompanies every Ashes contest remains a constant. From Plum Warner's assessment of England's thumping defeat in 1921, through EW Swanton's tutting at Lillee and Thomson's ferocious barrage in 1974–5, to readers' sharing of their gobsmacked delight at the drama of 2005, *The Cricketer* has seen it all.

Ashes to Ashes

The Ashes legend began with a mock obituary in the *Sporting Times*, following England's first defeat on home soil to Australia. While today we may view this as something of an overreaction, it's difficult to really see how anything has changed. Any particularly humbling defeat at the hands of Australia will be followed by a post-mortem of some type, and, since 1921, there has been no shortage of them to be found in *The Cricketer*. The formula is generally consistent – assert what is to be done, and if someone can be found to blame, so much the better.

Not to say Australia have not had their occasional troughs as well, and these too have been subjected to the same level of recrimination. *The Cricketer*'s predominantly English writers and readers have been almost schoolmasterly in their disappointment, as they have struggled not to cross the line from constructive criticism to gleeful conceit. Possibly because they are so much rarer, the logic has been to enjoy it while one can!

The Cricketer launched amidst the first prolonged period of Australian Ashes dominance, the inaugural issue coming shortly after Warwick Armstrong's Australia team had handed out the first Ashes whitewash to the ageing and war-weary England team in 1920–21.

In the wake of England's 3-0 defeat in the 1921 rematch with Warwick Armstrong's seriously impressive team, founding editor of *The Cricketer* 'Plum' Warner picked through the bones, trying hard not to point any fingers, but did suggest that England's faults lay in selection and they needed a more youthful side. For youthful, read under 35 ...

The Selection Committee have been blamed for the results which followed, but though no Selection Committee has ever been infallible in its judgement, or ever will be, I am of the opinion that our defeats were caused by one fact, and one fact only, namely, that we met a better side. Our selectors were faced with a difficult task. In any event it would have been difficult to pick an England XI, for we had not recovered from the long years of war, and the task of the selectors was made doubly hard by the fact that Hobbs, the best batsman in the world and a superb fieldsman at cover point, and JW Hearne, the second best batsman in England against the best bowling, were both *hors de combat* from illness and accidents.

Extenuating circumstances may, therefore, with justice be pleaded for our failures. We failed, and failed miserably, in the first and second Test matches, but though easily beaten at Leeds in the third game, we put up a fine fight in the face of heavy odds. Not only did we bat one short, and that one Hobbs, but the Hon. LH Tennyson sustained a severe injury while fielding, and had to bat with practically one hand, in spite of which he played two fine innings which will long be remembered.

It may be that the Selection Committee relied too much on the older generation, and did not give a chance to some of the younger men, such as H. Ashton, JL Bryan, and CH Gibson, of the Cambridge XI, while many had urged, including AC MacLaren, that M. Falcon, properly trained and in good condition, was the best fast bowler in England.

Everyone knows that our bowling today is nothing like up to the pre-war standard. There is no Richardson or Lockwood among the fast bowlers, nor is there a Barnes, a JT Hearne, or an Attewell among the medium-pace right-handed bowlers, and with our bowling at the low ebb it was, judged by the international standard, it became more than ever essential that the fielding should be excellent.

Many of our most successful batsmen today are past the age when activity and throwing power can be expected of them in the field, and moreover, the absence of Hobbs made an incalculable difference to the off-side fielding.

I would suggest that the General Committee of the MCC should be strengthened by the inclusion of younger blood – men actually playing in first-class cricket today.

We must also get rid of the idea that a Test match of necessity requires great experience. Everybody must make a beginning in Test matches, and I would go more for the young men who are naturally quicker and more active in the field, and who, given the opportunity, would train on into England cricketers.

There are today a large number of young cricketers of very great promise, and I hope that in picking future XIs to tour in Australia and in South Africa, and to represent England here, preference will be given to the men who are under 35 years of age, except in the case of geniuses like Hobbs and Barnes. The number of runs that Australia saved by their beautiful fielding is incalculable.

★

In 1956, Jim Laker and England consigned Australia to their third successive Ashes series defeat. It was, amazingly, only England's third home win against Australia since before the First World War, and the first time England had beaten Australia twice in a home series since 1905. While England only triumphed 2-1 in 1956, the margin of England's two victories and Australia's ineptness against Laker's spin were such that it was natural to view Australian cricket as in crisis. This was only eight years after Don Bradman's 'Invincibles' had swept aside everything in their path, after all. At any rate, Bill Bowes was not impressed.

One of the wettest seasons on record cannot excuse Australia's very ordinariness … Their failure against the turning ball and their inability to spin the ball themselves produced a harsh but general judgement that they were the worst balanced touring side for over 50 years.

To understand the Australian failures, I believe it is necessary to go back to the Hutton tour of Australia when the fast bowling partnership of Tyson and Statham carried all before it.

It called for a changed approach by the Australian selectors. Whereas the emphasis had been put on players who could hit the ball about in the manner of Bradman and score fast and entertaining runs there were, understandably, no players who had the Bradman technique. With the weakness exposed by speed bowling the pendulum swung the other way.

And let me pay the Australian selectors the compliment of saying they succeeded. Burke, MacDonald, Burge, Craig and Mackay certainly stood up to the ball. They were all players who, either playing forward or back, moved to the line of the flight of the ball and tried to play it with bat moving pendulum fashion by the side of the body.

But, oh dear, how difficult it is for a batsman who over-positions (who moves right in the line of flight of the ball) when the ball pitches and bends back.

So it was that we had an Australian side with fundamental weakness against off-spin. True [at Leeds and Manchester] the ball did not turn much, but Australian batsmen were so over-positioned that the slightest deviation had them in a tangle.

But from technical explanation let me now pass to criticism of team tactics, especially at the start of the tour. Using the excuse that the team was short of practice (because of the late arrival) the early matches were taken far too easily. Johnson explained the long succession of drawn matches by saying he wanted his batsmen in form.

He was careful not to have his speed men suffer injury, otherwise he would have found that Lindwall and Miller no longer had the ability to get victims by sheer speed and the fast Yorker as on previous tours. Not until 10 days before the first Test match at Nottingham did he take the cotton wool from his fast bowlers and tell them to prepare for the Test.

Bowes' sentiment was echoed by *The Cricketer*'s readers, hoping that Australia would soon shape up, for the sake of a competitive series next time around.

Dear Sir, – Let not the alleged spinner's pitches be blamed for the present failures of the tourists, for did not the batsmen 'fold up' on their own wickets against our speed merchants on our last tour? In short they are in the position which we were in when we were demoralised by the speed of Lindwall and Miller in 1948. The weakness of the batting is amply demonstrated when a batsman of Mackay's calibre is picked again after his fantastic attempts to play Laker at Leeds.

In conclusion, let us hope that the Australians, by diligent weeding out of prospective talent, can produce not another Bradman, but somebody with slightly less ability, and so even up the balance of strength for the next series – Yours faithfully, T. McAdam. Dumbarton, Scotland

★

In 1958–9, England visited Australia as, by common consent, the best side in world cricket, and fully expected to romp to another comfortable Ashes triumph. They were in for an extremely rude awakening, however, beaten 4-0, in an ill-tempered series, punctuated by rows over the questionable actions of some of the Australian bowlers. Bill Bowes reported on the tour, indicating that there was nothing so surprising in the result as some would believe.

From an England point of view it was a most disappointing tour. There was not one England player who enhanced a reputation, not one newcomer who made a reputation.

If there was one regrettable tendency on the part of the players as a whole it was towards complacency – in the early part of the tour. Seven years of success on the cricket field had not brought team spirit so much as a belief that, when needed, everything would come right.

There is one thing very certain in a change over from English to Australian playing conditions; batsmen in particular have to speed up their game. Pitches are harder and, from the slower bowlers in particular, the ball has a much higher bounce. It is much harder to speed up play than slow it down. The forward, defensive stroke, indeed, forward play generally, becomes a major part of batsmanship. The cut and the pull, two favourite strokes on the slower pitches of England, are not recommended in Australia.

'Keep that left foot moving to the ball,' is advice I've heard given by many successful batsmen in Australia. The bat has to meet the ball. It is fatal to wait for the ball to hit the bat.

The Australian batsmen, especially against fast bowling, make an early movement back towards the stumps in order to get as long as possible to watch the ball in flight and they seldom lift the bat more than an inch or two from the block hole. But having taken this position they play every stroke with the bat meeting the ball. They many times play 'half cock', as Yorkshire players term the stroke which is neither forward nor back, but seldom if ever do they play a backward defensive stroke.

Of the eight England players who had proved successful on previous tours of Australia, three fast bowlers, one wicket-keeper, and four batsmen, viz., May, Cowdrey, Graveney and

Bailey, there was sufficient experience ... and authority ... to make this point with the newcomers.

But was it ever made? And if it was made was it ever insisted upon?

Such was the complacency of the England party, so certain were they that things would come right, that serious practice at the start of the tour was never entertained ... The fresh air and gentle exercise of a golf course was much to be preferred. It was not unusual to see Trueman bowling left-handed and Tyson off-spinners. Not once did I see someone in authority standing behind the net and bringing a player to task for playing back when he should have gone forward.

The air of despondency filtered through into the correspondence pages as well, with one particular reader realising sooner than most that cricket's entertainment value was endangered. Unfortunately for Mr Toone and the rest of the cricketing public, this series was but a sign of things to come in the following decade.

Dear Sir, – All lovers of cricket must have been very disappointed by the miserable performances of the England team v. the Australians. Defeats by 8 wickets, 8 wickets, 10 wickets, 9 wickets and a draw speak for themselves. Plenty of excuses may be advanced for England's so-called bad luck, but the fact remains that the England team were simply no match for Australia. In the match at Brisbane it took nearly five days to score 665 runs, Bailey taking 7½ hours to score 68 runs, and on the third day of the match 106 runs were scored in five hours on what was an easy-paced wicket.

One way of preventing such displays of negative batting might be to revert to three-day Tests (with a possible fourth day in case of rain) as in the past. Modern cricket is being ruined by lack of proper footwork by batsmen and a purely negative and defensive attitude by batsmen and bowlers.

Let us get back to the good times when Tests and other matches really were worth watching. Unless some definite action is taken soon the fine old English game will lose its hold on the public to such an extent that the county clubs will cease to exist – Yours faithfully, WP Toone. Cepians, Dun Laoghaire, Eire

★

The 1986–7 series was probably the first time since 1956 that Australia had looked well and truly forlorn in an Ashes series. It was, in fact, the first time since then that a full-strength Australia side had lost back-to-back Ashes, if we discount the 1978–9 Packer-induced loss. Packer's impact on Australian cricket had been evident ever since – the increased demands of a TV schedule to fill up meant an exhausting programme of Test and one-day cricket. Christopher Martin-Jenkins was editor of *The Cricketer* and delivered a damning assessment of the state Australian cricket had come to.

Australian cricket is in pain. The same anxious questions about its health and the chances of a cure are being asked by well-wishers as were being asked of England only a few months ago. In Australia's case, like a sufferer from heart trouble, the only hope of a long life is to start cutting the excesses now. There is too much cholesterol. In other words, too much cricket.

Without wishing to sound smug, one has been saying and writing this for years, and this time one can only pray that the greedy controllers of Australian cricket will accept the truth and have the courage to admit that they have been wrong. Since that uneasy compromise between the Australian Cricket Board and World Series Cricket in 1979 there has been too much butter and cream every year: the flesh gets podgier and grosser with every series of hyped-up limited-overs international matches and with every rich mouthful, the vital organs, the heart and soul, are becoming rotten.

Moderation in all things! Butter and cream have their place, but only in a balanced diet. In England we are not much more sensible. There is still too much limited-overs domestic cricket being played and instead of finally having the sense to cut it down, those short-sighted and, yes, greedy, TCCB officials who met in December to discuss the eminently sensible conclusions of the Palmer Committee actually managed to increase the number of 40-over matches on Sundays. Then, in order to sell boxes to local companies, they included the Benson & Hedges Cup zonal rounds, which no one who knows cricket particularly wants to watch or to play, and cut out the quarter-finals, which have attracted very considerable support and interest. And, in first-class cricket, all the wise and experienced men who had called for a return to uncovered pitches were ignored. So England will look for spin bowlers in vain when Edmonds and Emburey grow longer of tooth and shorter of hair. (Even shorter!)

At least in England the one-day internationals have been kept to a maximum of four in a season. Each of these games, as a result, is a genuine occasion, well worth staging, playing and watching. Yet in Australia a meaningless series of internationals was starting in Perth even before the scheduled close of the fourth Test in Melbourne. Will Australian Board officials have the foresight to cut their programmes down next year? Do they have the power to make such decisions any more? Will the only answer be that people go to watch these games, so they must continue even if the standard is low and getting lower? Do PBL (Publishing and Broadcasting Limited) run Australian cricket? If so, will they still wish to do so when their 10-year contract ends in two years' time and they find themselves with a consistently losing side to promote? Or, having made profitable use of the raddled old body of Australian cricket, will they go off with their dollars and leave it to wither?

One must not overstate the case. The fact that England have won the Ashes is not all PBL's fault and it would be absurd to claim so. The disappearance to South Africa of several of the nation's best cricketers has left behind an inexperienced team, especially short of genuine Test bowlers. If they did not play so many matches the current malaise would be less obvious. Moreover, England have recovered nobly from their own traumas earlier this year and, once having taken the initiative at Brisbane, they have held it by dint of good disciplined cricket.

★

No era would bring half as much despair to English cricket as the 1990s. Each Ashes began with quiet hope and were rarely completely void of encouraging moments, but England were seriously lagging, as the long years of complacency in the Eighties came home to roost. Australia had put England firmly in the rear-view mirror and were not letting their foot off the gas. Each series seemingly brought a new Australian hero, while England fumbled from one meek remedy to another. In 1993, *The Cricketer* featured Michael Atherton's journal of the season, taking readers right to the coal-face of an Ashes summer on England duty.

Week beginning May 31: The first Test match of the Ashes series was a wonderful spectacle for the viewers; the pitch, whilst starting wet, did not do quite as much as expected. It did, however, help the spinners on the first two days. Peter Such bowled superbly for six wickets while Shane Warne announced his presence with a perfect leg-break to defeat Mike Gatting. As the pitch flattened out England were asked to bat for four and a half sessions to save the match, Graham Gooch's magnificent hundred not quite enabling England to achieve the feat.

Australia deserved to win being the more aggressive and assertive side, something we must watch to revive the series.

Week beginning June 14: Prior to the second Test Graham Gooch announces he will resign if there is little sign of improvement. Sadly, the Australians on a slow pitch amass a huge total. Of their first four batsmen only Mark Waugh failed to make a century, being bowled for 99. Michael Slater's was the best innings, a marvellous 157.

And thus England lose their seventh consecutive Test match with a performance none of us was proud of. I became the second batsman of the match to succumb on 99 – like the nightmare in which you are never making your ground, I ended scrambling on all fours in a fairly undignified exit. After the match, the chairman of selectors deflects much of the flak from the captain with an observation that Venus is in fact in a wrong juxtaposition. With what I'm not quite clear.

Week beginning June 28: Despite having so many new faces that a 'meet the players' drinks party was necessary, England put on a purposeful and confident performance at Trent Bridge finally to ignite the Ashes series. Favourites to win at tea, the Australians now realise they have a fight on their hands. The

England new caps have done themselves proud, particularly Graham Thorpe with a century on his long awaited debut.

Week beginning July 19: More bad news from the international front. England are beaten by an innings and plenty. Allan Border scores 200 and fittingly takes the catch to clinch the Ashes, and Paul Reiffel takes eight wickets in the match. Sadly, Graham Gooch, much respected and liked by the players, decides to bring a close to his reign as England captain. I go off to the Lake District for a small break only for it to be interrupted by the chairman of selectors who offers me the captaincy for two games.

Week beginning July 26: This week probably constitutes the most hectic of my life. Nothing quite prepares you for the press attention but within hours they had managed to find out where I live and about my girlfriend. Following the press conference there were endless interviews to conduct. Unfortunately, Lancashire are playing the Australians and I am resting and thus am an easy target.

Week beginning August 2: As England slip towards another defeat, the chairman of the England selectors Ted Dexter resigns, probably more hurt and battered than he would admit after the constant harpooning by the media. Every former captain, from 92-year-old Bob Wyatt, is mentioned for the job.

Week beginning August 16: What everyone had dreamed of all summer, an England victory, occurs. Maybe the Australians were tired, maybe Venus was in the right juxtaposition and maybe we got the rub of the green, but when it came it was an emotive moment, especially for those – and there were many – who had never beaten Australia or even won a Test match.

★

England's humbling whitewash in 2006–7 could not be said to have been unexpected. It was well known that England arrived in Australia in poor shape, and a number of their heroes from 2005 were either missing or just returning to the side with a serious lack of recent match practice behind them. Nonetheless the totality of the defeat, losing the urn in the shortest possible time after the glory and the euphoria of 2005, left England cricket fans dispirited and dejected. *The Cricketer*'s readers were sharpening their knives.

Duncan Fletcher has treated Chris Read unfairly. In Read's nine Test innings before being dropped in 2003–4 he scored 85 runs at 12. Not great but the averages of other players from the same Tests show that batting must have been difficult. Trescothick made 229 at 20, Hussain 184 at 23, Vaughan 314 at 29 and Flintoff 227 at 25. Read was dropped before he had a chance to prove himself on a flat wicket. Now Fletcher has picked a worse keeper who scored 143 runs at 14 in his last 11 innings before the Ashes, who had done little to justify his selection. – Julian Niblett, Nottingham

Last summer a scratch England team under Andrew Strauss gradually built self-belief and beat Pakistan. Though we still probably wouldn't have won, it should have been a solid basis for defending the Ashes as we would have momentum and confidence. Instead injured players came straight into the team with no recent cricket in the middle. The whole summer's achievements were thrown away. The discarded players were left feeling second-best and undervalued. Will the same mistake be made again, with Michael Vaughan brought straight back without having to prove he can bat and field? – Anne Rowntree, Wadeford, Somerset

Mike Selvey delivered the following assessment of the Ashes defence from hell, realising that, while sentimentality for 2005 still abounded, Duncan Fletcher's time had come.

It has not been edifying to watch England systematically destroyed, day by day and match by match, as if suffering death by a thousand cuts. But there has been an inevitability about it since Steve Harmison began the whole thing by firing the opening shot of the most hyped series in history straight towards second slip.

Despite protestations to the contrary, England arrived for the first Test in chaos. The build-up had been inadequate and ill-conceived, with key players such as Harmison and Ashley Giles woefully short of hard match-bowling. Duncan Fletcher's faith in the professional ability of Giles to pick up where he had left off was a leap too far as it transpired. Earlier the loss of Marcus Trescothick unbalanced not only the batting order (they missed the impetus he can provide) but their collective mental state.

The two teams' lead-ins to the series were in stark contrast. Australia, without Test cricket since April, were able to plan their campaign free of injury and then treating the Champions Trophy as an exercise in mugging up on the art of winning. For England that competition was an encumbrance, coming as it did after international cricket virtually non-stop since the start of March. However, the notion of returning to England for a week following their expected early elimination was crass and, apparently, contrary to the wishes of Andrew Flintoff. The extra time in Australia might not have made a material difference to the outcome but at least it would have given the impression that everything which could be done was being done.

Whether Flintoff was the right man to lead the side is something that will be debated *ad nauseam*. He had enjoyed some success against India and was promised the job when he returned to fitness after his ankle operation. Andrew Strauss, meanwhile, had done a fine job as locum. Hindsight suggests Flintoff might have benefited from not having the extra responsibility while ultimate responsibility for team performance might have curbed some of Strauss' batting excesses. More pertinent, though, was the lukewarm relationship between captain and coach on the rest of the side. Fletcher, a pragmatic man-manager, has in his seven-year tenure forged strong bonds with both Nasser Hussain and Michael Vaughan, but, so it is said, found Flintoff less receptive. Friction causes heat: Fletcher would have had an easier time with Strauss.

Mistakes were made in selection, although once again the rationale was sound. Selecting Panesar from the outset would have been a statement of intent but the coaching staff felt it would have utterly exposed the lower order. The choice of Geraint Jones or Chris Read proved marginal: both kept wicket well; neither looked remotely capable of getting runs.

Of the bowlers Harmison got better as the series progressed, serving to illustrate the amount of hard work he needs to get him right for the start of a series, while Flintoff and Matthew Hoggard bowled manfully. But the key to the 2005 success had been that England possessed *four* pace bowlers, each at the top of his game and offering no respite.

Much of the criticism that has been heaped on Fletcher has been unwarranted. Memories are short. When he took over the side they were a laughing stock and he managed them to an Ashes success and a ranking as the world's second-best side. If there is culpability, then he, as the top man, has to accept it, but by no means is it all down to him. However, as with many jobs, there is a natural shelf-life, after which things begin to go stale, the message losing its freshness. Fletcher has been a brilliant England coach but now the time is right to move on.

England cricket fans must have thought that nothing could possibly top that whitewash for sheer humiliation and deflation, but somehow the 2013–14 series did. Unlike in 2006–7, England went to Australia in the winter of 2013 with a strut to their step, having won the previous three Ashes series. The subsequent devastation of their assumed superiority over Australia was made all the worse by the undesirable animosity that had developed between the two teams and stories of dressing-room fractures in the England camp. Andrew Miller delivers the obituary for Alastair Cook's team.

Come back Graham Gooch, Mike Atherton, Alec Stewart, Nasser Hussain and even Andrew Flintoff. The performance of Alastair Cook's men was so startlingly devoid of character that an apology is owed to all the previous leaders of the past 25 years, who have travelled to Australia and been battered by the better side. There is no disgrace in losing, it tends to be a fact of sport, but aside from Ben Stokes' century at Perth, there is simply no positive to pick out of the remnants of this whitewash. No token victory with the series surrendered, as was the case in 1994/95, 1998/99 and 2002/03, no gallant final tilt as Gooch and David Gower instigated before their fall-out in 1990/91.

The blame game [has] begun, with Andy Flower confirming his intention to stay on as coach while at the same time denying that he had issued Kevin Pietersen any 'ultimatum' about his future. We've been here before with KP and this particular leopard is not about to change his spots.

Buried in the rubble is England's captain, Cook. Not so long ago it was being suggested that his job had been made all the easier by the wealth of back-room support available to the modern-day Test captain. Instead he's been left for dead by Michael Clarke's pro-active approach, which in turn has been made possible by the back-room harmony that Darren Lehmann has managed to instil. When push came to sledge, Australia's mavericks, metrosexuals and fair-dinkum ockers, the same diverse group of individuals who had been in disarray before the first Ashes leg, were able to come together in a common and, dare one say it, anachronistic cause.

Three years earlier, England had been to Australia and completed one of their most memorable Ashes triumphs with a ruthlessly executed 3-1 win. Amid the plethora of cock-a-hoop letters received from exuberant and, admittedly, smug England fans was this one:

Ian Chappell, Jason Donovan, Kylie Minogue, Evonne Goolagong, Germaine Greer, Paul Hogan, Barry Humphries, Ned Kelly, Rod Laver, Madge Bishop, Rolf Harris – can you hear me? Rolf Harris? Your boys took one hell of a beating! – Austin Baird, Cramlington, Northumberland

For Mr Baird, as so many other England fans, the 2010–11 series represented the exorcism of many a ghost of Ashes series past, not least the 5-0 nightmare of four years previously. And so for Mr Baird, the 2013–14 whitewash, far from being a crushing disappointment, was a welcome return to the norm.

Ah lads. You're back. I've been worried. After following you for 40 years with debacle following debacle, I was starting to think that alien doppelgangers were making a concerted effort at world domination. But no. Thankfully the England we all know and love has returned. Good old England. I can handle failure. It's the hope I can't stand. – Austin Baird, Cramlington, Northumberland

We are not amused!

The Ashes is one of those sporting rivalries that transcends the game in which it is played. Given that cricket is the national sport of both England and Australia, and that the Ashes underpins this more than anything else for the two countries, it is not surprising that the rivalry holds an almost sacrosanct position in the psyche of all English and Australian people who love cricket. And so, it becomes far more than about winning and losing. Losing an Ashes series heavily will cause disappointment and dissection, but even that pales in comparison to the disapproving or disgusted impeachments from beyond the boundary provoked by anything that seems an affront to the revered status the Ashes holds. Cricket that is overly aggressive, cricket that is not aggressive enough, administrators intervening when it is not unwarranted, administrators not intervening when it is warranted – these are all proverbial red rags to any cricket lovers where the Ashes are at stake.

The most famous example, of course, being the Bodyline series. Beyond the well-known toing and froing of cables between the Australian Board of Control and the MCC, and everything else that came with it, the tactics of Douglas Jardine's triumphant side caused more discussion and debate than anything else that ever happened in a sporting arena ever had.

The Bodyline aftermath, in fact, marked the first time that a serious volume of letters from readers regarding international cricket found their way onto the pages of *The Cricketer*. Pre-1933, a very typical contribution to the Correspondence section read something like this:

Dear Sir, – I venture to suggest that Mr T Collins is the oldest cricket Blue. Born on January 31, 1841, he played for Cambridge in 1863. He resides at Newport, Shropshire.

Post-Bodyline, however, every other letter seemingly was from a reader wishing to make his own feelings clear about the events in Australia.

Dear Sir, – Has Jardine been given enough credit for the success of the MCC Tour in Australia? I think he has been marvellous. Has anyone stressed the fact that the methods of Larwood and Voce were well known to the committee who selected them, and that they were picked because of those successful methods. Was Jardine supposed to alter those methods, even if they are considered wrong, which is much open to question? – Yours, BH Hill

Dear Sir, – It was, of course, inevitable, that Bodyline bowling would be banned by Australia, but I am sure we were all much intrigued to see what suggestions the sub-committee would present to the Australia Cricket Board of Control. Their remedy appears to me to be quite impracticable. How can the poor umpire be expected to decide if a ball is bowled 'with the intent of intimidating the batsman or injuring him'? To rabbits such as myself I am perfectly certain that all fast bowling, English or Australian, is intimidating. – Yours Faithfully, DG Draper

Sir, – The addition to the Laws of Cricket proposed by the Australian Board of Control to stop 'Leg-Theory' or 'Body-Line Bowling,' as it is called in Australia, places quite a grave responsibility on the umpire, and, further, does not appear a practicable suggestion. How is the umpire in the space of a fraction of a second, to decide on the bowler's 'intent'? Here, it seems to me, lie the seeds of much trouble.

Imagine the tension and the feeling engendered, if Larwood or Wall were forbidden to bowl another ball during an innings of a Test match because they had been 'called' twice, the bowler stoutly maintaining the while – backed up by his comrades on the field – that he had no intention of intimidating or injuring the batsman! All sorts of suggestions and innuendoes would be bandied about, and before the next Test one or other of the captains would be insisting on the discarding of the umpire or umpires in question. 'Warfare' of the most bitter kind would undoubtedly ensue, and few indeed would care to undertake the responsibility of acting as umpire. – Yours Faithfully, '1882'

Sir, – '1882' in his letter published in the last issue misses the whole point in the Australian suggestion with regard to 'leg-theory.'

If the bowler is bowling at the batsman his general attitude while doing so will give him away. Again, if the bowler does hit the batsman and thereby achieves his aim, let the umpire see what he does. If he is the first to run to the opponent and help him recover or does he do what certain members of our Test team did – stand easy and look on? He will soon see.

No. '1882', there is one thing that will stop all bickering – *Cut it right out of cricket*. This can be done.

If we did win the last series of Tests, we gave our opponents a grand tribute to their prowess in bowling such disgusting stuff.

If this 'leg-theory' in Australia was anything like witnessed at Lord's the other day – Bravo Australia! – Yours Faithfully, BHJ Trendell

And so it continued, throughout the 1933 season, and reared its head again the following year, with the coming of Australia for the next Ashes series. Australia ultimately won the series 2-1 amid much ill feeling over the omission of Harold Larwood, on the grounds of his refusal to apologise for his actions in 1932–3. By now, the supporters for bodyline bowling had all but died out, but the Larwood affair poured fuel on the embers.

Dear Sir, – I am, I feel, quite unqualified to write about such an important and pressing situation as the present body-line controversy, but I cannot bear to hear Larwood criticised. He is, I think, the fastest, finest, and fairest bowler of recent years.

If the Australians cannot properly deal with leg-theory, then they are not the class of team to be over here playing, since their chief object at the moment seems to be in picking our team and threatening horrible threats if we should play such a dangerous bowler as Larwood. To that question, 'What about Gregory and MacDonald?' there comes no answer, and it seems a wonder to me that the MCC do not impress this awkward point on the Australians, for they can find no suitable reply and reason for making such a fuss about Larwood.

It is the job of the English public to see that Larwood does not return to lower class cricket, and to get him back to let us show Australia that we choose our own team and bowl as we like, and to whatever field we wish. – Yours truly, GWS Walker.

Whether it was Mr Walker's intention or not, he certainly succeeded in stirring the pot.

Dear Sir, – Mr Walker has candidly stated that he is quite unqualified to write about the leg-theory controversy; this statement appears to be the only one in his letter that he has made any attempt to prove.

The various points he raises have been dealt with *ad nauseam*; including the obvious distinction between MacDonald and Gregory bowling to an orthodox field and Larwood bowling outside the leg stump with seven or eight fieldsmen on the on-side of the wicket.

Now that the vast proportion of cricketers have convinced themselves that fast leg-theory (with a packed field) is not in the best interests of the game, it can serve no useful purpose to resurrect the old arguments for and against it. As things stand, I don't suppose Mr Walker would like to see the English selectors grovelling before Larwood in an endeavour to persuade him to change his mind. He has had the effrontery to refuse to play unless he is allowed to usurp the functions of the captain and is given a free hand in deciding how he is to bowl and where he is to place his field. Unless and until he adopts a more reasonable attitude, there is obviously nothing more to be done about it. – Yours truly, 'Fairplay'.

Dear Sir, – I wish to congratulate Mr Walker on his very outspoken letter. I consider he sums up the whole situation very well.

There is no doubt that Jardine and Larwood have been let down very badly. Larwood is at present being criticised not only for his bowling (which is, and always has been perfectly fair) but for sticking up for himself and speaking his mind on the very unsatisfactory situation.

There seems to be no doubt that it is better to lose the Test matches than do anything the Australians do not like. After all, the Test matches at present being played are rather a farce, as we have a perfectly fair way of getting the Australians out and yet we do not use it simply because the Australians are unable as yet to cope with it. We have the finest captain England or any other country have had since the War and yet we do not play him. We have the finest fast bowler the world has ever known who is criticised so much by his own countrymen that he refuses to play, and no wonder.

How the Australians must laugh at our foolishness. The two bowlers who played in the third Test match, it might interest your readers to notice, are not even in the averages, and one of them bowled eight no-balls and three wides in a very short time on the second day. I wonder what would have been said had Larwood been guilty of this.

The crux of the whole matter is that Larwood is far too good for the majority of present-day batsmen, who are unable to stand up to his very accurate fast bowling, and so he must go, and some would stand idly by and see this injustice done, and let English cricket lose the finest, fairest fast bowler she has ever had. – Yours truly, John P Cheesebrough.

A lesser-known legacy of Bodyline, surely: that it inspired, in Mr Walker's controversial comments, what may well be one of the earliest known examples of trolling!

★

The 1960s, contrary to being the personification of freedom and revolution across so many fields of popular culture, were, in a cricketing sense, comatose. Of the 25 Ashes Tests played throughout the decade, 15 of them ended in draws. Many pieces featured in *The Cricketer* from this period have an undercurrent of misery running through them, reflective of the dreary, sophomoric cricket on display.

The 1961 series did at least produce a charismatic display from Australia under Richie Benaud's adventurous captaincy. It is simply a pity that it did not inspire England to raise their game any, as Bill Bowes describes:

Benaud was the tactician and at all times a driving force. He seldom indulged the 'umbrella' field placing and always made runs difficult to get. He brought menace and pressure to bear on the timid batsmen by going himself to field in the suicide position at short-leg or silly-point only a yard or so from the bats. He gave maximum effort himself, forced himself to bowl against doctor's orders, and set an example he expected every man in the side to follow.

Tactically, the batting approach of the Australians is very different from that of England. They never believe in getting bogged down at both ends. No matter how dogged and dour be the efforts of one batsman at the crease the other is always looking for runs.

This intention never to have both batsmen on the defensive can go awry. In the third Test at Leeds when Trueman cut down his pace and with fast-medium off-cutters captured 6 wickets for 30 runs, it would have been better had both batsmen concentrated on defence instead of making strokes ... But, in broad principle, Australia's method of 'keeping going at one end' is much to be preferred to England's. Many times the Australians hit themselves out of trouble.

It seems that our England batsmen are frightened of getting out. Even when comfortably established at the crease they are reluctant to play strokes, and the loss of a couple of quick wickets invariably means the end of all our entertainment for an hour.

This cautious approach, this lack of adventure, on the part of England batsmen has been a concern of the legislators for a long time ... The county selectors were asked to be generous towards any batsman who, trying to produce strokes, ran into a sequence of failures. Essentially, however, the final move must come from the players themselves. Batting, bowling or fielding the Australians showed a greater zest and enthusiasm for scoring or saving runs. They were better to watch, and with little to choose between the two sides in individual ability, these factors merited the Australian victory.

It would not continue unfortunately, as, if anything, England managed to drag Australia down to their level. As holders of the Ashes, Australia were often content to play out draws, while England proved completely incapable of forcing any initiative home. The following two series produced only three results across the 10 combined Tests. Ray Robinson, while, as an Australian, no doubt happy about his countrymen's safe retention of the Ashes in 1962–3, was not impressed with the display from either team, and called for swift action:

If good really can come out of evil, Test cricket could benefit from the stalemate series which ended here with half the paying customers hooting the last two batsmen off the field.

When two such captains as Richie Benaud and Ted Dexter – protagonists of lively cricket – find it beyond them to make a Test match look like a cricket match it is high time that the game's controllers rooted out the causes of tactics that led to the slow-clapping and booing.

A dead wicket discouraged driving, a patchy centre took pace off strokes and only half the slow outfield was cut daily. This helped Australia's fieldsmen to seem almost impenetrable.

Tactical clockwork is in need of a brisk winding-up when the first 23 hours of a Test are dawdled away before an attempt to win is crowded into part of the last seven hours.

This is the first time since the 30-hour time-limit began in Australia 16 years ago that three out of five Tests have been unfinished. In my view, the onus is squarely on the game's controllers to correct a state of affairs that is losing cricket friends by the drove.

Things got worse before they got better, however. The 1964 series took cricket's excitement value to untold lows, with four draws, the nadir being a 650-plays-600 struggle in five sunny days in Manchester, as the limitations of the bowling attacks on both sides came to a head. Jack Fingleton summed up:

Nobody seemed very happy about the fourth Test at Old Trafford. The spectators grumbled, and with justification … all in all, it was a pretty unhappy affair.

When one considers the standard of bowling of both sides, this pitch was much too good for a decision. George Duckworth told me that it was typical of Old Trafford pitches in the Twenties but that the weather then was allowed to obtrude because covers were not used. That might be the answer to a lot of things. I must say that, so far, I have not been impressed by the attempts to take grass from the pitch. It seems to have left the Test pitches I have seen pretty lifeless.

It was an unhappy Test, one almost best forgotten.

Needless to say, the readers were not amused either.

Sir, Much has been written about the Manchester Test. The match has provided the brighter-cricket boys with a fresh supply of acid, and in the course of their bitter attacks they have managed to malign batsmen, pitches, groundsmen, selectors, and administrators. The strange thing is that the villains of the piece – the bowlers – have slipped out through the back door unscathed.

It may be a little callous to knife those who laboured tenaciously in heart-breaking conditions, but there is no room for sentiment, and it is time we realised that in Test cricket, tenacity alone is not enough. This is not written as a personal attack but for the purpose of argument I wish to cite the bowling of Titmus and Cartwright. From Titmus, there was over upon over of gentle off-cut, and from Cartwright, over upon over of gentle in-swing. True, they were accurate, very accurate; and true, there was a certain amount of variation: but it was all so predictable – even the variation.

Any sequence of activity that occurs on a cricket field originates from the bowler's hand. As the bowler approaches the wicket, ball in hand, he is master of the field, for it is in his delivery that dictates all subsequent action that occurs prior to the next ball being bowled. He is the man with the initiative: in the interests of his own performance, and, more important, the balance of the game, it is an initiative he must not abuse.

And yet, it is an initiative that more and more bowlers do abuse. The aim of the present-day bowler, it seems, is to get the ball back before too much befalls, and subsequently, the maiden over is fast becoming the principal object of the exercise. Attrition – that is the thing.

The Manchester Test signalled not a triumph for Australia but a defeat for contemporary bowling. We have tampered with wickets and meddled with Laws, and all to little avail. It must now be abundantly clear that only a revision of bowling techniques will restore aggression to the game. – David W Hills, Woodford Green, Essex

A more balanced view was to be found, however, courtesy of Richie Benaud, writing regularly for *The Cricketer* at this time, who, from his vantage point of a recently retired player, was rather more sympathetic to the plight of the two teams.

A dull year – poor cricket – no interest in the county games and the Test matches even worse – this is the sort of thing I have been hearing from people following the conclusion of the final Test at The Oval.

I began to think perhaps I had been watching cricket in a different country for *most* of the cricket I saw during the season was interesting and even at times wonderfully exciting.

Others have mentioned during the year that I seem a bit cynical about aspects of play on the field and some writing off it and if this is true then in the main it is because I have had a taste of both and I hope am able to appreciate the game even more because of this. Perhaps this is why I cannot agree with those who knock this year of cricket in England … it wasn't always easy to sit in the press box or grandstand and watch cricket six days a week but I am happy to say that generally speaking I really enjoyed watching Simpson's side and Dexter's England side.

It was not a good series of Test matches simply because the captains were unable to control the weather and three of the five games were washed out.

For England the bright spot of the year was Boycott. His determination and application are clearly visible but I was amused to read that the Australians are responsible for his developing a hunger for runs. The theme of this piece was that Boycott after Manchester was determined that when he got the chance to make runs against Australia he would never throw his innings away. Perhaps I am a trifle cynical but I must confess to having had a good chuckle at this one.

The next two series both produced 1-1 draws, closing out the miserable decade, but, thankfully, help was on the way. Both teams were about to experience a serious upturn in the calibre of their bowling attacks, and with them came a nastier, more aggressive brand of cricket that would dominate the following decade and bring the supporters flooding back. But it still would not be to everyone's liking.

★

The 1970s were dominated by two things – pugnacious fast bowling and seismic controversy, the two usually proving symptomatic of one another. Beginning in 1970–71, the Ashes and Test cricket at large experienced a golden era, as both countries produced teams full of charismatic cricketers who captured the public's imagination as few had since the immediate post-war years. John Snow had bumped and bounced his way to 31 wickets in 1970–71, not making any friends while doing it – as if he cared – before Dennis Lillee announced himself in 1972 with 31 of his own in England. By 1974–5, Lillee had overcome a career-threatening back injury to spearhead Australia's charge. He was joined by one Jeff Thomson – a hurricane of a fast bowler with a lethal slingshot action who got fit for the series by hunting wild pigs in the bush with his bare hands. Between them, they regained the Ashes, with a bruising 4-1 win, and captured the Australian public's imagination as no two fast bowlers had since Lindwall and Miller.

Nonetheless, this new brand of shoulders-back-chest-out cricket was not for everyone, not least some of the more establishment-type figures in the journalistic fraternity, such as EW Swanton, then *The Cricketer*'s editorial director, who commented on the many volatile incidents during this period with a haughty frown. Here are his thoughts on the first Test of the 1974–5 series.

Jeff Thomson will not sweep through the series picking up nine wickets a time but equally I doubt whether his performance will turn out to be a mere flash in the pan. He is lusty and well-built and obviously has the mechanics for the job. It remains to see how he will react to hard work on plumb pitches when he is not encouraged by the abnormal lift that was to be had from one end throughout the match.

While on the subject of fast bowling, which seems likely to dominate this series if only because neither side is fully equipped with much else, I trust that the Australian Board will react firmly whether in public or private to the words both written and spoken over the air by Dennis Lillee. Lillee in his book *Back to the Mark* makes the astonishing admission that 'I bowl bouncers for one reason and that is to hit the batsman and thus intimidate him'... the slim hopes of his having been misquoted were dispelled when during the Brisbane Test he blithely admitted on TV that he bowled to hit.

Thomson incidentally has been reported in literally blood-thirsty terms before the season started but there is evidence that he may have been misreported. He gave a more civilised impression when interviewed immediately after the first Test. I will say no more now except echo the pleas of Jack Fingleton to call a halt to bumper tactics. He refers, of course, to both teams. Was not Snow warned in three Tests out of six in Australia four years ago? Bill O'Reilly expressed similar sentiments. I have often noticed that it is those both in the press box and outside who have scarcely been in the middle themselves who relish and egg on those who 'hit the batsman and thus intimidate him'.

Passions are always excited when real speed becomes a factor. At this point I cannot say I am exactly happy but at least it provokes confidence both that the first Test umpires, Tom Brooks and Robin Bailache, seem to wear their authority firmly and wisely, and also, most importantly, that there are two strong and sensible fellows in ultimate control of the two camps, Tim Caldwell, who succeeded Sir Donald Bradman as chairman of selectors of the Australian Cricket Board, and Alec Bedser.

Another prominent voice was that of *The Cricketer*'s editor David Frith. Frith sensed that there was a line in the sand, which some of the players were not above stepping over.

The Greig–Lillee clashes have been a kind of cricket parallel to the Ali–Foreman mini-pantomimes without the sense of spoof that would have taken some of the heat out of them. Greig signalling his own boundaries was genuinely funny until one examined the cost. It was, of course, high provocation, a red rag. The bull can't be blamed for charging at it.

The foul language from several players, the glares, the waving of arms, the pointing towards the dressing room. This is not entertainment. It is the petulance of the immature, and nothing more can be said of it than that in this turbulent age it merely makes a change from abrasions of a racial, political, or a religious kind.

Many of the readers similarly disapproved.

Sir, – Mr Lillee recently made it clear that he intends to direct his bowling at the bodies of batsmen. Mr Thomson now informs us that Mr Cowdrey 'is going to cop it as quick as anyone'. Clearly this duo are no respecters of persons – it is too much to hope they will show some respect for the game they are fortunate enough to play at the highest level – at the moment?

I have never subscribed to the view that the bumper was the legitimate ploy of any fast bowler. Nothing has happened to make me change that view; clearly the Australians believe that there is no substitute for skill other than violence and intimidatory (and possibly questionable) bowling actions.

We are well aware of the apparent natural aggressiveness of the average Australian and his forthright manner of speech, bordering frequently upon rudeness, but if they do not wish to bring the game into disrepute they really will have to exercise more self-control and grow up! – WM Sutton, Blackburn, Lancs

Sir, – The evidence from Australia suggests that recent criticisms of conduct on the field are far from a 'blimpish' reaction.

One of the major figures involved is Tony Greig. Come reports from Australia of his pointing a dismissed batsman to the pavilion and making a most unnecessary reaction to Lillee after he was hit by fast bowling. This is not the behaviour expected of a county captain and a previous MCC vice-captain.

Only a few years ago, John Snow, then England's leading bowler, was dropped for disciplinary reasons relating to on-the-field conduct. The authorities must take similarly strong measures to combat this growing incivility. It is becoming difficult to tell the difference in our modern cricketer between 'gamesmanship' and mere 'bad sportsmanship'. – Peter E Hodgkinson, Durham City

A case for the defence must be heard, though, and later that year, as the 1975 series was wrapping itself up, Ian Chappell, in his own inimitable fashion, made one – by collaring an unsuspecting David Frith who had had the nerve to step into the Aussie dressing room to offer them his best.

'What's all this garbage you've been writing about us, Dave?' Ian Chappell challenged me when I called in during the Oval Test.

Ian was referring to something I wrote in the September *Cricketer*: that his team had not been 'the sweetest opponents' in recent years.

'Out there,' he said, pointing to the middle, 'is no place to be amicable.'

Point taken – up to a point.

There seems to have developed during the Seventies a conviction – in many walks of life – that courtesy is alien to masculinity; ergo, those jealous of their manliness need to be impassive except when 'needling' opponents.

Lately there have been illustrations of this from almost every cricketing country in the world and, while it might – just *might* – be allowable at international level, since this is a branch of show business, it will, and indeed has, spread to other areas.

I learned last week that there were frequent instances of verbal abuse in the middle during Surrey Clubs Championship matches last season.

If these fellows had possessed reasonable self-control all their lives, why has their behaviour changed now?

Are they apeing their betters?

Surely the field of *club* cricket *is* a place to be amicable?

An Australia v West Indies series is coming up, and the six Test matches between two strong and very attractive teams should provide much to interest a vast worldwide following.

Yet perhaps the most fervid hope should be for the series to be played in the play-induced climate of chivalry as was that memorable contest 15 years ago in Australia by Benaud and Worrell in the sides they led.

The numerous newcomers to Australia's cricket grounds last year deserve to see something less one-sided than the Tests of 1974/75 and they deserve to experience international cricket of high quality and free of petulance and childish 'niggles'.

If they see this kind of cricket I promise – no 'garbage'!

The glory

For all the pain and disappointment that accompanies a mal-functioning Ashes campaign, by the same token moments of glory bring joy, pleasure and exuberance like little else can in sport. Essentially, when things go well, they go very, very well.

In 1926, it had been 14 years since England had won an Ashes series, and, given that four of those were the years of the First World War, it probably felt a lot longer than that. And, boy, had England had a miserable time of it in the immediate post-war series, losing the first eight Test matches spanning two series, before managing a couple of draws. England showed improvement in 1924–5 but still ended up leaving Australia with a 4-1 defeat. So to 1926, where England and Australia met at The Oval after a combination of rain and three-day Test matches meant the first four matches were all drawn. England's gradual post-war recovery was about to be affirmed in a mem-orable encounter that would set the standard for the excitement and delight of Ashes finales in south London. Writing about the match 42 years later for *The Cricketer*, Sir Neville Cardus recalled the events as clearly as if they had been played the week before.

Between 1920 and 1926, England won a solitary Test and Australia won 12; this during a period in which we could put into the field cricketers as splendid as Hobbs, Woolley, Hendren, JWHT Douglas (nobody today is as dangerous with a new ball as 'Johnny' was); Hearne, Tate, Sutcliffe, AER Gilligan, Kilner. At last, in 1926, came sweet revenge and unforgettable achievement, all taking place at The Kennington Oval. The first four Tests of this 1926 rubber were drawn or rained off, and the fifth encounter was arranged to be fought to a finish.

England batted first, reaching 280. Australia retaliated with 302. On a mellowing Monday evening of August 16, Hobbs and Sutcliffe opened England's second innings. We all imagined that this innings would be Hobbs' last for England. He was in his 44th year. As I recall the scene, I am still touched the Australians applauded the Master as he came to the wicket. The entire crowd, the packed Oval, stood up, in veneration. The westering sun graced the scene, rendering it one to cherish in the picture-gallery of memory.

In the afternoon's declining hour England – Hobbs and Sutcliffe – scored 49 without loss. But during the midnight and subsequent hours, a terrific thunderstorm occurred in London. Next morning a soaked wicket, drying rapidly under a scorching sun. Wickets became deadly in those seasons. As the crowd gathered on the Tuesday morning, I stood near The Oval pavilion entrance, and Herbert Sutcliffe arrived. 'A bad look out, Herbert,' I said. He gave me a blank expression. 'Why,' he responded, 'I don't follow?' 'Well,' I said, 'the thunderstorm. There'll be a hell of a wicket.' 'I didn't hear any thunderstorm,' said Herbert, 'I'm a sound sleeper. But don't worry. Everything will be all right – *if Jack doesn't get out.*'

Well, Jack didn't get out. He and Sutcliffe both made hundreds in England's second innings of 436 (extras had the third highest score with 37) before England stormed home, bowling Australia out for 125, thanks mainly to Harold Larwood, playing in his second Test, and Wilfred Rhodes, of apocryphal 'We'll get 'em in singles' fame from 1902, who had been recalled only two months shy of his 50th birthday. Plum Warner, often so reserved in his writing, could hardly contain his elation at the victory.

At five minutes past six on the evening of Wednesday August 18, at Kennington Oval, Geary bowled down Mailey's wicket, and after many long years of waiting and disappointment English cricket came into its own again.

As soon as it was realised that England had won the vast crowd gave a yell of delight and swarmed in front of the pavilion, a huge mass which extended right back to the pitch itself. There they stayed for half an hour, shouting themselves hoarse.

The crowd unmistakeably interpreted what all those who take an interest in English cricket and who are concerned for its welfare feel, and that is that the tide of misfortunate had turned at last, and the turn of the tide is welcomed with fervent enthusiasm.

This victory means everything for English cricket. Had we been beaten, despondency would have crept over the land. As it is, our cricket will be fortified and refreshed by this great victory.

To Chapman all England will offer her warmest congratulations. He is the happy warrior of the cricket field, and he led his side with spirit, with judgement, and with imagination.

The youngest member of the side, Larwood, of Notts, took six wickets in the match for 116 runs, and fielded well. He should have a big future before him, but he must guard against bowling just short of a length. The bowling, fielding, and wicket-keeping was of a high class, and we won on our merits.

August 18, 1926, was a great day for English cricket – a landmark, I venture to think, in our cricket history, and if I may be allowed to say so, it brought joy to my heart.

I believed in our men, and my confidence in their ability to defeat a powerful and generous foe has never wavered. Therefore, 'I die happy,' I had my whole soul and heart on our beating the Australians this year, and our success has been made a thousand times more pleasant by the perfectly charming way in which our doughty opponents took their defeat.

Maybe I have waxed sentimental, but there can be no good cricket without sentiment, a quality which enriches life and refines it and gives it zest.

★

Parallels between England's Ashes fortunes after the two world wars are certainly interesting. In both cases they went winless in the first two series, recovered somewhat in the third to at least score a heartening victory when the series were already lost, before triumphantly regaining the Ashes in the following series with a win at The Oval after four draws. *The Cricketer*'s resident statistician, Roy Webber, took note of this prior to the fifth Test in 1953, using it as a sign that victory surely awaited England at The Oval. He even pointed out that England's consolation victories in 1924–5 and 1950–1 both came at Melbourne, and that, among the draws in both 1926 and 1953, the Lord's Test was the only one to be played through without weather interruptions. Thankfully for English cricket, Webber's proclamation proved well-founded, as, once again, England scampered home to victory at The Oval. Instead of the dominance in the middle of Hobbs and Sutcliffe, it was the spinning combo of Laker and Lock that proved the difference, and instead of Plum Warner exuberantly celebrating the victory in *The Cricketer*, it was Bill Bowes doing the honours.

The afternoon session saw Hassett and Morris set about the England bowling to the tune of 19 runs in as many minutes. Eight runs came from Bedser's first over. Trueman, with a shot sounding like the crack of a revolver, was pulled for four by Morris, who then slashed Bedser square with a similar powerful stroke.

Visions of a tremendous Australian score forced themselves into the mind but Hutton, even though Trueman had just bowled a maiden over, and the ball was still new, brought on the off-spinner Laker for the fast bowler.

With only another four runs added to the score Laker had Hassett lbw and then Bedser, too, after bowling only three overs, was taken off for Lock.

Taking runs with the well-placed single and the occasional boundary, Morris and Hole had 50 runs on the board in 55 minutes. Other than an odd delivery beating the batsman there was still nothing untoward. Hutton persisted in his spin attack.

It was at 59 when the real fun began, with Hole lbw to Laker.

The left-handed Harvey, a player calculated to pulverise a slow spin attack, came to the crease. He took a quick single from Laker, but playing forward to the first ball he received from Lock, missed, and was bowled. Three down for 60.

Miller played the rest of the over, ran a single for Morris, and then, completely at sea against Laker, pushed a catch to Trueman in the leg trap.

The two Surrey spin bowlers, Laker and Lock, were in rare fettle. They fairly danced with delight at each success, and above all, they were brimful of confidence and spinning the ball vigorously.

Morris, forced into defence, stuttered across his stumps and was lbw to Lock. From a scoreboard showing one wicket down for 59 it now showed five down for 61. The Oval crowd were yelling themselves hoarse. It was rare stuff.

To my delight I noted that both Laker and Lock had decided to bowl to a definite theory instead of to a general field placing. Laker bowled leg-theory with only three men on the off-side, Lock bowled off theory with only three fieldsmen on the leg. This tightening up brought results.

Australia's last four wickets fell for only 31 runs and England were in the splendid position of needing only 132 for victory. The Ashes were England's for the taking.

The last morning of the match, in spite of the fact that three hours of play would be certain to see a decision one way or another, brought another splendid crowd. It was a morning of splendid sunshine too.

Johnston bowled beautifully, that is, so far as length, direction, and variations in pace were concerned, but only occasionally did he manage to spin one and make it bite. May made one lucky slash which sent the ball over the top of slips for a four. On another occasion he edged between the wicket-keeper and Miller at first slip for four more, and one he edged through the slips for a two.

They were the only blemishes in batsmanship which was equal to every call. Neither man was worried at playing the maiden over. When the opportunity to hit came along both did so. May made some excellent strokes to the covers, hitting with the force of a battering-ram; and Edrich, on an occasion when Lindwall departed from his role of negative attack so much as to bowl a couple of bouncers, cracked each one of them decisively to the boundary.

The score was taken to 88 before Australia had a success. Bowling to a leg-theory field placing, Miller made May snick a catch to Davidson at leg slip. May had scored 37 valuable runs. Compton came out to join his Middlesex captain with 44 runs wanted to win.

Not until England were within nine runs of victory and still eight wickets to fall did Hassett give in. He bowled an over himself, which realised four runs. Morris bowled at the other end, where Compton finally took four to square leg to bring England the victory. What a yell went up. England had won the Ashes for the first time in 19 years. Thousands of spectators flocked across the pitch to take up position outside the dressing-rooms and there they chanted 'We want Len.'

★

What was surely one of the most spectacular occasions in the long history of cricket matches between England and Australia in fact came when the Ashes were not even at stake. The two teams met at the MCG in May 1977 to commemorate 100 years of Test cricket, and what a party it was.

The Centenary Test would have been a momentous occasion even if a ball had never been bowled. A five-day festival in the Melbourne sun celebrating 100 years of rivalry with more than double that number's worth of former Test cricketers in attendance. That a game of cricket was also thrown in and that it turned out to be an absolute doozy was a bonus, as David Frith reported.

With the impressive opening ceremony over, Greg Chappell spun the specially-minted gold medallion and Greig called correctly. Australia were told to bat, and the exuberant crowd of 61,316 watched stunned, as Australia were bowled out soon after tea. Some of the strokes suggested nervousness and some incompetence against the fast, short ball. Davis went first, and soon McCosker left, having played on after hooking Willis into his jaw.

Australia were rotting away at 45 for 4, and when Walters was caught off the top edge trying to hook, it was 51 for 5, with only the allrounders to support Chappell. The Australian captain was playing one of his tightest grimmest innings: indeed, during his four hours at the crease he hit no boundary. At lunch, with only 16 overs bowled, Australia were 57 for 5.

Marsh drove Old for two fours to start the afternoon, and he and his captain doubled the score before the fifth wicket fell, when the vice-captain was dazzlingly caught by Knott off the inside-edge. It was the first of three inspired catches. The disappointing Gilmour was taken by Greig at slip, full-stretch, and O'Keefe saw a flying Brearley hold an edge with the fingertips of his left hand. Underwood, immaculate in length and direction, then induced Chappell to swing wildly, and the clatter of stumps marked his 250th wicket in Test cricket. Walker fell 15 minutes later and it was all over. Woolmer was lost that evening, but Underwood filled the breach cumbersomely yet safely to help England to 29 for 1.

Within 25 overs England were out. Lillee was the chief executioner, earning 6 for 26 with ferocity and flair – his best Test figures. He owed no more to the pitch than to the waves of encouragement which roared across from the thousands of beer-filled 'ockers' in the Southern Stand. The jittery batting may have had something to do with the rareness of the occasion.

There were fears that the game wouldn't live to see the players' reception with the Queen at tea time on the final day. Doug Walters proclaimed: 'We'll be fishing by 2.30 Day Three!' A big Australian total and then an extraordinary performance from Derek Randall for England ensured the contest went right to the wire.

Australia were reassured by contrasting but high-quality innings by the youngsters Davis and Hookes, and Marsh then became the first wicketkeeper to make a century for Australia against England. That might have been the end of the excitement, with England expected to exceed their dismal first innings but not to come anywhere within sight of their target of 463. Now, though, it was the turn of a young English batsman to set the cricket world abuzz. Randall, just 26, from Nottingham, not only became the 14th England batsman to record a hundred on debut against Australia but he brought gusts of fun and animation as well as vibrant strokeplay into the game.

The morning session [of the final day] had seen Randall to his hundred, reached off Lillee's bowling; within minutes the bowler had hit him on the skull and caught the rebound. Then when the new ball was taken Lillee thought Marsh had caught Randall, who pointed to his shoulder. Words were exchanged. The batsman managed to carry on grinning. When he fell out of the way of another bouncer he did a backward roll and shot to his feet again. It was one of the most stirring and lengthy personal duels in the 225-match history of these Tests, and everyone loved it.

Randall's 174 was not quite enough. After Lillee took the final wicket of Knott to seal the match in Australia's favour, it was several minutes before anyone realised that the margin of victory of 45 runs was exactly the same as it had been 100 years previously. The result barely even mattered. To paraphrase Frith, 'It was that kind of match.'

As perfect an occasion as the Centenary Test was, it makes for almost sentimental value when remembered now with the knowledge that there was a storm brewing behind the scenes that would shake cricket to its core unlike anything that had ever been witnessed or even imagined, as Frith recalled 40 years later:

> Over the five days' play just on a quarter of a million people had come through the turnstiles, none of them aware that beneath the jubilant proceedings an amazing plot was secretly developing. Players were signing up for big money to play what seemed a preposterous series of matches to be known as SuperTests. Television coverage would be beamed on the commercial network owned by someone largely unrecognised: Kerry Packer.
>
> The age of innocence was about to end. The Money Age was upon us. A mellow and poignant light hung over the glorious festival Test match.

★

The 2005 Ashes series rightly holds an unparalleled place in Test cricket history. In terms of non-stop entertainment, universal contemporary fascination, and long-term impact on the game at large, 2005 was a joy. It was like living in some kind of dream world for two months, as readers' gooey-eyed letters to *The Cricketer* testify.

Thank you Freddie Flintoff for your performance in the Edgbaston Test. Anyone who was lucky enough to watch it will never forget it. It was the best all-round sporting performance I have witnessed. His batting and bowling were incredible and swung the match. To me though, his conduct stood above everything else. His bravery batting on after hurting his shoulder was awe-inspiring and his approach to Brett Lee after the victory left a lump in the throat. – Jon Berridge, by email

I have just returned from an unforgettable Ashes supporters' tour, where I was privileged to be at every day of the Lord's, Edgbaston and Old Trafford Tests. Obviously the cricket was exceptional with mind-blowing tension but I will never forget the genuine good-natured bantering and support for each side and the expressions of goodwill offered to us as visitors to the wonderful country of England. Huge thanks to the players and umpires who performed so admirably under enormous pressure; surely the image of Freddie Flintoff consoling Brett Lee must go down as one of the all-time great sporting images – of any sport let alone cricket. – Greg Morrissey, Parkes, NSW, Australia

Ian Botham ignited my interest in cricket 24 years ago, when I was 14, by putting the Australians to the sword. It has continued to burn ever since. I hope there are kids all over the country, who have watched Freddie and the rest of the great England team, inspired to embrace this wonderful game. The Ashes has demonstrated the best sportsmanship throughout the gripping summer. Forget displays of Wayne Rooney petulance. England proved that talent does not have to come with a disturbing level of aggression. – Matt Broad, Weymouth, Dorset

Watching Michael Vaughan lift the Ashes after 16 long years – wonderful. Watching thousands of people celebrate victory in Trafalgar Square – even better. Watching 12 children playing cricket in my local park – football goalposts redundant – best of all! – John Gordon, Bideford, Devon

As evident as it was at the time what a special event the 2005 Ashes was, its stature would only grow the further away from it we moved. Recalling the series eight years later, Andrew Miller examined just why it mattered so much.

On Sunday, August 7 2005, in a parallel galaxy not so far away, English cricket died a painful, public death in the corner of a Birmingham field. England, powered by the brilliant Freddie Flintoff, had grappled their way to a winning position only for their fingers to be prised from the prize, one defiant run after another, by Australia's redoubtable tail.

With three runs left to defend, a lifter from Steve Harmison caught the glove through to Geraint Jones but Michael Kasprowicz, sensing that all was not right, turned to the third umpire for a review. After much deliberation Channel 4's zoom lens made it clear. At the crucial moment of impact, the offending hand had already loosened its grip on the bat.

Umpire Billy Bowden crossed his arms on his chest to overturn his decision and one ball later, a crestfallen Harmison fired a wild leg-side delivery past the despairing Jones for four byes. Australia had triumphed by one wicket in a match unanimously pronounced as the most devastating defeat in English history.

Punch drunk and defenceless, England barely competed for the rest of the summer. Little more than a month later, Ricky Ponting's men completed only the second whitewash in Ashes history with a crushing victory at The Oval.

In a mournful edition of *Wisden Cricketers' Almanack*, the editor, Matthew Engel, lamented England's missed opportunity before he restated his very grave fear for the future of the country's summer game.

'Let's not go through all this again because it really is too awful,' he wrote. '[From this summer onwards] English cricket will be shown live only on Sky Sports ... live cricket has now disappeared from the screens of more than half the homes in the country ... the damage will be incalculable.'

The greatest legacy of the greatest series of all time is that nothing so apocalyptic came to pass. But it was a desperately close-run thing. It is easy to assume now that the Ashes has never been challenged as Test cricket's most alluring peak. However, such assumptions had been far from obvious in the 18 years leading up to that seismic summer.

In 43 Ashes Tests since 1989 Australia had won 28 to England's seven, a ratio entirely in keeping with the 4-1 score-line that typified the era. Of those seven wins, six had come with the Ashes already out of reach and Australia, restless for new challenges, had long since allowed their eyes to stray to the horizon. Or more specifically to India, a country where Australia had not won a series since 1969–70 and which Steve Waugh christened 'The Final Frontier'.

In March 2001, shortly before another of those 4-1 Ashes squibs, Australia and India had contested arguably the greatest three-match Test series of all time, a contest transformed by VVS Laxman's epic 281 at Kolkata. A dramatic shared series down under was the prelude to Australia's return visit in October 2004. This time they triumphed 2-1.

In the early years of the 2000s India–Australia was Test cricket's new Blue Riband rivalry, fuelled by the excellence of the contests and underpinned by India's fiscal dominance that

Cricket Australia has not been shy in courting. Not for the last time in the decade, English cricket was playing gooseberry to the game's new power-brokers.

No pressure then, as Michael Vaughan's team arrived at Lord's on July 21 tasked with reigniting passions in the sport's most ancient rivalry. The players were undeniably ready. They had picked up seven wins on the bounce in the summer of 2004 ahead of a thrilling 2-1 victory in South Africa. But unseen amid the hype was the frailty in England's team that would become abundantly clear in the subsequent 18 months. The physical breakdowns of Michael Vaughan and Simon Jones, the mental traumas that beset Marcus Trescothick and Steve Harmison; all of these were held in check, just, but the warning signs were everywhere.

All of England's players were in a single 11-man basket and the handle was coming loose before our eyes. That, of course, made the desperate brilliance of their campaign all the more riveting. Such tangible human drama was the hook, the line and the sinker for a captivated British public.

By the summer's end all such existential angst could go hang. The 10,000 fans who packed into Trafalgar Square were not there to dwell on any averted disaster. The only thing which mattered was the spectacle to which they had been treated.

The Ashes had provided English cricket with the ultimate redundancy package: enough goodwill, exposure and income to see the sport through the shock of severance from terrestrial TV, plus the mother of all leaving dos to send it on its way.

The hurricane of goodwill had knock-on effects elsewhere in cricket's community. In May 2005, the charity Chance to Shine was launched in east London, seeking to arrest cricket's decline in state schools – a problem that the elitism of the Sky deal was never designed to tackle. The project may well have succeeded in its own right – it certainly deserved to – but the winds of 2005 enabled it to soar.

Miracles require no context to be glorious. In its hour of need cricket's prayers were answered. Nothing can ever detract from the glory.

★

While not on the same level as that of a decade earlier – nothing is – England's victory in 2015 was a heartening and at times euphoric revenge mission for Alastair Cook's side after the brutal whitewash of 2013–14. The third series in the space of two years – an indictment of the increased burden the Ashes must shoulder to generate much-needed interest and revenue for Test cricket – was in no way short of excitement, and brought as much interest as could possibly be expected to an English public, when one remembers that, on an average day, barely half a million watched the action live. Simon Hughes sums up why, in 2015, the Ashes continues to matter as much as it ever did.

Six millimetres of grass. Half a fingernail. That's what it took for England to regain the Ashes and save 25 people their jobs. That is how fine the margins are in the business of cricket and in sport generally. People support a winning team and castigate one that is losing. The viewing figures for Channel 5's Test match highlights exceeded 2m during the Trent Bridge Test. Unprecedented. Sponsors and advertisers are delighted. Yet when England are poor, viewers switch off in droves and the airwaves turn blue. It is very black and white.

Failure, especially in the Ashes, stirs up acrimony, navel

gazing and a hunt for scapegoats. People – captains, players, coaches, trainers, even analysts – are sacked. Managers resign and sponsors assess their impact and reconsider their support. Working parties are set up to consider what is wrong at all levels. The conclusion, invariably, is to invest in 'the grassroots'.

And that is exactly what England did. In this case, literally. The groundsmen let the grass grow. Not to meadow levels, but enough to give the locally bred seam and swing bowlers something to work with. Is tailoring home conditions to your advantage justified? Absolutely. Particularly with some much at stake. What is the point of calling it 'home' otherwise?

For all the traditions of rivalry – the curious dynamic between the two countries and the sporting theatre that this inspires – in an early 21st-century world the continued significance of the Ashes in world sport will be measured ultimately by numbers: viewing figures, advertising revenue, social-media exposure. While David Frith astutely described 1977 as the symbolic beginning of the Money Era, the fact is that the Ashes has come with a price tag certainly since the MCC were prepared to throw Harold Larwood under a bus to stave off fears that the 1934 visit by Australia wouldn't go ahead. Maybe even earlier.

Does this give cause for concern for the future of the Ashes? Probably not.

In a world where the vast majority of international cricket appears to exist purely for its own sake, Test series between England and Australia have no such contextual problems. Everyone watching knows why it is being played, why it matters and the ramifications of each potential result.

With its unparalleled history, that little urn, the assured

legendary status that a great innings with the bat or a destructive spell with the ball will receive, the Ashes is Test cricket's premium product. It will be respected and preserved accordingly.

The Ashes by Numbers

Philip Bailey

SERIES BY SERIES

All statistics within this chapter pertain to Ashes cricket only.

Ashes series results and captains

Host	Season	Matches	Australia	England	Drawn	Ashes holder	Aus captain	Eng captain	Other Aus captain		Other Eng captain	
Australia	1882/83	3	1	2	0	E	TP Horan	IFW Bligh	JM Blackham, HH Massie, WL Murdoch	1		
England	1884	3	0	1	2	E	WL Murdoch	Lord Harris			AN Hornby	1
Australia	1884/85	5	2	3	0	E	WL Murdoch	A Shrewsbury				
England	1886	3	0	3	0	E	HJH Scott	AG Steel				
Australia	1886/87	2	0	2	0	E	PS McDonnell	A Shrewsbury				
Australia	1887/88	1	0	1	0	E	PS McDonnell	WW Read				
England	1888	3	1	2	0	E	PS McDonnell	WG Grace			AG Steel	1
England	1890	2	0	2	0	E	WL Murdoch	WG Grace				
Australia	1891/92	3	2	1	0	A	JM Blackham	WG Grace				
England	1893	3	0	1	2	E	JM Blackham	WG Grace			AE Stoddart	1
Australia	1894/95	5	2	3	0	E	G Giffen	AE Stoddart	JM Blackham	1		
England	1896	3	1	2	0	E	GHS Trott	WG Grace				
Australia	1897/98	5	4	1	0	A	GHS Trott	AE Stoddart				
England	1899	5	1	0	4	A	J Darling	AC MacLaren			WG Grace	1
Australia	1901/02	5	4	1	0	A	J Darling	AC MacLaren	H Trumble	2		
England	1902	5	2	1	2	A	J Darling	AC MacLaren				
Australia	1903/04	5	2	3	0	E	MA Noble	PF Warner				
England	1905	5	0	2	3	E	J Darling	FS Jackson				
Australia	1907/08	5	4	1	0	A	MA Noble	AO Jones			FL Fane	3
England	1909	5	2	1	2	A	MA Noble	AC MacLaren				
Australia	1911/12	5	1	4	0	E	C Hill	JWHT Douglas				
England	1912	3	0	1	2	E	SE Gregory	CB Fry				
Australia	1920/21	5	5	0	0	A	WW Armstrong	JWHT Douglas				
England	1921	5	3	0	2	A	WW Armstrong	LH Tennyson			JWHT Douglas	2

Host	Season	Matches	Australia	England	Drawn	Ashes holder	Aus captain	Eng captain	Other Aus captain		Other Eng captain	
Australia	1924/25	5	4	1	0	A	HL Collins	AER Gilligan	W Bardsley	2		
England	1926	5	0	1	4	E	HL Collins	AW Carr			APF Chapman	1
Australia	1928/29	5	1	4	0	E	J Ryder	APF Chapman			JC White	1
England	1930	5	2	1	2	A	WM Woodfull	APF Chapman			RES Wyatt	1
Australia	1932/33	5	1	4	0	E	WM Woodfull	DR Jardine				
England	1934	5	2	1	2	A	WM Woodfull	RES Wyatt			CF Walters	1
Australia	1936/37	5	3	2	0	A	DG Bradman	GOB Allen				
England	1938	4	1	1	2	A	DG Bradman	WR Hammond				
Australia	1946/47	5	3	0	2	A	DG Bradman	WR Hammond			NWD Yardley	1
England	1948	5	4	0	1	A	DG Bradman	NWD Yardley				
Australia	1950/51	5	4	1	0	A	AL Hassett	FR Brown				
England	1953	5	0	1	4	E	AL Hassett	L Hutton				
Australia	1954/55	5	1	3	1	E	IWG Johnson	L Hutton	AR Morris	1		
England	1956	5	1	2	2	E	IWG Johnson	PBH May				
Australia	1958/59	5	4	0	1	A	R Benaud	PBH May				
England	1961	5	2	1	2	A	R Benaud	PBH May	RN Harvey	1	MC Cowdrey	2
Australia	1962/63	5	1	1	3	A	R Benaud	ER Dexter				
England	1964	5	1	0	4	A	RB Simpson	ER Dexter				
Australia	1965/66	5	1	1	3	A	RB Simpson	MJK Smith	BC Booth	2		
England	1968	5	1	1	3	A	WM Lawry	MC Cowdrey	BN Jarman	1	TW Graveney	1
Australia	1970/71	6	0	2	4	E	WM Lawry	R Illingworth	IM Chappell	1		
England	1972	5	2	2	1	E	IM Chappell	R Illingworth				
Australia	1974/75	6	4	1	1	A	IM Chappell	MH Denness			JH Edrich	1
England	1975	4	1	0	3	A	IM Chappell	AW Greig			MH Denness	1
England	1977	5	0	3	2	E	GS Chappell	JM Brearley				
Australia	1978/79	6	1	5	0	E	GN Yallop	JM Brearley				

Host	Season	Matches	Australia	England	Drawn	Ashes holder	Aus captain	Eng captain	Other Aus captain	Other Eng captain
England	1981	6	1	3	2	E	KJ Hughes	JM Brearley		IT Botham 2
Australia	1982/83	5	2	1	2	A	GS Chappell	RGD Willis		
England	1985	6	1	3	2	E	AR Border	DI Gower		
Australia	1986/87	5	1	2	2	E	AR Border	MW Gatting		
England	1989	6	4	0	2	A	AR Border	DI Gower		
Australia	1990/91	5	3	0	2	A	AR Border	GA Gooch		AJ Lamb 1
England	1993	6	4	1	1	A	AR Border	GA Gooch		MA Atherton 2
Australia	1994/95	5	3	1	1	A	MA Taylor	MA Atherton		
England	1997	6	3	2	1	A	MA Taylor	MA Atherton		
Australia	1998/99	5	3	1	1	A	MA Taylor	AJ Stewart		
England	2001	5	4	1	0	A	SR Waugh	N Hussain	AC Gilchrist 1	MA Atherton 2
Australia	2002/03	5	4	1	0	A	SR Waugh	N Hussain		
England	2005	5	1	2	2	E	RT Ponting	MP Vaughan		
Australia	2006/07	5	5	0	0	A	RT Ponting	A Flintoff		
England	2009	5	1	2	2	E	RT Ponting	AJ Strauss		
Australia	2010/11	5	1	3	1	E	RT Ponting	AJ Strauss	MJ Clarke 1	
England	2013	5	0	3	2	E	MJ Clarke	AN Cook		
Australia	2013/14	5	5	0	0	A	MJ Clarke	AN Cook		
England	2015	5	2	3	0	E	MJ Clarke	AN Cook		
Australia	total	162	82	56	24					
England	total	163	48	50	65					
TOTAL		325	130	106	89					
Series results			Series	Australia	England	Drawn				
				69	32	32	5			

Longest period Ashes held by each side

Australia	19 years	1934 to 1953
England	9 years	1882/83 to 1891/92

Longest winning streak for each side

Australia	8 Tests	1920/21 to 1921
England	7 Tests	1884/85 to 1887/88

Longest winless streak for each side

Australia	12 Tests	1968 to 1972
England	17 Tests	1986/87 to 1993

Number of days Ashes have been held by each side

Australia	27,912
England	21,181

Most wins as captain for each side

Australia	13 Tests	AR Border
England	11 Tests	JM Brearley

Narrowest victory margins in Ashes Tests

England won by 1 wicket	Australia	324 and 121	England	183 and 263-9	The Oval	1902
England won by 1 wicket	Australia	266 and 397	England	382 and 282-9	Melbourne	1907/08
Australia won by 3 runs	Australia	299 and 86	England	262 and 120	Manchester	1902
England won by 3 runs	England	284 and 294	Australia	287 and 288	Melbourne	1982/83
England won by 2 runs	England	407 and 182	Australia	308 and 279	Birmingham	2005

Largest victory margins in Ashes Tests

675 runs	England	521 and 342-8 dec	Australia	122 and 66	Brisbane	1928/29
An innings and 579 runs	England	903-7 dec	Australia	201 and 123	The Oval	1938
562 runs	Australia	701 and 327	England	321 and 145	The Oval	1934
409 runs	Australia	350 and 460-7 dec	England	215 and 186	Lord's	1948
405 runs	Australia	566-8 dec and 254-2 dec	England	312 and 103	Lord's	2015

ASHES BATTING RECORDS

Most Ashes career runs		Matches	Innings	Not outs	Runs	HS†	Hundreds	Average
DG Bradman	Australia	37	63	7	5028	334	19	89.78
AR Border	Australia	42	73	15	3222	200*	7	55.55
SR Waugh	Australia	45	72	18	3173	177*	10	58.75
C Hill	Australia	41	76	1	2660	188	4	35.46
MA Taylor	Australia	33	61	2	2496	219	6	42.30
RT Ponting	Australia	35	58	2	2476	196	8	44.21
RN Harvey	Australia	37	68	5	2416	167	6	38.34
VT Trumper	Australia	40	74	5	2263	185*	6	32.79
MJ Clarke	Australia	35	62	7	2241	187	7	40.74
WM Lawry	Australia	29	51	5	2233	166	7	48.54
ME Waugh	Australia	29	51	7	2204	140	6	50.09
SE Gregory	Australia	52	92	7	2193	201	4	25.80
WW Armstrong	Australia	42	71	9	2172	158	4	35.03
GS Chappell	Australia	30	55	6	2154	144	8	43.95
AR Morris	Australia	24	43	2	2080	206	8	50.73
DC Boon	Australia	30	55	7	2041	164*	6	42.52
IM Chappell	Australia	28	52	3	1986	192	4	40.53
SJ McCabe	Australia	24	43	3	1931	232	4	48.27
KD Walters	Australia	35	60	6	1911	155	4	35.38
MA Noble	Australia	39	68	6	1905	133	1	30.72

*

		Matches	Innings	Not outs	Runs	HS†	Hundreds	Average
JB Hobbs	England	41	71	4	3636	187	12	54.26
DI Gower	England	38	69	3	3037	215	9	46.01
WR Hammond	England	33	58	3	2852	251	9	51.85
H Sutcliffe	England	27	46	5	2741	194	8	66.85
JH Edrich	England	32	57	3	2644	175	7	48.96
G Boycott	England	34	63	7	2579	191	6	46.05
GA Gooch	England	39	73	0	2436	196	4	33.36
MC Cowdrey	England	43	75	4	2433	113	5	34.26
L Hutton	England	27	49	6	2428	364	5	56.46
KP Pietersen	England	27	50	2	2158	227	4	44.95
AN Cook	England	30	55	1	2117	235*	4	39.20
KF Barrington	England	23	39	6	2111	256	5	63.96
IR Bell	England	33	60	4	1983	115	4	35.41
AC MacLaren	England	35	61	4	1931	140	5	33.87
MA Atherton	England	33	66	2	1900	105	1 ·	29.68
DCS Compton	England	28	51	8	1842	184	5	42.83
AJ Stewart	England	33	65	6	1810	107	1	30.67
TW Hayward	England	29	51	2	1747	137	2	35.65
EH Hendren	England	28	48	4	1740	169	3	39.54
W Rhodes	England	41	69	14	1706	179	1	31.01

* denotes a not-out score
† Highest score

Ashes career batting averages		Matches	Innings	Not outs	Runs	HS	Hundreds	Average
AE Trott	Australia	3	5	3	205	85*	0	102.50
DG Bradman	Australia	37	63	7	5028	334	19	89.78
SG Barnes	Australia	9	14	2	846	234	2	70.50
MEK Hussey	Australia	15	24	2	1304	195	4	59.27
SR Waugh	Australia	45	72	18	3173	177*	10	58.75
A Jackson	Australia	4	6	0	350	164	1	58.33
A Symonds	Australia	3	4	0	232	156	1	58.00
MTG Elliott	Australia	6	10	0	556	199	2	55.60
AR Border	Australia	42	73	15	3222	200*	7	55.55
CL McCool	Australia	5	7	2	272	104*	1	54.40
AG Fairfax	Australia	5	6	2	215	65	0	53.75
GRJ Matthews	Australia	10	16	5	589	128	1	53.54
DM Jones	Australia	16	26	2	1240	184*	3	51.66
RG Gregory	Australia	2	3	0	153	80	0	51.00
AR Morris	Australia	24	43	2	2080	206	8	50.73
KR Stackpole	Australia	13	24	1	1164	207	3	50.60
JL Langer	Australia	21	38	5	1658	250	5	50.24
RB Simpson	Australia	19	31	3	1405	311	2	50.17
ME Waugh	Australia	29	51	7	2204	140	6	50.09
RM Cowper	Australia	9	15	1	686	307	1	49.00

*

E Paynter	England	7	11	4	591	216*	1	84.42
H Sutcliffe	England	27	46	5	2741	194	8	66.85
KF Barrington	England	23	39	6	2111	256	5	63.96
DS Steele	England	3	6	0	365	92	0	60.83
RE Foster	England	5	9	1	486	287	1	60.75
KS Duleepsinhji	England	4	7	0	416	173	1	59.42
LH Tennyson	England	4	5	1	229	74*	0	57.25
M Leyland	England	20	34	4	1705	187	7	56.83
L Hutton	England	27	49	6	2428	364	5	56.46
JB Hobbs	England	41	71	4	3636	187	12	54.26
CAG Russell	England	6	11	2	474	135*	3	52.66
CP Mead	England	7	10	2	415	182*	1	51.87
WR Hammond	England	33	58	3	2852	251	9	51.85
BC Broad	England	7	13	2	569	162	3	51.72
RT Robinson	England	7	11	1	502	175	2	50.20
CF Walters	England	5	9	1	401	82	0	50.12
G Brown	England	3	5	0	250	84	0	50.00
JH Edrich	England	32	57	3	2644	175	7	48.96
FS Jackson	England	20	33	4	1415	144*	5	48.79
IJL Trott	England	12	21	2	917	168*	3	48.26

minimum 100 runs

* denotes a not-out score

Highest individual score

334	DG Bradman	Australia	Leeds	1930
311	RB Simpson	Australia	Manchester	1964
307	RM Cowper	Australia	Melbourne	1965/66
304	DG Bradman	Australia	Leeds	1934
270	DG Bradman	Australia	Melbourne	1936/37
266	WH Ponsford	Australia	The Oval	1934
254	DG Bradman	Australia	Lord's	1930
250	JL Langer	Australia	Melbourne	2002/03
244	DG Bradman	Australia	The Oval	1934
234	SG Barnes	Australia	Sydney	1946/47
234	DG Bradman	Australia	Sydney	1946/47
364	L Hutton	England	The Oval	1938
287	RE Foster	England	Sydney	1903/04
256	KF Barrington	England	Manchester	1964
251	WR Hammond	England	Sydney	1928/29
240	WR Hammond	England	Lord's	1938
235*	AN Cook	England	Brisbane	2010/11
231*	WR Hammond	England	Sydney	1936/37
227	KP Pietersen	England	Adelaide	2010/11
216*	E Paynter	England	Nottingham	1938
215	DI Gower	England	Birmingham	1985

* denotes a not-out score

Fastest 50s	Balls faced			
JT Brown	34	England	Melbourne	1894/95
GN Yallop	35	Australia	Manchester	1981
DA Warner	35	Australia	Birmingham	2015
KP Pietersen	36	England	The Oval	2013
MJ Prior	37	England	Lord's	2009

Fastest 100s*	Balls faced			
AC Gilchrist	57	Australia	Perth	2006/07
GL Jessop	76	England	The Oval	1902
IT Botham	86	England	Manchester	1981
IT Botham	87	England	Leeds	1981
RR Lindwall	88	Australia	Melbourne	1946/47

** J Darling reached his 100 in approximately 85 balls at Sydney 1897/98
but this is only an estimate with the exact data not available.*

Slowest 50s	Balls faced			
TE Bailey	350	England	Brisbane	1958/59
AC Bannerman	330	Australia	Sydney	1891/92
C Kelleway	296	Australia	Lord's	1912
DR Jardine	260	England	Adelaide	1932/33
JW Trumble	250	Australia	Melbourne	1884/85

Slowest 100s	Balls faced			
WM Woodfull	372	Australia	Melbourne	1928/29
Nawab of Pataudi	366	England	Sydney	1932/33
D Randall	353	England	Sydney	1978/79
DCS Compton	349	England	Adelaide	1946/47
WR Hammond	339	England	Adelaide	1928/29
H Sutcliffe	339	England	Melbourne	1928/29

Most runs in a series			Matches	Innings	Not outs	Runs	HS	Average	Hundreds	Fifties
DG Bradman	1930	Australia	5	7	0	974	334	139.14	4	0
WR Hammond	1928/29	England	5	9	1	905	251	113.12	4	0
MA Taylor	1989	Australia	6	11	1	839	219	83.90	2	5
DG Bradman	1936/37	Australia	5	9	0	810	270	90.00	3	1
AN Cook	2010/11	England	5	7	1	766	235*	127.66	3	2
DG Bradman	1934	Australia	5	8	0	758	304	94.75	2	1
H Sutcliffe	1924/25	England	5	9	0	734	176	81.55	4	2
DI Gower	1985	England	6	9	0	732	215	81.33	3	1
AR Morris	1948	Australia	5	9	1	696	196	87.00	3	3
DG Bradman	1946/47	Australia	5	8	1	680	234	97.14	2	3

* denotes a not-out score

Most 100s		Matches	Innings	Hundreds
DG Bradman	Australia	37	63	19
JB Hobbs	England	41	71	12
SR Waugh	Australia	45	72	10
DI Gower	England	38	69	9
WR Hammond	England	33	58	9
GS Chappell	Australia	30	55	8
AR Morris	Australia	24	43	8
RT Ponting	Australia	35	58	8
H Sutcliffe	England	27	46	8
AR Border	Australia	42	73	7
MJ Clarke	Australia	35	62	7
WM Lawry	Australia	29	51	7
MJ Slater	Australia	20	37	7
JH Edrich	England	32	57	7
M Leyland	England	20	34	7

ASHES BOWLING RECORDS

Most Ashes wickets		Matches	Balls	Maidens	Runs conceded	Wickets	Average	Best bowling	Five in innings	Ten in match
SK Warne	Australia	36	10757	488	4535	195	23.25	8-71	11	4
GD McGrath	Australia	30	7280	332	3286	157	20.92	8-38	10	0
H Trumble	Australia	31	7895	448	2945	141	20.88	8-65	9	3
DK Lillee	Australia	24	6998	302	2858	128	22.32	7-89	7	2
MA Noble	Australia	39	6895	353	2860	115	24.86	7-17	9	2
RR Lindwall	Australia	29	6728	216	2559	114	22.44	7-63	6	0
CV Grimmett	Australia	22	9164	427	3439	106	32.44	6-37	11	2
WJ O'Reilly	Australia	19	7864	439	2587	102	25.36	7-54	8	3
G Giffen	Australia	26	6292	427	2737	101	27.09	6-72	7	1
CTB Turner	Australia	17	5179	457	1670	101	16.53	7-43	11	2
TM Alderman	Australia	17	4717	192	2117	100	21.17	6-47	11	1
GF Lawson	Australia	21	5460	196	2763	97	28.48	7-81	7	1
JR Thomson	Australia	20	4759	160	2318	97	23.89	6-46	5	0
GD McKenzie	Australia	25	7486	233	3009	96	31.34	6-48	6	0
MG Johnson	Australia	19	3765	117	2246	87	25.81	7-40	5	0
KR Miller	Australia	29	5717	225	1949	87	22.40	7-60	3	1
AA Mailey	Australia	18	5201	90	2935	86	34.12	9-121	6	2
AK Davidson	Australia	25	5993	221	1996	84	23.76	6-64	5	0
CJ McDermott	Australia	16	3838	104	2145	84	25.53	8-97	8	1
R Benaud	Australia	27	7284	289	2641	83	31.81	6-70	4	0

Most Ashes wickets		Matches	Balls	Maidens	Runs conceded	Wickets	Average	Best bowling	Five in innings	Ten in match
IT Botham	England	32	7252	232	3590	128	28.04	6-95	7	1
RGD Willis	England	31	6466	174	2998	123	24.37	8-43	7	0
W Rhodes	England	41	5790	234	2616	109	24.00	8-68	6	1
SF Barnes	England	20	5749	262	2288	106	21.58	7-60	12	1
AV Bedser	England	21	7065	209	2859	104	27.49	7-44	7	2
R Peel	England	20	5216	444	1715	101	16.98	7-31	5	1
J Briggs	England	31	4941	335	1994	97	20.55	6-45	7	3
T Richardson	England	14	4498	191	2220	88	25.22	8-94	11	4
DL Underwood	England	25	6848	356	2311	88	26.26	7-50	4	2
JM Anderson	England	26	5686	212	3121	87	35.87	6-47	4	1
SCJ Broad	England	22	4291	138	2326	84	27.69	8-15	6	1
JA Snow	England	20	5073	168	2126	83	25.61	7-40	4	0
MW Tate	England	20	7686	330	2540	83	30.60	6-99	6	1
JC Laker	England	15	4010	204	1444	79	18.27	10-53	5	2
FS Trueman	England	19	4361	83	1999	79	25.30	6-30	5	1
GA Lohmann	England	15	3310	326	1002	77	13.01	8-35	5	3
JE Emburey	England	23	6960	318	2404	76	31.63	7-78	3	0
D Gough	England	17	3909	124	2280	74	30.81	6-49	4	0
JB Statham	England	22	5405	131	2138	69	30.98	7-57	3	0
AR Caddick	England	18	4089	107	2560	64	40.00	7-94	4	1
H Larwood	England	15	4053	120	1912	64	29.87	6-32	3	1

Best bowling average		Matches	Balls	Maidens	Runs conceded	Wickets	Average	Best bowling	Five in innings	Ten in match
TP Horan	Australia	7	289	39	102	9	11.33	6-40	1	0
MF Malone	Australia	1	342	24	77	6	12.83	5-63	1	0
JJ Ferris	Australia	8	2030	224	684	48	14.25	5-26	4	0
JB Iverson	Australia	5	1108	29	320	21	15.23	6-27	1	0
CJ Eady	Australia	2	223	14	112	7	16.00	3-30	0	0
JP Faulkner	Australia	1	166	4	98	6	16.33	4-51	0	0
SP Jones	Australia	9	186	17	82	5	16.40	4-47	0	0
CTB Turner	Australia	17	5179	457	1670	101	16.53	7-43	11	2
RM Hogg	Australia	11	2629	94	952	56	17.00	6-74	5	2
I Meckiff	Australia	4	898	24	292	17	17.17	6-38	1	0
F Martin	England	1	287	21	102	12	8.50	6-50	2	1
RM Ellison	England	2	455	20	185	17	10.88	6-77	2	1
GA Lohmann	England	15	3310	326	1002	77	13.01	8-35	5	3
W Bates	England	10	1184	136	411	31	13.25	7-28	4	1
W Barnes	England	18	2102	256	706	49	14.40	6-28	3	0
H Dean	England	2	324	19	97	6	16.16	4-19	0	0
F Morley	England	2	376	51	101	6	16.83	4-47	0	0
R Peel	England	20	5216	444	1715	101	16.98	7-31	5	1
G Ulyett	England	15	1508	184	566	31	18.25	7-36	1	0
JC Laker	England	15	4010	204	1444	79	18.27	10-53	5	2

minimum 5 wickets

Best bowling figures

	Figures			
RAL Massie	16-137	Australia	Lord's	1972
MA Noble	13-77	Australia	Melbourne	1901/02
BA Reid	13-148	Australia	Melbourne	1990/91
AA Mailey	13-236	Australia	Melbourne	1920/21
CTB Turner	12-87	Australia	Sydney	1887/88
H Trumble	12-89	Australia	The Oval	1896
SCG MacGill	12-107	Australia	Sydney	1998/99
H Trumble	12-173	Australia	The Oval	1902
HV Hordern	12-175	Australia	Sydney	1911/12
SK Warne	12-246	Australia	The Oval	2005
JC Laker	19-90	England	Manchester	1956
H Verity	15-104	England	Lord's	1934
W Rhodes	15-124	England	Melbourne	1903/04
AV Bedser	14-99	England	Nottingham	1953
W Bates	14-102	England	Melbourne	1882/83
SF Barnes	13-163	England	Melbourne	1901/02
T Richardson	13-244	England	Manchester	1896
JC White	13-256	England	Adelaide	1928/29
F Martin	12-102	England	The Oval	1890
GA Lohmann	12-104	England	The Oval	1886

Most wickets in an innings

	Figures			
AA Mailey	9-121	Australia	Melbourne	1920/21
FJ Laver	8-31	Australia	Manchester	1909
GD McGrath	8-38	Australia	Lord's	1997
AE Trott	8-43	Australia	Adelaide	1894/95
RAL Massie	8-53	Australia	Lord's	1972
H Trumble	8-65	Australia	The Oval	1902
SK Warne	8-71	Australia	Brisbane	1994/95
RAL Massie	8-84	Australia	Lord's	1972
CJ McDermott	8-97	Australia	Perth	1990/91
CJ McDermott	8-141	Australia	Manchester	1985
JC Laker	10-53	England	Manchester	1956
JC Laker	9-37	England	Manchester	1956
SCJ Broad	8-15	England	Nottingham	2015
GA Lohmann	8-35	England	Sydney	1886/87
H Verity	8-43	England	Lord's	1934
RGD Willis	8-43	England	Leeds	1981
GA Lohmann	8-58	England	Sydney	1891/92
W Rhodes	8-68	England	Melbourne	1903/04
LC Braund	8-81	England	Melbourne	1903/04
T Richardson	8-94	England	Sydney	1897/98

Most wickets in a series			Balls	Maidens	Runs conceded	Wickets	Best bowling	Average	Five in innings	Ten in match
JC Laker	1956	England	1703	127	442	46	10-53	9.60	4	2
TM Alderman	1981	Australia	1950	76	893	42	6-135	21.26	4	0
RM Hogg	1978/79	Australia	1740	60	527	41	6-74	12.85	5	2
TM Alderman	1989	Australia	1616	68	712	41	6-128	17.36	6	1
SK Warne	2005	Australia	1517	37	797	40	6-46	19.92	3	2
DK Lillee	1981	Australia	1870	81	870	39	7-89	22.30	2	1
AV Bedser	1953	England	1591	58	682	39	7-44	17.48	5	1
MW Tate	1924/25	England	2528	62	881	38	6-99	23.18	5	1
MG Johnson	2013/14	Australia	1132	51	517	37	7-40	13.97	3	0
AA Mailey	1920/21	Australia	1465	27	946	36	9-121	26.27	4	2
GD McGrath	1997	Australia	1499	67	701	36	8-38	19.47	2	0

ASHES WICKETKEEPING RECORDS

Most career dismissals		Matches	Catches	Stumpings	Dismissals
IA Healy	Australia	33	123	12	135
RW Marsh	Australia	37	124	7	131
AC Gilchrist	Australia	20	89	7	96
WAS Oldfield	Australia	38	59	31	90
BJ Haddin	Australia	20	79	1	80
APE Knott	England	33	93	8	101
AFA Lilley	England	32	65	19	84
AJ Stewart	England	26	76	2	78
TG Evans	England	31	64	12	76
MJ Prior	England	18	62	1	63

Most dismissals in an innings	Dismissals	Catches	Stumpings			
IA Healy	6	6	0	Australia	Birmingham	1997
RW Marsh	6	6	0	Australia	Brisbane	1982/83
AC Gilchrist	5	5	0	Australia	Leeds	2001
AC Gilchrist	5	4	1	Australia	Nottingham	2005
AC Gilchrist	5	4	1	Australia	Sydney	2002/03
AC Gilchrist	5	5	0	Australia	Sydney	2006/07
ATW Grout	5	5	0	Australia	Lord's	1961
ATW Grout	5	5	0	Australia	Sydney	1965/66
BJ Haddin	5	5	0	Australia	Lord's	2013
BJ Haddin	5	5	0	Australia	Manchester	2013
IA Healy	5	5	0	Australia	Melbourne	1990/91
IA Healy	5	5	0	Australia	Adelaide	1990/91
IA Healy	5	5	0	Australia	Perth	1998/99
IA Healy	5	5	0	Australia	Brisbane	1994/95
IA Healy	5	5	0	Australia	Melbourne	1994/95
GRA Langley	5	5	0	Australia	Lord's	1956
JA Maclean	5	5	0	Australia	Brisbane	1978/79
RW Marsh	5	5	0	Australia	Manchester	1972
RW Marsh	5	5	0	Australia	Nottingham	1972
WAS Oldfield	5	1	4	Australia	Melbourne	1924/25
MJ Prior	6	6	0	England	Melbourne	2010/11
CMW Read	6	6	0	England	Melbourne	2006/07
CMW Read	6	5	1	England	Sydney	2006/07
RC Russell	6	6	0	England	Melbourne	1990/91
AJ Stewart	6	6	0	England	Manchester	1997

Most dismissals in a match	Dismissals	Catches	Stumpings			
AC Gilchrist	9	8	1	Australia	Sydney	2006/07
IA Healy	9	9	0	Australia	Brisbane	1994/95
GRA Langley	9	8	1	Australia	Lord's	1956
RW Marsh	9	9	0	Australia	Brisbane	1982/83
ATW Grout	8	8	0	Australia	Lord's	1961
BJ Haddin	8	8	0	Australia	Perth	2013/14
IA Healy	8	7	1	Australia	Melbourne	1994/95
JJ Kelly	8	8	0	Australia	Sydney	1901/02
RW Marsh	8	8	0	Australia	Adelaide	1982/83
AJ Stewart	8	8	0	England	Manchester	1997
TG Evans	7	6	1	England	Lord's	1956
JT Murray	7	7	0	England	Manchester	1961
MJ Prior	7	7	0	England	Melbourne	2010/11
MJ Prior	7	7	0	England	Sydney	2010/11
SJ Rhodes	7	7	0	England	Adelaide	1994/95
RW Taylor	7	7	0	England	Leeds	1981

Most dismissals in a series	Dismissals	Catches	Stumpings	Matches		
BJ Haddin	29	29	0	5	Australia	2013
RW Marsh	28	28	0	5	Australia	1982/83
IA Healy	27	25	2	6	Australia	1997
AC Gilchrist	26	24	2	5	Australia	2006/07
AC Gilchrist	26	24	2	5	Australia	2001
IA Healy	26	21	5	6	Australia	1993
APE Knott	24	21	3	6	England	1970/71
APE Knott	23	22	1	6	England	1974/75
MJ Prior	23	23	0	5	England	2010/11
AJ Stewart	23	23	0	6	England	1997
SJ Rhodes	21	20	1	5	England	1994/95

Highest team totals			
729-6 dec	Australia	Lord's	1930
701	Australia	The Oval	1934
695	Australia	The Oval	1930
674-6 dec	Australia	Cardiff	2009
659-8 dec	Australia	Sydney	1946/47
656-8 dec	Australia	Manchester	1964
653-4 dec	Australia	Leeds	1993
645	Australia	Brisbane	1946/47
641-4 dec	Australia	The Oval	2001
632-4 dec	Australia	Lord's	1993
604	Australia	Melbourne	1936/37
602-6 dec	Australia	Nottingham	1989
602-9 dec	Australia	Brisbane	2006/07
601-8 dec	Australia	Brisbane	1954/55
601-7 dec	Australia	Leeds	1989
600	Australia	Melbourne	1924/25
586	Australia	Sydney	1894/95
584	Australia	Leeds	1934
582	Australia	Adelaide	1920/21
581	Australia	Sydney	1920/21
903-7 dec	England	The Oval	1938
658-8 dec	England	Nottingham	1938
644	England	Sydney	2010/11
636	England	Sydney	1928/29
627-9 dec	England	Manchester	1934
620-5 dec	England	Adelaide	2010/11
611	England	Manchester	1964
595-5 dec	England	Birmingham	1985
592-8 dec	England	Perth	1986/87
589	England	Melbourne	1911/12
577	England	Sydney	1903/04
576	England	The Oval	1899
558	England	Melbourne	1965/66
551	England	Sydney	1897/98
551-6 dec	England	Adelaide	2006/07
548	England	Melbourne	1924/25
538	England	The Oval	1975
533	England	Leeds	1985
529	England	Melbourne	1974/75
524	England	Sydney	1932/33

Lowest all-out team totals

36	Australia	Birmingham	1902
42	Australia	Sydney	1887/88
44	Australia	The Oval	1896
53	Australia	Lord's	1896
58#	Australia	Brisbane	1936/37
60	Australia	Lord's	1888
60	Australia	Nottingham	2015
65	Australia	The Oval	1912
66#	Australia	Brisbane	1928/29
68	Australia	The Oval	1886
70	Australia	Manchester	1888
74	Australia	Birmingham	1909
78#	Australia	Lord's	1968
80	Australia	The Oval	1888
80#	Australia	Sydney	1936/37
81	Australia	Manchester	1888
82	Australia	Sydney	1887/88
83	Australia	Sydney	1882/83
84	Australia	Sydney	1886/87
84	Australia	Manchester	1956
45	England	Sydney	1886/87
52	England	The Oval	1948
53	England	Lord's	1888
61	England	Melbourne	1901/02
61	England	Melbourne	1903/04
62	England	Lord's	1888
65#	England	Sydney	1894/95
72#	England	Sydney	1894/95
75	England	Melbourne	1894/95
77	England	Sydney	1884/85
77	England	Lord's	1997
79#	England	Brisbane	2002/03
84	England	The Oval	1896
87#	England	Leeds	1909
87	England	Melbourne	1958/59
92	England	Melbourne	1994/95
95	England	Manchester	1884
99	England	Sydney	1901/02
100	England	The Oval	1890
101#	England	Melbourne	1903/04
101	England	Birmingham	1975

Note: *# indicates because of injury not all 10 wickets fell*

Highest partnership for each wicket

Wicket	Runs					
1	329	GR Marsh	MA Taylor	Australia	Nottingham	1989
2	451	WH Ponsford	DG Bradman	Australia	The Oval	1934
3	276	DG Bradman	AL Hassett	Australia	Brisbane	1946/47
4	388	WH Ponsford	DG Bradman	Australia	Leeds	1934
5	405	SG Barnes	DG Bradman	Australia	Sydney	1946/47
6	346	JHW Fingleton	DG Bradman	Australia	Melbourne	1936/37
7	165	C Hill	H Trumble	Australia	Melbourne	1897/98
8	243	MJ Hartigan	C Hill	Australia	Adelaide	1907/08
9	154	SE Gregory	JM Blackham	Australia	Sydney	1894/95
10	163	PJ Hughes	AC Agar	Australia	Nottingham	2013
1	323	JB Hobbs	W Rhodes	England	Melbourne	1911/12
2	382	L Hutton	M Leyland	England	The Oval	1938
3	262	WR Hammond	DR Jardine	England	Adelaide	1928/29
4	310	PD Collingwood	KP Pietersen	England	Adelaide	2006/07
5	206	E Paynter	DCS Compton	England	Nottingham	1938
6	215	L Hutton	J Hardstaff	England	The Oval	1938
6	215	G Boycott	APE Knott	England	Nottingham	1977
7	143	FE Woolley	J Vine	England	Sydney	1911/12
8	124	EH Hendren	H Larwood	England	Brisbane	1928/29
9	151	WH Scotton	WW Read	England	The Oval	1884
10	130	RE Foster	W Rhodes	England	Sydney	1903/04

Highest successful fourth innings run chases

404-3	Australia	Leeds	1948
315-6	Australia	Adelaide	1901/02
287-5	Australia	Melbourne	1928/29
276-4	Australia	Sydney	1897/98
275-8	Australia	Sydney	1907/08
332-7	England	Melbourne	1928/29
315-4	England	Leeds	2001
298-4	England	Melbourne	1894/95
282-9	England	Melbourne	1907/08
263-9	England	The Oval	1902

Result record for each captain		Matches	Won	Lost	Drawn
AR Border	Australia	28	13	6	9
DG Bradman	Australia	19	11	3	5
RT Ponting	Australia	19	8	6	5
J Darling	Australia	18	5	4	9
MA Taylor	Australia	16	9	4	3
IM Chappell	Australia	16	7	4	5
MJ Clarke	Australia	16	7	7	2
MA Noble	Australia	15	8	5	2
WM Woodfull	Australia	15	5	6	4
R Benaud	Australia	14	6	2	6
WW Armstrong	Australia	10	8	0	2
AL Hassett	Australia	10	4	2	4
GS Chappell	Australia	10	2	4	4
SR Waugh	Australia	9	8	1	0
IWG Johnson	Australia	9	2	4	3
WL Murdoch	Australia	9	1	6	2
WM Lawry	Australia	9	1	2	6
GHS Trott	Australia	8	5	3	0
HL Collins	Australia	8	4	2	2
JM Blackham	Australia	8	3	3	2
RB Simpson	Australia	8	2	0	6
PS McDonnell	Australia	6	1	5	0
GN Yallop	Australia	6	1	5	0
KJ Hughes	Australia	6	1	3	2
C Hill	Australia	5	1	4	0
J Ryder	Australia	5	1	4	0
G Giffen	Australia	4	2	2	0
HJH Scott	Australia	3	0	3	0
SE Gregory	Australia	3	0	1	2
H Trumble	Australia	2	2	0	0
TP Horan	Australia	2	0	2	0
W Bardsley	Australia	2	0	0	2
BC Booth	Australia	2	0	1	1
HH Massie	Australia	1	1	0	0
RN Harvey	Australia	1	1	0	0
AR Morris	Australia	1	0	1	0
BN Jarman	Australia	1	0	0	1
AC Gilchrist	Australia	1	0	1	0
AC MacLaren	England	22	4	11	7
JM Brearley	England	15	11	1	3
AN Cook	England	15	6	7	2
MA Atherton	England	15	4	9	2
WG Grace	England	13	8	3	2
PBH May	England	13	3	6	4

Result record for each captain		Matches	Won	Lost	Drawn
JWHT Douglas	England	12	4	8	0
DI Gower	England	12	3	5	4
R Illingworth	England	11	4	2	5
AJ Strauss	England	10	5	2	3
L Hutton	England	10	4	1	5
ER Dexter	England	10	1	2	7
APF Chapman	England	9	6	1	2
AE Stoddart	England	8	3	4	1
N Hussain	England	8	2	6	0
WR Hammond	England	8	1	3	4
GA Gooch	England	8	0	5	3
A Shrewsbury	England	7	5	2	0
MC Cowdrey	England	6	1	2	3
MH Denness	England	6	1	4	1
NWD Yardley	England	6	0	5	1
DR Jardine	England	5	4	1	0
PF Warner	England	5	3	2	0
FS Jackson	England	5	2	0	3
GOB Allen	England	5	2	3	0
MW Gatting	England	5	2	1	2
MP Vaughan	England	5	2	1	2
AER Gilligan	England	5	1	4	0
RES Wyatt	England	5	1	2	2
FR Brown	England	5	1	4	0
MJK Smith	England	5	1	1	3
RGD Willis	England	5	1	2	2
AJ Stewart	England	5	1	3	1
A Flintoff	England	5	0	5	0
AG Steel	England	4	3	1	0
AW Carr	England	4	0	0	4
IFW Bligh	England	3	2	1	0
FL Fane	England	3	1	2	0
CB Fry	England	3	1	0	2
LH Tennyson	England	3	0	1	2
AW Greig	England	3	0	0	3
Lord Harris	England	2	1	0	1
AO Jones	England	2	0	2	0
IT Botham	England	2	0	1	1
WW Read	England	1	1	0	0
AN Hornby	England	1	0	0	1
JC White	England	1	0	1	0
CF Walters	England	1	0	1	0
TW Graveney	England	1	0	0	1
JH Edrich	England	1	0	1	0
AJ Lamb	England	1	0	1	0

CHAPTER ONE: ALL-TIME ASHES XI

Greatest Ashes XI career records		Matches	Innings	Not outs	Runs	HS	Average
JB Hobbs	England	41	71	4	3636	187	54.26
L Hutton	England	27	49	6	2428	364	56.46
DG Bradman	Australia	37	63	7	5028	334	89.78
WR Hammond	England	33	58	3	2852	251	51.85
AR Border	Australia	42	73	15	3222	200*	55.55
IT Botham	England	32	52	1	1486	149*	29.13
AC Gilchrist	Australia	20	28	4	1083	152	45.12
SK Warne	Australia	36	48	5	946	90	22.00
JC Laker	England	15	23	4	277	63	14.57
DK Lillee	Australia	24	33	12	384	73*	18.28
GD McGrath	Australia	30	33	16	105	20*	6.17

* denotes a not-out score

Greatest Ashes XI		Matches	Won	Lost	Drawn
JB Hobbs	England	41	14	19	8
L Hutton	England	27	6	12	9
DG Bradman	Australia	37	17	11	9
WR Hammond	England	33	13	12	8
AR Border	Australia	42	17	12	13
IT Botham	England	32	16	8	8
AC Gilchrist	Australia	20	14	4	2
SK Warne	Australia	36	24	7	5
JC Laker	England	15	3	7	5
DK Lillee	Australia	24	8	7	9
GD McGrath	Australia	30	22	4	4

Hundreds	Fifties	Catches	Stumpings	Balls	Maidens	Runs conceded	Wickets	Average
12	15	11		124	5	53	0	
5	14	22		54	1	60	1	60.00
19	12	20		92	2	51	1	51.00
9	7	43		3958	136	1612	36	44.77
7	19	51		1070	53	351	4	87.75
3	6	54		7252	232	3590	128	28.04
3	6	89	7					
0	4	30		10757	488	4535	195	23.25
0	1	0		4010	204	1444	79	18.27
0	1	6		6998	302	2858	128	22.32
0	0	10		7280	332	3286	157	20.92

CHAPTER TWO: THE FIVE GREATEST ASHES SERIES

Greatest Ashes series averages			Matches	Innings	Not outs	Runs	HS	Average	Hun- dreds	Fifties
1932/33	Australia	HH Alexander	1	2	1	17	17*	17.00	0	0
1932/33	Australia	DG Bradman	4	8	1	396	103*	56.57	1	3
1932/33	Australia	EH Bromley	1	2	0	33	26	16.50	0	0
1932/33	Australia	LS Darling	2	4	0	148	85	37.00	0	1
1932/33	Australia	JHW Fingleton	3	6	0	150	83	25.00	0	1
1932/33	Australia	CV Grimmett	3	6	0	42	19	7.00	0	0
1932/33	Australia	H Ironmonger	4	8	3	13	8	2.60	0	0
1932/33	Australia	AF Kippax	1	2	0	27	19	13.50	0	0
1932/33	Australia	PK Lee	1	2	0	57	42	28.50	0	0
1932/33	Australia	HSB Love	1	2	0	8	5	4.00	0	0
1932/33	Australia	SJ McCabe	5	10	1	385	187*	42.77	1	1
1932/33	Australia	LE Nagel	1	2	1	21	21*	21.00	0	0
1932/33	Australia	LPJ O'Brien	2	4	0	87	61	21.75	0	1
1932/33	Australia	WAS Oldfield	4	7	2	136	52	27.20	0	1
1932/33	Australia	WJ O'Reilly	5	10	0	61	19	6.10	0	0
1932/33	Australia	WH Ponsford	3	6	0	141	85	23.50	0	1
1932/33	Australia	VY Richardson	5	10	0	279	83	27.90	0	1
1932/33	Australia	TW Wall	4	8	1	42	20	6.00	0	0
1932/33	Australia	WM Woodfull	5	10	1	305	73*	33.88	0	3
1932/33	England	GOB Allen	5	7	0	163	48	23.28	0	0
1932/33	England	LEG Ames	5	8	1	113	69	16.14	0	1
1932/33	England	WE Bowes	1	2	2	4	4*		0	0
1932/33	England	WR Hammond	5	9	1	440	112	55.00	2	2
1932/33	England	DR Jardine	5	9	0	199	56	22.11	0	1
1932/33	England	H Larwood	5	7	1	145	98	24.16	0	1
1932/33	England	M Leyland	5	9	0	306	86	34.00	0	2
1932/33	England	TB Mitchell	1	1	0	0	0	0.00	0	0
1932/33	England	Nawab of Pataudi	2	3	0	122	102	40.66	1	0
1932/33	England	E Paynter	3	5	2	184	83	61.33	0	2
1932/33	England	H Sutcliffe	5	9	1	440	194	55.00	1	3
1932/33	England	H Verity	4	5	1	114	45	28.50	0	0
1932/33	England	W Voce	4	6	2	29	8	7.25	0	0
1932/33	England	RES Wyatt	5	9	2	327	78	46.71	0	3
1954/55	Australia	RG Archer	4	7	0	117	49	16.71	0	0
1954/55	Australia	R Benaud	5	9	0	148	34	16.44	0	0
1954/55	Australia	PJP Burge	1	2	1	35	18*	35.00	0	0
1954/55	Australia	JW Burke	2	4	0	81	44	20.25	0	0
1954/55	Australia	AK Davidson	3	5	0	71	23	14.20	0	0
1954/55	Australia	LE Favell	4	7	0	130	30	18.57	0	0
1954/55	Australia	RN Harvey	5	9	1	354	162	44.25	1	1
1954/55	Australia	GB Hole	3	5	0	85	57	17.00	0	1
1954/55	Australia	IWG Johnson	4	6	4	116	41	58.00	0	0

denotes a not-out score

Catches	Stumpings	Balls	Maidens	Runs conceded	Wickets	Average	Best bowling	Five in innings	Ten in match
0	0	276	3	154	1	154.00	1-129	0	0
3	0	72	1	44	1	44.00	1-23	0	0
1	0	60	4	19	0		0-19	0	0
2	0	66	5	14	0		0-3	0	0
3	0								
1	0	882	41	326	5	65.20	2-94	0	0
2	0	1471	96	405	15	27.00	4-26	0	0
0	0	12	1	3	0		0-3	0	0
0	0	316	14	163	4	40.75	4-111	0	0
3	0								
4	0	557	17	215	3	71.66	2-40	0	0
0	0	262	9	110	2	55.00	2-110	0	0
2	0								
6	1								
1	0	2302	144	724	27	26.81	5-63	2	1
0	0								
7	0								
4	0	1021	33	409	16	25.56	5-72	1	0
0	0								
7	0	1026	29	593	21	28.23	4-50	0	0
8	2								
0	0	138	2	70	1	70.00	1-50	0	0
6	0	725	27	291	9	32.33	3-21	0	0
9	0								
2	0	1322	42	644	33	19.51	5-28	2	1
2	0								
1	0	126	5	60	3	20.00	2-49	0	0
0	0								
0	0								
1	0								
3	0	810	54	271	11	24.63	5-33	1	0
3	0	801	24	407	15	27.13	4-110	0	0
2	0	12	0	12	0		0-12	0	0
4	0	782	32	215	13	16.53	4-33	0	0
3	0	935	23	377	10	37.70	4-120	0	0
1	0								
2	0	16	0	7	0		0-7	0	0
5	0	568	16	220	3	73.33	2-34	0	0
2	0								
3	0								
3	0								
3	0	888	37	243	12	20.25	3-46	0	0

Greatest Ashes series averages			Matches	Innings	Not outs	Runs	HS	Average	Hun-dreds	Fifties
1954/55	Australia	WA Johnston	4	6	2	25	11	6.25	0	0
1954/55	Australia	GRA Langley	2	3	0	21	16	7.00	0	0
1954/55	Australia	RR Lindwall	4	6	2	106	64*	26.50	0	1
1954/55	Australia	CC McDonald	2	4	0	186	72	46.50	0	1
1954/55	Australia	LV Maddocks	3	5	0	150	69	30.00	0	1
1954/55	Australia	KR Miller	4	7	0	167	49	23.85	0	0
1954/55	Australia	AR Morris	4	7	0	223	153	31.85	1	0
1954/55	Australia	WJ Watson	1	2	0	21	18	10.50	0	0
1954/55	England	KV Andrew	1	2	0	11	6	5.50	0	0
1954/55	England	R Appleyard	4	5	3	44	19*	22.00	0	0
1954/55	England	TE Bailey	5	9	1	296	88	37.00	0	2
1954/55	England	AV Bedser	1	2	0	10	5	5.00	0	0
1954/55	England	DCS Compton	4	7	2	191	84	38.20	0	1
1954/55	England	MC Cowdrey	5	9	0	319	102	35.44	1	2
1954/55	England	WJ Edrich	4	8	0	180	88	22.50	0	1
1954/55	England	TG Evans	4	7	1	102	37	17.00	0	0
1954/55	England	TW Graveney	2	3	0	132	111	44.00	1	0
1954/55	England	L Hutton	5	9	0	220	80	24.44	0	1
1954/55	England	PBH May	5	9	0	351	104	39.00	1	2
1954/55	England	RT Simpson	1	2	0	11	9	5.50	0	0
1954/55	England	JB Statham	5	7	1	67	25	11.16	0	0
1954/55	England	FH Tyson	5	7	1	66	37*	11.00	0	0
1954/55	England	JH Wardle	4	6	1	109	38	21.80	0	0
1972	Australia	GS Chappell	5	10	1	437	131	48.55	2	1
1972	Australia	IM Chappell	5	10	0	334	118	33.40	1	2
1972	Australia	DJ Colley	3	4	0	84	54	21.00	0	1
1972	Australia	R Edwards	4	7	1	291	170*	48.50	1	1
1972	Australia	BC Francis	3	5	0	52	27	10.40	0	0
1972	Australia	JW Gleeson	3	4	1	37	30	12.33	0	0
1972	Australia	RJ Inverarity	3	5	1	61	28	15.25	0	0
1972	Australia	DK Lillee	5	7	4	10	7	3.33	0	0
1972	Australia	AA Mallett	2	3	0	34	20	11.33	0	0
1972	Australia	RW Marsh	5	9	2	242	91	34.57	0	2
1972	Australia	RAL Massie	4	5	0	22	18	4.40	0	0
1972	Australia	AP Sheahan	2	4	2	90	44*	45.00	0	0
1972	Australia	KR Stackpole	5	10	1	485	114	53.88	1	5
1972	Australia	KD Walters	4	7	0	54	20	7.71	0	0
1972	Australia	GD Watson	2	4	0	21	13	5.25	0	0
1972	England	GG Arnold	3	5	2	28	22	9.33	0	0
1972	England	G Boycott	2	4	0	72	47	18.00	0	0
1972	England	BL D'Oliveira	5	9	1	233	50*	29.12	0	1

* denotes a not-out score

Catches	Stumpings	Balls	Maidens	Runs conceded	Wickets	Average	Best bowling	Five in innings	Ten in match
1	0	1132	37	423	19	22.26	5-85	1	0
9	0								
2	0	1046	28	381	14	27.21	3-27	0	0
1	0								
7	0								
1	0	708	28	243	10	24.30	3-14	0	0
0	0								
0	0								
0	0								
4	0	632	22	224	11	20.36	3-13	0	0
2	0	588	8	306	10	30.60	4-59	0	0
1	0	296	4	131	1	131.00	1-131	0	0
0	0								
4	0								
3	0	24	0	28	0		0-28	0	0
13	0								
4	0	48	0	34	1	34.00	1-34	0	0
2	0	6	0	2	1	2.00	1-2	0	0
6	0								
0	0								
1	0	1147	16	499	18	27.72	5-60	1	0
2	0	1208	16	583	28	20.82	7-27	2	1
1	0	566	15	229	10	22.90	5-79	1	0
8	0	338	17	125	2	62.50	1-28	0	0
6	0	90	7	27	1	27.00	1-26	0	0
1	0	729	20	312	6	52.00	3-83	0	0
1	0								
1	0								
0	0	460	28	157	3	52.33	2-45	0	0
1	0	366	26	90	4	22.50	3-26	0	0
0	0	1499	83	548	31	17.67	6-66	3	1
0	0	618	32	269	10	26.90	5-114	1	0
21	2								
0	0	1195	58	409	23	17.78	8-53	2	1
0	0								
4	0	102	7	35	0		0-35	0	0
1	0	30	1	7	0		0-7	0	0
1	0	240	14	92	3	30.66	1-23	0	0
0	0	665	25	279	13	21.46	4-62	0	0
0	0								
3	0	498	23	176	5	35.20	1-13	0	0

Greatest Ashes series averages			Matches	Innings	Not outs	Runs	HS	Average	Hun-dreds	Fifties
1972	England	JH Edrich	5	10	0	218	49	21.80	0	0
1972	England	KWR Fletcher	1	1	0	5	5	5.00	0	0
1972	England	N Gifford	3	5	1	50	16*	12.50	0	0
1972	England	AW Greig	5	9	1	288	62	36.00	0	3
1972	England	JH Hampshire	1	2	0	62	42	31.00	0	0
1972	England	R Illingworth	5	8	2	194	57	32.33	0	1
1972	England	APE Knott	5	8	0	229	92	28.62	0	2
1972	England	P Lever	1	1	0	9	9	9.00	0	0
1972	England	BW Luckhurst	4	8	1	168	96	24.00	0	1
1972	England	PH Parfitt	3	6	1	117	51	23.40	0	1
1972	England	JSE Price	1	2	1	23	19	23.00	0	0
1972	England	MJK Smith	3	6	0	140	34	23.33	0	0
1972	England	JA Snow	5	8	0	111	48	13.87	0	0
1972	England	DL Underwood	2	3	2	8	5	8.00	0	0
1972	England	B Wood	1	2	0	116	90	58.00	0	1
1981	Australia	TM Alderman	6	9	5	22	12*	5.50	0	0
1981	Australia	AR Border	6	12	3	533	123*	59.22	2	3
1981	Australia	RJ Bright	5	9	0	127	33	14.11	0	0
1981	Australia	TM Chappell	3	6	1	79	27	15.80	0	0
1981	Australia	J Dyson	5	10	0	206	102	20.60	1	0
1981	Australia	RM Hogg	2	3	1	0	0*	0.00	0	0
1981	Australia	KJ Hughes	6	12	0	300	89	25.00	0	1
1981	Australia	MF Kent	3	6	0	171	54	28.50	0	2
1981	Australia	GF Lawson	3	5	1	38	14	9.50	0	0
1981	Australia	DK Lillee	6	10	3	153	40*	21.85	0	0
1981	Australia	RW Marsh	6	11	0	216	52	19.63	0	1
1981	Australia	DM Wellham	1	2	0	127	103	63.50	1	0
1981	Australia	MR Whitney	2	4	0	4	4	1.00	0	0
1981	Australia	GM Wood	6	12	1	310	66	28.18	0	2
1981	Australia	GN Yallop	6	12	0	316	114	26.33	1	1
1981	England	PJW Allott	1	2	1	66	52*	66.00	0	1
1981	England	IT Botham	6	12	1	399	149*	36.27	2	1
1981	England	G Boycott	6	12	0	392	137	32.66	1	1
1981	England	JM Brearley	4	8	0	141	51	17.62	0	1
1981	England	GR Dilley	3	6	2	150	56	37.50	0	1
1981	England	PR Downton	1	2	0	11	8	5.50	0	0
1981	England	JE Emburey	4	7	2	134	57	26.80	0	1
1981	England	MW Gatting	6	12	0	370	59	30.83	0	4
1981	England	GA Gooch	5	10	0	139	44	13.90	0	0
1981	England	DI Gower	5	10	0	250	89	25.00	0	1
1981	England	M Hendrick	2	3	3	6	6*		0	0
1981	England	APE Knott	2	4	1	178	70*	59.33	0	2

denotes a not-out score

Catches	Stumpings	Balls	Maidens	Runs conceded	Wickets	Average	Best bowling	Five in innings	Ten in match
1	0								
0	0								
2	0	204	6	116	1	116.00	1-18	0	0
8	0	975	44	398	10	39.80	4-53	0	0
1	0								
6	0	528	28	197	7	28.14	2-32	0	0
17	0								
0	0	270	11	137	1	137.00	1-61	0	0
3	0	5	0	5	0		0-5	0	0
5	0	12	0	10	0		0-10	0	0
0	0	199	5	115	3	38.33	2-87	0	0
4	0								
2	0	1235	46	555	24	23.12	5-57	2	0
0	0	750	49	266	16	16.62	6-45	1	1
0	0								
8	0	1950	76	893	42	21.26	6-135	4	0
12	0								
4	0	1150	82	390	12	32.50	5-68	1	0
2	0								
2	0								
1	0	244	8	123	4	30.75	3-47	0	0
3	0								
6	0								
0	0	637	30	285	12	23.75	7-81	1	0
1	0	1870	81	870	39	22.30	7-89	2	1
23	0								
0	0								
0	0	468	16	246	5	49.20	2-50	0	0
4	0								
7	0	48	2	17	0		0-17	0	0
0	0	138	4	88	4	22.00	2-17	0	0
12	0	1635	81	700	34	20.58	6-95	3	1
2	0	18	2	2	0		0-2	0	0
4	0								
1	0	588	24	275	14	19.64	4-24	0	0
2	0								
1	0	1163	58	399	12	33.25	4-43	0	0
8	0	18	1	13	0		0-13	0	0
1	0	60	4	28	0		0-28	0	0
3	0								
0	0	602	28	221	6	36.83	4-82	0	0
6	0								

Greatest Ashes series averages			Matches	Innings	Not outs	Runs	HS	Average	Hundreds	Fifties
1981	England	W Larkins	1	2	0	58	34	29.00	0	0
1981	England	CM Old	2	4	1	63	29	21.00	0	0
1981	England	PWG Parker	1	2	0	13	13	6.50	0	0
1981	England	CJ Tavaré	2	4	0	179	78	44.75	0	2
1981	England	RW Taylor	3	6	0	23	9	3.83	0	0
1981	England	P Willey	4	8	0	179	82	22.37	0	1
1981	England	RGD Willis	6	10	2	43	13	5.37	0	0
1981	England	RA Woolmer	2	4	0	30	21	7.50	0	0
2005	Australia	MJ Clarke	5	9	0	335	91	37.22	0	2
2005	Australia	AC Gilchrist	5	9	1	181	49*	22.62	0	0
2005	Australia	JN Gillespie	3	6	0	47	26	7.83	0	0
2005	Australia	ML Hayden	5	10	1	318	138	35.33	1	0
2005	Australia	MS Kasprowicz	2	4	0	44	20	11.00	0	0
2005	Australia	SM Katich	5	9	0	248	67	27.55	0	2
2005	Australia	JL Langer	5	10	1	394	105	43.77	1	2
2005	Australia	B Lee	5	9	3	158	47	26.33	0	0
2005	Australia	GD McGrath	3	5	4	36	20*	36.00	0	0
2005	Australia	DR Martyn	5	9	0	178	65	19.77	0	1
2005	Australia	RT Ponting	5	9	0	359	156	39.88	1	1
2005	Australia	SW Tait	2	3	2	8	4	8.00	0	0
2005	Australia	SK Warne	5	9	0	249	90	27.66	0	1
2005	England	IR Bell	5	10	0	171	65	17.10	0	2
2005	England	PD Collingwood	1	2	0	17	10	8.50	0	0
2005	England	A Flintoff	5	10	0	402	102	40.20	1	3
2005	England	AF Giles	5	10	2	155	59	19.37	0	1
2005	England	SJ Harmison	5	8	2	60	20*	10.00	0	0
2005	England	MJ Hoggard	5	9	2	45	16	6.42	0	0
2005	England	GO Jones	5	10	1	229	85	25.44	0	1
2005	England	SP Jones	4	6	4	66	20*	33.00	0	0
2005	England	KP Pietersen	5	10	1	473	158	52.55	1	3
2005	England	AJ Strauss	5	10	0	393	129	39.30	2	0
2005	England	ME Trescothick	5	10	0	431	90	43.10	0	3
2005	England	MP Vaughan	5	10	0	326	166	32.60	1	1

* denotes a not-out score

Catches	Stumpings	Balls	Maidens	Runs conceded	Wickets	Average	Best bowling	Five in innings	Ten in match
0	0								
0	0	504	27	175	5	35.00	3-44	0	0
0	0								
1	0								
13	0								
0	0	96	3	35	1	35.00	1-31	0	0
2	0	1516	56	666	29	22.96	8-43	1	0
2	0								
2	0	12	0	6	0		0-6	0	0
18	1								
1	0	402	6	300	3	100.00	2-91	0	0
10	0								
3	0	312	6	250	4	62.50	3-80	0	0
4	0	72	1	50	1	50.00	1-36	0	0
2	0								
2	0	1147	25	822	20	41.10	4-82	0	0
1	0	804	22	440	19	23.15	5-53	2	0
4	0								
4	0	36	2	9	1	9.00	1-9	0	0
0	0	288	5	210	5	42.00	3-97	0	0
5	0	1517	37	797	40	19.92	6-46	3	2
8	0	42	2	20	0		0-8	0	0
1	0	24	0	17	0		0-17	0	0
3	0	1164	32	655	24	27.29	5-78	1	0
5	0	960	18	578	10	57.80	3-78	0	0
1	0	967	22	549	17	32.29	5-43	1	0
0	0	733	15	473	16	29.56	4-97	0	0
15	1								
1	0	612	17	378	18	21.00	6-53	2	0
0	0								
6	0								
3	0								
2	0	30	0	21	0		0-21	0	0

MISCELLANEOUS ASHES STATISTICS

Most ducks in career		Ducks	Innings
SE Gregory	Australia	11	92
GD McGrath	Australia	10	33
SK Warne	Australia	10	48
D Gough	England	9	29
AFA Lilley	England	9	47
J Briggs	England	9	48

Most balls without scoring	Score	Balls faced			
AP Sheahan	0*	44	Australia	Lord's	1968
AR Caddick	0*	37	England	The Oval	1997
GG Arnold	0	34	England	Adelaide	1974/75
MR Whitney	0	32	Australia	Manchester	1981
H Verity	0*	31	England	Nottingham	1934

Most Ashes Tests without a victory				
RA Smith	England	15 matches	11 lost	4 drawn
NWD Yardley	England	10 matches	7 lost	3 drawn
CH Parkin	England	9 matches	7 lost	2 drawn
RC Russell	England	9 matches	6 lost	3 drawn
RJ Bright	Australia	8 matches	5 lost	3 drawn

Most Ashes Tests without a defeat				
CE Pellew	Australia	9 matches	7 won	2 drawn
ERH Toshack	Australia	9 matches	6 won	3 drawn
TR Veivers	Australia	9 matches	2 won	7 drawn
EA McDonald	Australia	8 matches	6 won	2 drawn
EJ Smith	England	7 matches	5 won	2 drawn
RH Spooner	England	7 matches	2 won	5 drawn

Most catches in the field		Matches	Catches
IT Botham	England	32	54
AR Border	Australia	42	51
GS Chappell	Australia	30	48
MA Taylor	Australia	33	46
H Trumble	Australia	31	45
ME Waugh	Australia	29	43
WR Hammond	England	33	43
RT Ponting	Australia	35	41
MC Cowdrey	England	43	40
WW Armstrong	Australia	42	37
LC Braund	England	20	37
AN Cook	England	30	37

Most catches in the field in a series			Matches	Catches
JM Gregory	Australia	1920/21	5	15
GS Chappell	Australia	1974/75	6	14
AR Border	Australia	1981	6	12
IT Botham	England	1981	6	12
LC Braund	England	1901/02	5	12
AW Greig	England	1974/75	6	12
WR Hammond	England	1934	5	12

Most common bowler/fielder combinations			
DK Lillee	RW Marsh	Australia	27
B Lee	AC Gilchrist	Australia	24
JM Anderson	MJ Prior	England	23
CV Grimmett	WAS Oldfield	Australia	22
GD McGrath	AC Gilchrist	Australia	20
SK Warne	IA Healy	Australia	20
MG Hughes	IA Healy	Australia	19
GF Lawson	RW Marsh	Australia	19
GD McKenzie	ATW Grout	Australia	18
IT Botham	RW Taylor	Australia	18
GD McGrath	IA Healy	Australia	18

Most common batsman/bowler dismissals		Batsman country	
MA Atherton	GD McGrath	England	19
AR Morris	AV Bedser	Australia	18
TW Hayward	H Trumble	England	15
AFA Lilley	MA Noble	England	14
DI Gower	GF Lawson	England	14
AJ Stewart	SK Warne	England	14
AC MacLaren	H Trumble	England	13
VT Trumper	SF Barnes	Australia	13
AFA Lilley	H Trumble	England	12
AL Hassett	DVP Wright	Australia	12
RN Harvey	AV Bedser	Australia	12
KD Walters	DL Underwood	Australia	12

Shortest matches with a definite result

Balls

788	Manchester	1888
792	Lord's	1888
911	Sydney	1894/95
1034	Brisbane	1950/51
1049	The Oval	1896

Most appearances as umpire

RM Crockett	27
J Phillips	24
Aleem Dar	19
GE Borwick	15
F Chester	14
HD Bird	14
SA Bucknor	14

Hundred before lunch on Day 1	Runs in session	Final score			
VT Trumper	103	104	Australia	Manchester	1902
CG Macartney	112	151	Australia	Leeds	1926
DG Bradman	105	334	Australia	Leeds	1930

Most runs conceded in an innings

	Overs	Maidens	Runs	Wickets			
LO Fleetwood-Smith	87	11	298	1	Australia	The Oval	1938
IAR Peebles	71	8	204	6	England	The Oval	1930
CV Grimmett	64	14	191	2	Australia	Sydney	1928/29
WJ O'Reilly	59	9	189	7	Australia	Manchester	1934
AA Mailey	43.6	2	186	4	Australia	Melbourne	1924/25

Most runs in a day by an individual	Runs in day	Day	Final score			
DG Bradman	309	1	334	Australia	Leeds	1930
DG Bradman	271	2	304	Australia	Leeds	1934
DG Bradman	244	1	244	Australia	The Oval	1934
RE Foster	214	3	287	England	Sydney	1903/04
SJ McCabe	213	3	232	Australia	Nottingham	1938
WR Hammond	210	1	240	England	Lord's	1938
WH Ponsford	205	1	266	Australia	The Oval	1934

Most runs in a day	Wickets in day	Day			
475	2	1	Australia 475-2	The Oval	1934
471	9	3	Australia 162-3 to 389, England 244-2	The Oval	1921
458	3	1	Australia 458-3	Leeds	1930
455	1	2	Australia 39-3 to 494-4	Leeds	1934
447	17	5	England 247-4 to 377, Australia 111-6d, England 206-5	The Oval	2013
436	7	2	England 129-4 to 403-8d, Australia 162-3	The Oval	1921
435	4	1	England 435-4	The Oval	1899
429	12	1	Australia 407, England 22-2	Leeds	1921
427	12	1	England 294, Australia 133-2	Birmingham	2001
427	5	3	Australia 119-1 to 527-5d, England 19-1	Perth	2006/07

About the authors

Simon 'Yozzer' Hughes is editor of *The Cricketer* magazine. He was a lively fast bowler who played for more than a decade in Middlesex's Championship-winning team before joining Durham for his last seasons. He had a Botham-esque bowling arm and was knocking on England's door in his early 20s. He then forged successful careers in journalism and television. He wrote the award-winning *A Lot of Hard Yakka*, and followed that with *Yakking around the World, Jargonbusting, And God Created Cricket* and *Morning Everyone: An Ashes Odyssey*. His latest book is *Who Wants to Be a Batsman?* On television he is known as The Analyst. He pioneered innovative coverage of the game as part of Channel 4's Bafta-winning team (winning the Royal Television Society's Sports Pundit of the Year award in 2002), and has since transferred his skills to *Cricket on 5*.

Gideon Haigh has been a journalist since 1984, contributed to more than 100 newspapers and magazines, and written 32 books. He lives in Melbourne, where he is a spare parts cricketer, committeeman, life member and the games record holder of the South Yarra CC. He is married with a daughter, a great many cricket books and bats.

James Coyne joined *The Cricketer* as assistant editor in May 2016, after working on six editions of *Wisden Cricketers' Almanack*. His journalism career started in his native Bedford, where barely anyone his age seemed to like cricket (perhaps no surprise given that England were getting pummelled by Australia every two years or so). He is a fan of taking the game to non-traditional locations, going on tours across mainland Europe, and more recently Latin America, where he was researching a book on the sport's long and inglorious history there. He still contributes to *Wisden*'s 'Cricket Round the World' section, and plays league cricket in Bedfordshire and Hertfordshire to a modest level.

Huw Turbervill has been writing professionally about cricket for 23 years, and for the last three years has been managing editor and writer at *The Cricketer*. His career started at the *East Anglian Daily Times*. He then spent 15 years on the *Sunday* and *Daily Telegraph*, as well as the *Express*. He has worked alongside Scyld Berry, Mike Atherton and Steve James, and reported from Bangladesh, New Zealand, Sri Lanka and Zimbabwe. While at the *Telegraph* he wrote *The Toughest Tour: The Ashes Away Series Since the War*. He has been running Carpediems Cricket Club for 14 years. As a seam-bowling allrounder, he reached the heady heights of Suffolk IIs.

Jamie Crawley is a budding writer and cricket fanatic, enjoying his first foray in print with this book. He joined *The Cricketer* in November 2016 and was tasked with exhaustively scouring *The Cricketer*'s 96 years' worth of Ashes coverage to unearth the finest writing and hidden gems. Jamie lives in North London, and spends his spare time umpiring in the Middlesex County Cricket League.

Philip J Bailey is an English cricket statistician. He was educated at Eltham College and Cambridge University. He is the chief statistician and records compiler for *Wisden Cricketers' Almanack* and contributes the career records section to *Playfair Cricket Annual*. He has previously worked for the Cricinfo website before co-founding Cricket Archive where he is editor.

Bailey is acknowledged to be one of the major statisticians of his generation. The former *Wisden* editor Matthew Engel credits him with taking 'this abstruse branch of science to levels that in other fields win Nobel Prizes'.

Index